Stress & Release in an Urban Estate

Stress & Release
in an
Urban Estate

A STUDY IN ACTION RESEARCH

JOHN SPENCER

with the collaboration of

JOY TUXFORD & NORMAN DENNIS

TAVISTOCK PUBLICATIONS

First published in 1964
by Tavistock Publications (1959) Limited
11 New Fetter Lane, London E.C.4

Printed in Great Britain
in 12 point Bembo
by Fletcher & Son Limited, Norwich

Contents

Contents

vi

Preface

THIS BOOK is a greatly abbreviated version of the report on the Bristol Social Project presented to the Carnegie Trustees in 1961. Its main focus is that part of the Project which falls under the heading of action research. To have included in the same volume the two studies of the neighbourhoods (the Neighbourhood Study) and of a sample of ordinary families (the Family Study) would have produced a book of excessive length. It is therefore planned to give an account of these two studies in a second volume.

The Director of the Project took the main responsibility for the preparation of the report, but the work which has gone into it is essentially the product of the Project team. In the case of the Neighbourhood Study and the Family Study the work is that of Mr. Norman Dennis and Miss Joy Tuxford. They also had the task of writing up these two studies.

It is impossible to do justice to the contributions made by all the eleven members of the team and invidious perhaps to select particular individuals for special mention. A description of their functions, with their names and the dates of their appointments, is given in Appendices IV and V. Each member of the team kept a diary of his or her work and the Director has made extensive use of this material in writing the report. Nevertheless, special mention must be made of the diary kept by the group worker while working with the Espressos (Part III). The reader will recognize how greatly dependent on her own descriptive material is the account of her work presented in that section.

Preface

A copy of the complete report to the Trust, together with a number of the supporting papers, has been placed in the library of the Institute of Education at Bristol University. It is available for consultation by *bona fide* research workers on application to the Librarian of the Institute.

In the course of five years the Project team received assistance from a wide range of people connected with the work. We are unable to express adequately our gratitude to all the many people from whom help and acts of kindness were received. We should, however, like to express our thanks to the following for their help:

Mr. C. Beales; Mr. C. Beedell; Miss G. Bennett; Clr. A. Bowden; Dr. H. Bracey; the staff of the Bristol Council of Social Service; Mr. R. A. Brooks; Mr. C. Burt; the Clergy of the two estates; Bishop F. A. Cockin; Mr. J. Connell; Mr. K. H. Cox; Professor A. Curle; Miss E. H. L. Duncan; Mr. B. M. Dyer; the General Practitioners of the two estates; Miss E. M. Goldberg; Dr. E. Hare; the Head Teachers of the two estates; Alderman W. H. Hinton; Dr. Portia Holman; the staff of the Institute of Community Studies; the staff of the Bristol Institute of Education; Mr. A. W. Jefford; Sister J. Laver; Mr. W. Lelean; Dr. Kate Liepmann; Mr. S. MacFarlane; Mr. John Mack; Alderman J. J. Milton; Mr. F. Morton; Alderman F. A. Parish; Miss E. M. Parry; Mr. T. Pascoe; Dr. T. Phillips; Mr. A. Pollock; Dr. Rhona Rapoport; Dr. J. Sandler; the Save the Children Fund; Mr. R. Sawyer; Dr. D. H. Stott; Mr. A. Strange; Dr. F. K. Taylor; Miss V. A. Thick; Mrs. N. Thompson; Dr. Sarah Walker; Clr. W. J. Waring; Miss R. G. Watkins; Mr. N. Whicheloe.

And to all those members of the Main and Executive Committees who gave us assistance on many occasions. We should mention particularly Professor Roger Wilson and Dr. Robert Barbour who also helped during the preparation of the report.

We must acknowledge also our gratitude for the services of:

Mr. Peter Kuenstler (September 1953 – December 1954)

Mr. Richard Mills (September 1953 – April 1957)

viii

Mr. Edgar Simpkins (January – February 1954)
Mrs. Pauline Morris (June – July 1954)
Miss Jennifer Stevenson (June – December 1954)
Mrs. Leonora Gay (March 1955 – September 1958)
Professor Raymond Fisher (September 1955 – August 1956)
Mrs. Dorothy Brown (March – December 1956)
Mr. Bernard Crix (June – July 1956)
Mrs. Jean Reiss (January – April 1957)
Miss Agnes Ross (June – July 1957)
Mr. Tony Lynes (July – September 1957)
Mr. Ralph Braunholtz (September – December 1957)
Dr. Lumsden Walker (consultant psychiatrist during the Family Study).

In addition we enjoyed having with us at varying stages in the Project's work:

Mr. Martin Russell	Mrs. Deirdre Stanley
Miss Jane Compton	Miss Claire Follett
Mrs. Varda Clegg	Miss Winifred Apelt
Mr. Andrew Thomas	Miss Carmel Barnett

A special debt of thanks is due to the Harry M. Cassidy Memorial Research Fund under the direction of Professor Charles E. Hendry, School of Social Work, University of Toronto, for making available in the preparation of the report for book publication the invaluable editorial help of Mrs. Florence C. Strakhovsky, Research Secretary of the Fund.

Wherever possible in this report we have concealed the identity of people and places by the use of pseudonyms.

Toronto, July 1962   JOHN SPENCER

Introduction

As CHAIRMAN of the Bristol Social Project Executive Committee (a misleading name for what as it transpired would have been better called a steering committee), I wish to preface the report which follows with some introductory observations.

The Project was a very difficult operation. Some of those associated with it expected this, since the purpose of the exercise was exploration in a region not even mapped in outline. It was impossible to define objectives or even methods in advance, and it was clear that this would make explanation difficult and arouse anxiety. The reality was more difficult than anybody had anticipated. The Project was beset not merely by the normal hazards of social surveying; it was committed to action in public on highly charged issues; the curiosity of the uncommitted social scientist does not move parallel with the presuppositions of city government and social services based on the day-by-day and year-by-year realities of political thought and democratic responsibility; the passionate insight of experimentally-minded social workers was not always in easy harness with the experience of those with equal concern working in the everyday world. And the press was always interested. All these elements are entirely legitimate. But to study 'the stresses and strains of family life and to take part in the developing life of a community' in these circumstances is like trying to elucidate the principles of navigation in a hurricane while experimenting with the engines under the gaze of television. It can be done, and because of the tempestuous nature of contemporary social change it is worth doing, even though the principal lesson learned is how to do it better next time.

It is appropriate here to say something about the Project team. Just as the Project was itself unorthodox, so none of the team members was 'orthodox' or 'safe' in any conventional sense. Those of them concerned with analysis and interpretation combined austere academic standards with warm convictions about human relationships. The members concerned primarily with field operations were all highly original people who were much better at understanding those among whom they worked at Upfield than at explaining what they did in everyday terms that would be understandable to local residents or members of lay committees. (This may have been because they were not given enough chance to explain their work.) All of the team were strong characters, drawn to the Project by their profound personal interest in social relationships and in what a better understanding of them might mean for the development of social policy. All of them came with diverse but rich and authentic experience of wrestling with these issues in settings other than the public life of a great city. Each of them had a disciplined integrity of concern which did not make it easy for them to be welded into a working team.

The Director would have had no easy job to pull the various team contributions together in any event. To do it in the particular setting of the Project, with its emphasis on lay participation, set an additionally difficult task, for none of the team, except perhaps the field worker, Bill Miller, was working in terms familiar to laymen. And when it came to preparing the report, those team members who were articulate at all (and not all of them were) would have found it easier to write for their fellow professionals than to translate what they had to say in terms which may be generally understandable without bringing the authors into contempt with their colleagues.

The report which follows (in two volumes) is the report of the Project team under the direction of Dr. John Spencer. The authors of its sections are himself, Mr. Norman Dennis, and Miss Joy Tuxford, who have drawn on their own material and also on that of other team members. Drafts of the sections and of the whole report were submitted to the Executive Committee, to the Main Project Committee, and to various individuals; in particular, I went through the whole draft as it then stood in some detail, making suggestions which I believed might increase the possibility and value of publication, without impairing the points which the authors felt constrained to make. In this way, the team members have received a mass of comments which they have incorporated in their redrafting in such ways as they think justifiable. But the report remains a team and not a Committee document.

With regard to the contents of the report, we believe it presents data and ideas of importance to those whose business it is to ana-lyse the influences at work in society and in individuals as mem-bers of society; to those, in statutory and voluntary service, whose business it is to formulate social policy and to carry out field operations; and to those who venture into the difficult and con-troversial field of attempting to relate social research and social policy.

This last activity becomes both more difficult and more neces-sary as our society overcomes the material obstacles to a good life for all. By the planned use of limited resources we have discovered what remarkable progress can be made in raising standards of housing, nutrition, health, and education. Human wretchedness for the most part will not in future be inescapable by reason of sheer lack of physical opportunity; where it exists it will be by reason of the inability of persons to establish satisfying human re-lationships in the contemporary pattern of society. The demands which society makes on individuals involve a much subtler analysis and a more perceptive response than the physical shortcomings which have been the focus of social policy over the last century and a quarter in general and the last fifty years in particular. It may be, of course, that contemporary society demands the wrong things. We hope that other public citizens and other social scient-ists will engage together in the risky enterprise of considering the nature of human need and how to meet it. And we hope that this report will help them to find the way.

ROGER WILSON
Professor of Education in the
University of Bristol
Chairman of the Main and
Executive Committees of the
Bristol Social Project

PART I

The Project

CHAPTER 1

The Project in Outline

Whatever is attempted without previous certainty of success, may be considered as a Project, and amongst narrow minds may, therefore, expose its author to censure and contempt; and if the liberty of laughing be once indulged, every man will laugh at what he does not understand, every Project will be considered as madness, and every great or new design will be considered as a Project.

SAMUEL JOHNSON

In 1952 a committee of Bristol's leading citizens drawn from a wide range of public life in the city submitted certain proposals for an action-research project in the following terms:

To investigate and take part in the life of a developing community in Bristol in an attempt to establish practical means of tackling those stresses and strains which arise in such a community in the form of delinquency and other disturbances. The main emphasis of the Project will be on encouraging local initiative and on getting local residents to take a greater degree of responsibility for their community life.

The present study (in two volumes) is a condensed version of the detailed report submitted to the Carnegie Trust by the small team of social scientists and social workers employed in this Project during the five-year period from 1953 to 1958. In this first volume are included the phases of the Project's work that fall under the label of 'action research'. The second volume will contain the Neighbourhood Study and the Family Study.

The idea of an action-research project in a local community was a rather new concept in English social policy and there were few precedents upon which to build. The vagueness of the initial statement of purpose above contained the seeds of both strength and weakness, since a general statement accepted by a committee is likely to carry a diversity of interpretations according to the different ways of thinking of the members.

The initial problem from which the Project arose was juvenile delinquency. Among the social problems which have been a source of public anxiety and concern in the post-war world, juvenile delinquency has occupied a prominent place. For this there are many reasons, some valid, others founded on rather dubious arguments. In 1948 current statistics had shown a marked rise over the pre-war years – for the juvenile court age-group (8–17 years) an increase of 58 per cent in indictable offences between 1938 and 1948. The year 1948 was in fact one of the peak years of the cyclical fluctuations in delinquency with the highest figure in the post-war period.

In setting up the Bristol Social Project the Committee had the advantage of discussions with Mr. John Mack, Stevenson Lecturer in Citizenship at the University of Glasgow, and in particular of the argument and recommendations of his private report to the Carnegie Trust written at the conclusion of a general survey of juvenile delinquency. In that report he argued that the main problem revealed by delinquency was *family disorganization* – the failure of families, and particularly of parents, to give children the two things they most need, assurance of continuing love and moral discipline made acceptable by love. He suggested that from a general survey of investigations made into delinquency this was the only thing on which investigators were all agreed, but that in spite of so obvious a statement it had little influence on preventive policy, which was still primarily concerned with the individual delinquent rather than with the family group.

From this he arrived at two conclusions: (i) the attempt to detect delinquency proneness at an early stage in the individual is unlikely to succeed; and (ii) in spite of the immense volume of literature on juvenile delinquency, no agreement has been or is likely to be reached on the 'causes of delinquency'. Those two conclusions led to a practical recommendation that attention should be shifted from the delinquent to the deeper problems of which delinquency is an indicator – family disorganization.

Mack then considered the useful work done by a variety of pioneering organizations, such as the Family Service Units and the Marriage Guidance Councils, by way of education for family life. A weakness, he thought, was the concentration of attention on families in trouble and our lack of knowledge about ordinary families, particularly on the more intangible and delicate question of relationships. But, he pointed out:

> . . . families are no more self-sufficient than individuals. They depend for their civil and economic security on the political institutions of a wider society. They depend likewise for moral and emotional sustenance on the intangible fabric of custom and tradition, and on the close network of informal social and neighbourly relationships, which are to be found most strongly developed in well-established communities.

This observation led him to the central theme in his diagnosis – the effect of social isolation on the family. In a growing industrial and urban society the family is no longer dependent on those close local ties of neighbourhood and kinship which previously had supported it in the day-to-day business of living and in the bringing-up of children. Side by side with this change has gone an increasing dependence on outside forces of control.[1] Mack emphasized the development of this attitude, particularly in new housing estates where the residents, after an initial period of social

---

[1] Dr. A. T. M. Wilson (1949) writes in an article on marital problems: 'the atomization of society—the inadequacy of kinship and neighbourhood and community relations and the functional isolation of the family – appeared to be accompanied by a passive amenability to remote impersonal control.'

activity and enterprise, tend to become self-centred and isolated as well as passive and fearful of giving offence to people in the remote city centre.

This social isolation places a strain on the small family of today. Lacking a wider circle of friends and relations, they seek within the family satisfactions which it cannot supply. The problem which Mack proposed for investigation was the effect of social isolation, or what has been called the process of 'atomization' or 'desocialization', on the family. The method he recommended was that of 'operational research', and the essential feature of this method he took to be the co-operation between social scientists in an experimental solution of community and family problems. Such co-operation would be dependent on the agreement and understanding of the people involved, both in local government and in public affairs, but also in the areas in which the social experiment would be carried out. The social scientists he saw as interpreters and advisers helping the people directly concerned to work the thing out for themselves.

Mack's ideas on a plan of 'operational research', or 'action research' as we decided to call it, are described at some length because of the influence which they have had on the design and planning of the Project. His emphasis on the effect of social isolation on the family and on 'operational research' as a method of work, though loosely formulated in his report, nevertheless provided the groundwork for much of our subsequent thinking during the early planning stage.

Action research, at least in our interpretation, is essentially problem-centred. This means that in the course of the Project, as ideas were clarified and reformulated in the team and in the Committee, our understanding of the problem grew and developed. In a project concerned with change it would be naïve to suppose that the understanding of the specialist members of the team remained unaltered throughout the course of five years. The nature of this change we shall try to describe later on.

The Project was envisaged as having three main stages: Stage I would be an initial phase of general planning and discussion with

6

a quite specific and limited survey mainly to help the Committee in the choice of areas for the operation of the team. It was perfectly clear that a process of selection would be essential. Our resources made it impossible to consider working in the whole of Bristol (population 440,000). Stage II would consist of the main body of the work; and Stage III would be devoted to the writing of a report and the very difficult task of evaluation.

The method, as we have said, was that of action research. Action research, as we understand it, is concerned with the bringing about of social change. It stands in marked contrast to the conventional method of applied research, and is open to criticism from those social scientists who, for various reasons, prefer to have no direct association with social action. A fundamental principle in action research is collaboration between layman and social scientist. The relationship between them is based on the assumption that through this collaboration the social scientist can gain insight into the problems which trouble and perplex humanity and may be able to help the layman to deal more effectively with them.

Mack and the Project team, however, differ from one another in certain respects in their interpretation of the idea of action research. For Mack, the research process was itself involved in the action: 'The main object of any experiment will be practical and not theoretical.' Mack saw the success of the experiment in terms of the achievement of more adequate relationships and forms of association in the life of the community as a whole.

Without denying the relevance of this method, we included in the Project a 'built-in' programme of research (using that phrase in the conventional sense) focused mainly on the social structure of the neighbourhoods and the group and family life of the three areas selected for our work. Action and research took place together side by side. Some members of the team have had mainly an 'action' and others a predominantly research role.

Closeness of collaboration between the Project team and the layman varied according to the situation. In the action programme our aim was to maintain as close a relationship between the two as

possible, whereas the planning and direction of the research programme into stresses and strains in the family and the neighbourhood were largely in the hands of the professional members.

The initial focus of the Project was the local community.
Three areas of Bristol were selected for the research, two of them
housing estates on the periphery of the city, and the third an old
central area. Of the two housing estates selected – Upfield (population 12,000) and Boltwood (population 4,000) – the former
ranks high on symptoms of problem behaviour, whereas the latter
appears little more than average. When speaking of Upfield, however, we refer sometimes to Old Upfield and sometimes to New
Upfield. The estate was in fact built in two stages – the old part
during the inter-war years, and the new part following the end of
the second world war. It is in the old part that the symptoms of
problem behaviour are mainly located. The third area chosen was
Mount View (classified as a Neighbourhood Unit in the City
Development Plan) with a population of 11,000.

In this way the problems of 'developing communities' were
studied alongside an older area. But it was in Upfield particularly
that action and research were interwoven in an action programme
designed to help the neighbourhood in dealing with some of the
problems which concerned its leaders and residents. Limitation of
resources made it necessary to confine the action programme to
Upfield alone. The study of the Mount View area occupied only
a very small part of our time.

The Project in its early stages was never specifically called an
experiment in community organization, yet the similarity between some of the basic ideas of action research in a local community and the process of community organization (Ross, 1955,
p. 38) deserves careful study. We shall later consider some of the
implications of the Project for community organization in urban
areas.

The Project team was qualified mainly in the field of sociology
and social work, though we were greatly assisted by professional
psychiatric advice. None of the eleven members, with the single
exception of the Director, was associated with the Project through-

out the whole of its existence. Their appointments were related to the needs of the Project at the various stages of work.

The two disciplines which provided the framework of our thinking in the Project were sociology and psychiatry. Our observations of the family and the community were based on certain assumptions about the social and emotional behaviour of individuals and society, which we shall describe later. The task of interrelating the insights derived from these two disciplines proved to be particularly difficult.

But the Project team did not see itself only as a staff of specialists. The contribution of the field worker, whose previous experience had included work as a tinker, tramp, hardware roundsman, youth leader, and organizer of the unemployed during the 1930s, was especially valuable, not only in bringing the specialists down to earth and in deflating their theories, but also through the perception and sensitivity of his observations as an ordinary resident of Upfield. He contributed the insight which comes from living close to the 'grass roots'.

The sociologist on the team, like the field worker, lived with his family as ordinary residents at both Upfield and Boltwood. The rest of the team lived outside the three Project areas, in various parts of the city.

Responsibility for the Project rested formally with the Main Committee representative of public life in the city, but it was the smaller Executive Committee which was closest to the Project team.[1] The Executive met frequently to discuss the main lines of policy and administration and also had opportunity for informal meetings in which the members could speak in a more personal way. In addition to these, two sub-committees were set up, one to advise on the strains and stresses of family life and ways of studying and dealing with them, and the other to examine the 'problems of co-ordination of social work and social workers at the local and field-work level'.

During the planning stage of the Project (Stage I) the concern

---

[1] Hereafter when we mention 'the Committee' or 'the Project Committee' it is usually the Executive Committee to which we refer, unless otherwise specified.

9

The Project

of the Committee was with Bristol as a whole, and for this purpose a wide range of interest and functions represented by the members was particularly useful in a general survey of the problem. In Stage II, however, when the focus of work shifted from a general survey of the city to three particular neighbourhoods, the need arose for an advisory group more closely concerned with the life of those areas. It was fortunate that both Upfield and Boltwood already possessed local Councils representative of the professional, social, and religious life of the estate; otherwise it would have been necessary to create them.

Our approach to the three areas took several forms: general surveys; the provision of physical amenities at Upfield that could meet local needs; work with groups; and studies of neighbourhood and family.

GENERAL SURVEYS

In Stage I a survey was made of the distribution in Bristol of certain overt symptoms of social disorganization, such as crime, juvenile delinquency, and child deprivation, as a preliminary step to the selection of the three areas. There were also two small surveys of the rate of mobility of tenants from the estates and the reasons behind this movement. In the old central area of Mount View a questionnaire focused primarily on neighbour relationships was given to a random sample of families with children of primary school age and a short survey made through the use of local leaders, newspapers, and materials obtained from the Registrar General and the local Planning Department.

THE PROVISION OF PHYSICAL AMENITIES

The Adventure Playground

The experience of the Adventure Playground, described in Part IV, illustrates two facets of estate life – the problems of children with widely differing standards of behaviour growing up in a single locality, and the obstacles to establishing new and unfamiliar methods of work in new areas.

The users of the Playground came from families with very varied standards in the upbringing of their children. For some, aggressiveness, destructiveness, or bad language were a natural feature of family life. Other users came from homes with very different standards. To the latter and their parents the rough behaviour on the Playground was both unwelcome and resented.

This variety in standards was reflected in the diversity of views on the responsible committee as to the Playground's main function. To some, including the Project workers, the prime need was for a tolerant and helpful Playground leader who would have a long-term influence on the antisocial users. To others on the committee the main need was for adventurous play opportunities for ordinary children, as an extension of the educational opportunities of the neighbourhood. The members of the Playground committee gave generously of their time, and the arduous work done by them brought out the human problems involved when social and antisocial families live in close proximity.

The Meeting Rooms

The importance of meeting places for small groups has achieved some general recognition in recent years. The New Town of Harlow, for example, has developed a successful policy of Tenants Common Rooms in pursuit of the aim of creating a vigorous social life in the town. The London County Council in the building of large blocks of flats has also included Tenants Club Rooms in the plans.

As the Project team became familiar with the estate and its social life they came to recognize that an important missing amenity was a place where small groups could meet in comfort and dignity. Hence the decision to formulate the latent wishes of people on the estate for a well-designed meeting place for small groups and to present proposals to the Carnegie Trustees. The

The Project

Upfield Community Council accepted responsibility for detailed planning and subsequent running, and the Carnegie Trustees very generously gave a grant towards the cost.

The rooms were built and furnished within the available finance and to a very much tighter time schedule than might have been possible with a regular building firm.[1] Within twelve months of a decision in principle the rooms were actually in use – a remarkable achievement at a time when building firms were preoccupied with profitable commercial work.

WORK WITH GROUPS

But physical amenities were not ends in themselves. They helped groups to come together and facilitated the Project team's policy of work and study in group relationships. For this policy there were several reasons. First and foremost, an assumption on which we continually relied was that it is through active group relationships that people of all ages can and do learn responsible social behaviour. We must make a distinction, however, between the groups which individuals in the Project team joined as part of their ordinary role as residents on the estates and those groups initiated for the specific purpose of helping the members to improve their social relationships and common understanding. The field worker, for example, was a member of the Upfield Labour Party, and the sociologist of the Boltwood Community Association. Their role was that of the ordinary estate resident, though the fact that they were known to be members of the Project team with a special interest in the social and political life of the estate must not be overlooked.

By work with groups, therefore, we refer primarily to the work carried out by the social group worker, in her professional role, but also to the work done by the psychiatric social worker with two groups of social workers and teachers, described in

[1] A full report on the Meeting Rooms, together with a technical report from the architect, has been sent to the Carnegie Trust. These documents may be seen by anyone interested on application to the Trust.

Part II of this study. All the work in this second category was concerned with Upfield leaders and residents.

The choice of groups was of necessity diverse, deliberately so. We were constantly reminded of the variety of levels at which housing estate life is lived, and an action-research team must penetrate local life at many points. The choice, moreover, was determined mainly by the situation on the estate, not by consideration of the claims of research. We did not, for example, confine membership of the groups to particular people as part of an experiment to test certain hypotheses about behaviour in groups, although the criticism was in fact made that groups were formed for this particular purpose.

The choice was also influenced by the hope that the work would continue after the termination of the Project – in Mack's words, 'the advisers will have succeeded if, when they move out, the operation is a going concern'. Empirical considerations, therefore, such as local needs, appropriate opportunities for the entry of the worker, and the likelihood of continuation after the conclusion of the Project, were the main grounds for the selection of groups, and particularly for the formation of new groups, rather than theoretical or academic questions.

In addition to work with professional leaders, work was concentrated on mothers, toddlers, and adolescents. For this there are excellent reasons, not only supported by a growing body of social and psychological knowledge, but also arising from the special problems of a housing estate which contains a large proportion of young families.

The Mothers Group

For a period of eighteen months the group worker worked with a small group of ten mothers who had been prevented by difficult family problems from making a positive social relationship with other women outside their homes (see Chapter 5). At first they came together in the Meeting Rooms, but at a later stage they met in each other's homes. There is no doubt that membership of this

13

group provided the mothers with a real opportunity for support and security in the face of considerable difficulties. We must emphasize, however, the long-term nature of work of this kind, and we should have welcomed an opportunity for securing the continuation of this group for a much longer period.

The Goslings Club

The objects of this Club for toddlers were fourfold: (i) to enable a group of mothers to have a free afternoon each week to do shopping, visit friends, etc.; (ii) to help the toddlers to play in a social group with adult supervision; (iii) to provide the mothers with an opportunity for informal discussion about their own and their children's experiences; and (iv) to help the local community through the working of a steering committee to take part in an activity which fulfils a very practical need of mothers on the estate.

The Goslings Club (described in some detail in Chapter 6) proved to be a useful achievement, supported by a vigorous and enthusiastic committee of Upfield women and helped after the ending of the Project by the Save the Children Fund. About fifteen mothers bring their children on one afternoon each week and when collecting them stay for tea and talk together in a group with the worker. The schools spoke confidently of the children whom they received from the Club, and a small minority of difficult children were helped by the warm and positive response shown by the Club to them and to their mothers.

But the Club did not, in spite of our intentions, draw into its membership the low-status and disorganized families who give rise to those symptoms of strain and stress which formed the focus of our initial survey. The local committee was happiest when working for the needs of the ordinary child.

The Adolescents

Group work with adolescents (as with toddlers) was the responsibility of the group worker. Her initial contact was through an established youth club on the estate, which has separate sections for girls and boys. For the first eighteen months she worked with two groups of girls within the girls' club, contrasted in status and standards of behaviour (see Chapter 9). They called themselves the 'Toffs' and the 'Bums'. For the last nine months of her appointment with the Project team the group worked independently with an exceptionally difficult group of some twenty-six girls and boys in late adolescence, of whom the majority reflected, by their anti-social and destructive behaviour, not only the disturbed relationships within their families, but also the pressure exerted from many different social situations at work and in the wider society. This group we shall call the 'Espressos'. We write at some length about them in Part III because they illustrate very vividly the problems involved in group work with that minority of adolescents who disturb and anger society by their behaviour.

NEIGHBOURHOOD AND FAMILY[1]

Although the main emphasis of the Project was on the collaboration between layman and professional social worker and social scientist in effecting social change in a selected area, it was certainly not exclusively so. The 'stresses and strains' described in the initial proposals are to be observed at various levels – the individual, the family, the neighbourhood, and also in the wider society.

The Neighbourhood Study

This was the work of the sociologist. It consists of three main sections. The first section is a systematic study of the three neighbourhoods selected by the Project – the two estates of Upfield and Boltwood and the old central area of Mount View. In this study the sociologist sets out to answer such questions as: What is the character of each neighbourhood; how does it compare with others in the city? What are the houses like? What services are available – workplace, shops, churches, pubs and clubs, transport

[1] This phase of the Project's work will be written up in the second volume.

facilities, the health and welfare services? What is the age structure of the population, the distribution of the sexes, the size of the households, the crime rate, and the occupational structure?

The second section is an analysis of the concepts of neighbourliness and the local community. Interest in the idea of the neighbourhood community is widespread – among administrators, town planners, religious leaders, philanthropists, and social scientists. But 'community' on close examination turns out to be an ambiguous word, used in a variety of senses. The sociologist examines the reasons for the popularity of the idea and the obstacles to the creation of the local community in a modern industrial city.

The third section is a study of the Community Association and Joint Council at Boltwood, of both of which the sociologist was an active member. The method, therefore, was that of participant observation. Among their stated objectives, community associations have given an important place to the goal of fostering neighbourliness and helping in the creation of the local community. The sociologist studies the experience of Boltwood against the general background of the changing urban neighbourhood.

The Family Study

We see the family as one of the crucial areas in which 'stresses and strains' are generated. To focus attention only on the neighbourhood and to neglect the family is not only to distort the evidence which we already possess, but to assume that measures for the prevention and alleviation of these stresses and strains are primarily to be sought in a neighbourhood context.

Our need, therefore, as Mack argued, is for greater understanding of ordinary families. It is a common complaint that much of the knowledge of the structure and behaviour of families comes from families that are functioning badly, from the disordered and the pathological. These are the families whose troubles bring them to the notice of the social services, who so frequently arouse public hostility or anxiety, and to whom so much attention is given. And rightly so, since our knowledge of them is still inadequate to provide the skilled understanding which is an essential basis for constructive help.

But we still know little of *ordinary families* seen in the context of their daily life in the neighbourhood where they live. What are the factors in modern society which give rise to the 'stresses and strains' which are the common experience of family living? To secure evidence from three selected areas which would provide answers to the general statements about the so-called 'decline of the family' is clearly impossible. But our aim was more modest. We wished to know more about ordinary families in the setting of the two estates in which the Project team was at work, and particularly about the stresses and strains to which they were subject.

Unlike research into the neighbourhood, the method of participant observation, that is, of observing the life of the community through sharing in its everyday experiences, was a method inappropriate to the study of the family. Other methods had to be devised by the sociologist and the psychiatric social worker, who set out to make a systematic study of a random sample of families living at Upfield and Boltwood.

This Family Study was built in, as it were, to the main body of the Project. We cannot, however, apply to it the label of action research in the sense in which we used the term. The object was that of greater understanding and we never claimed that the families who so generously gave their time in the interviews would gain any benefit directly for themselves. Our experience, however, suggests that many of them enjoyed the opportunity of talking about themselves to the two field workers.

In the Family Study the emphasis was on the family as a group in all its many aspects. It is often said that social workers and general practitioners tend to see the problems or sickness of the individual member in the family but not the family in its totality. Research workers also tend to concentrate on certain aspects of family behaviour demanding study, for example, the ties of

17

kinship, or methods of child-rearing, and to neglect the family working together, whether in harmony or discord, as a group. To look at the family as a group involves not only the relationships of the various members with one another, but also the relationships of the family with the wider society outside it.

Difficulties of personality do undoubtedly prevent adequate behaviour in the various roles of husband, wife, father, mother, neighbour, wage-earner, etc., and psychotherapy or intensive case work may do much to free the personality to perform the role more effectively. In many areas of behaviour, however, little is known about the kind of 'role performance' which is required in a given situation, and this is particularly true of the family in the environment of the new estate. In a rapidly changing world many individuals do not know what is appropriate behaviour as husbands or wives, mothers or fathers, especially in the diverse standards of the estate, confused by the varying opinions of experts and authorities, bawled at by mass newspapers and advertising, television, and the cinema, affected by the changing education of their children and an apparent instability of values in society at large.

Because the implications of the Family Study for social action are so important, though no simple conclusions can be drawn from it, and because this phase of the Project was not, strictly speaking, action research, on which we are reporting here, we have left the task of writing up this phase, as well as the Neighbourhood Study, for the second volume.[1]

[1] The detailed report on both these studies is, of course, on file with the Carnegie Trust and in the Library of the Institute of Education, University of Bristol.

CHAPTER 2

Action Research: Aims and Methods

*It was a great step in science when men became convinced
that, in order to understand the nature of things they must
begin by asking, not whether a thing is good or bad,
noxious or beneficial, but of what kind is it? And how
much is there of it?*

J. C. MAXWELL to the British Association, 1871

THESE are the main features of the Project's approach to the
task in hand and the sequence of events as they occurred. At first
sight perhaps they give the impression of a rather bewildering
diversity. The focus of attention appears fragmented and diffuse.
But this diversity is inescapable. In many different forms – of
standards of behaviour, of social relationships, of work and leisure,
and of ways of living – diversity is the characteristic element of
the two estates and the old central area selected for our work.

But it is not only a characteristic of the problem, it is also
essential to the method of action research. The approach of action
research is in marked contrast to the conventional methods of
social research which depend on the isolation of the problem
under investigation. The conventional social scientist relies on the
systematic testing of hypotheses, sometimes under experimental
conditions, controlling whenever possible the variables in his experiment so as to isolate the particular behaviour under investigation, whereas in action research such a process is impossible. For

this inability to test hypotheses, action research has been severely criticized, and the conclusion has been drawn that as a method of adding to our knowledge of society it has little claim to respect (cf. Argyle, 1957). In our view this is quite an erroneous conclusion.

In adopting the method of action research we have never implied that it is a method of establishing laws about human behaviour. We do maintain, however, that in the particular circumstances of the Project it was the only procedure to adopt. The Bristol Social Project was not planned as an alternative to the rigorous and exact methods of pure research which constitute a normal and essential part of university departments, in which research and teaching are linked together as closely related functions where new knowledge is communicated by the teacher to successive generations of students. Indeed, the policy of the Carnegie Trust, whose support made the Project possible, prohibits direct assistance to universities in this way.

The three main aspects of action research as understood in the Bristol Social Project we take to be:

1. close collaboration between the layman and the professional team;
2. the use of a problem-centred approach; and
3. the intention of helping to bring about change in an existing situation.

Each of these three features will be developed in subsequent sections of this report. We confine ourselves at this stage to a discussion of the major issues.

COLLABORATION

The essential element of our interpretation of action research is collaboration between laymen and the professional team of social scientists and social workers. We start from a conviction that collaboration of this kind can contribute both to action and to knowledge in a way that is mutually helpful to both layman and professional.

The reasons for this conviction arise not only from our belief in the general value, in the conduct of social affairs, of knowledge about human behaviour but also from our awareness of the wide gap which exists between knowledge and action and of the lack of effect of research and inquiry on the course of social action. To quote, for example, an editorial from the journal of the National Council of Social Service:

> There is no lack of social data presented to the public these days in the pages of the reports of Royal Commissions, official committees, white papers and blue books, but how few of the findings and recommendations result in legislative or administrative action! An instructive and useful piece of research might well be made into the reasons why, after months – sometimes years – of enquiry and study by able and well-informed people, their reports are consigned to oblivion in the dusty archives of Whitehall (*Social Service Quarterly*, 1957, p. 99).

On a national scale there is abundant evidence of the existence of this gap. The question remains as to how best we can take steps to narrow it. The answer to this question is not simply a matter of saying in more intelligible form what is already known in the jargon of the trade. It is not sufficient to plead for more popular accounts of the results of research, for less use of jargon, or for studies that are more relevant to the practical needs of administrators who, faced with conflicting claims and policies, have to take daily decisions in an imperfect society. All this is true enough and the social scientist would agree that there is plenty of work to be done in communicating his findings more effectively. The mass media of press, radio, and television at their best already serve to communicate the work of social scientists to a wider public. But the social scientist is generally content to leave the task of communication to those whose business it is to explain and to simplify. His concern is to work out a better theoretical framework for understanding social behaviour and to concentrate on the development of what is usually called pure research as distinct from any form of applied research, including action research, the method of the Bristol Project. Social scientists are naturally anxious to disown the idea that their studies can be used as 'how-to-do-it' manuals (cf. Mair, 1956, p. 121). Social anthropologists, for example, have tried to avoid commitment to policy decisions in colonial territories and some of them have grown sceptical of attempts to relate knowledge to practical affairs.

By adopting a different approach in the Bristol Project we do not wish to deny the validity of the cogent arguments in favour of well-established methods. But these arguments do not in themselves provide grounds for the rejection of action research. What they do is to underline the difficulties which are likely to arise through the commitment of social scientists to collaboration with laymen in social action.

Collaboration between the laymen and our professional team in the context of the community took several forms, and the roles of individual team members varied according to the laymen with whom various forms of collaboration took place.

The channel of communication between the team and the Bristol Social Project Committee was through the Director, who discussed the policy and operation of the Project at the weekly staff meetings of the team and at the meetings of the Main and Executive Committees. The meetings of each committee varied in frequency and character but it was with the members of the much smaller Executive (thirteen members) that the Director's relations were closest. Members of the team made reports to these two committees on twenty-four occasions.

The other team members, on the other hand, were particularly close to the estate. Two members of the team (George Harris and Bill Miller) lived with their families on the estates, Mr. Miller at Upfield and Mr. Harris at both Boltwood and Upfield. The division of their roles between that of team member and that of resident of the estate has inevitably presented difficulties for the individuals involved when the standards and aims implied in their membership of the Project have conflicted with the standards and aims of their other roles in the localities.

At both Boltwood and Upfield there were already in existence local Community Councils containing the leaders of the estates whether professionals or representatives of local groups and associations. For the Director and for the two members of the team just mentioned this was an invaluable method of gaining contact. But it was contact *at one particular level* of the life of the estate: the two Community Councils provided a formal method of entry to the estate at the level of the 'leaders' only. Again and again we return to this point – the diversity and fragmentation of the social relationships of the estates; no single point of entry is adequate.[1]

Other necessary methods of collaboration took various forms. It was Mr. Miller who came closest, perhaps, to the grass roots of the life of Upfield. His work, for example, as editor of the *Upfield Echo* (a local newspaper published by arrangement with the Upfield Community Council) brought him into contact with a wide variety of people in informal situations. His role as field worker did not carry with it a status which was likely to inhibit the creation of good informal relationships in a predominantly working-class community.

The group worker, Mrs. Andes, felt her primary responsibility was to the members of the three groups with whom she worked: to the adolescents, to the toddlers, and to the mothers. Her closest relationship was with them, but her professional role also involved contact and discussion with the leaders of the estate, for example, with the committee of the Wood Grove Girls Club and also with the Committee of the Project. Miss Cassidy, the psychiatric social worker, also worked with two groups, teachers and social workers, at the professional level, but her primary role was that of research worker in the Families Research.

These examples provide some illustration of the variety of ways in which the Project team understood the need for collaboration. First and foremost was the realization that we were birds of passage, a temporary disturbance in the continuity of the estates,

[1] cf. Simey (1949, pp. 47-8): 'If the researcher has to accept a responsibility for studying this problem in its total social context, he may find it hard to make a beginning. It is impossible to study everything at once. He must seek a profitable point of penetration, and this cannot be the condition of social relationships as a whole.'

and that one test of the measure of our achievement would be the stability of the estates after the disappearance of the team.

Collaboration took several forms, only some of which, we must emphasize, were of direct benefit to the estates and to the leading citizens of Bristol whose position gives them responsibility – in greater or less degree – for the life of the estates. The members of the Project team had several roles – as observers and interpreters of behaviour, as contributors to a general report designed to throw light on the 'stresses and strains of a developing community' from which readers other than those actually concerned with the Project might benefit, as enablers or facilitators, and as social therapists.

But we did not see ourselves as 'back-room boys' and it is for this reason that collaboration between layman and professional assumes primary importance among the aims of action research.

THE PROBLEM-CENTRED APPROACH

Action research is essentially problem-centred. Mack's initial suggestion that the Project 'should start from some situation which strikes the community in question as a live problem-situation' constitutes an essential feature of action research. In pure research the selection of the subject and the design of the research are related primarily to the theoretical interests of the worker. In action research, on the other hand, it is the problem as seen by the community which constitutes the starting-point of the experiment. Without this actual feeling of a problem to be solved there can be no basis for the collaboration of which we have written above.

Juvenile delinquency was the initial problem and the starting-point of the Project. This problem, however, was constantly reformulated through subsequent reflection and experience. The terms of reference of the Project pointed to 'stresses and strains in a developing community', and, of these stresses and strains, delinquency was included as one among others. In his short survey in the first year, the Director interpreted this phrase in terms of certain overt signs of stress and strain, such as juvenile delinquency, truancy, child neglect, and adult crime. One of the two estates and the old central area were selected because they appeared heavily weighted with symptoms of this kind.

It is a comparatively simple task to make an analysis of the symptoms; but to help the patient to understand the nature of the sickness itself and to take the appropriate medicine is entirely another matter. And so it proved to be. The patient wanted neither the doctor nor the medicine which was offered. He hadn't asked for it. Moreover, he was sceptical of the doctor's diagnosis. It was one thing for leading Bristol citizens to say that they would like Bristol to be the site of an investigation, and quite another to locate the work in a particular area which is self-consciously aware of its selection. To many citizens in the selected area, the very fact of selection was a threat to their already troubled state of mind. The articulate residents of Upfield were certainly sceptical about our choice: 'Why choose us?' 'Why not Wellesley or Great Barton?' 'Why must we endure the stigma of yet another group of outsiders?' 'Why not leave us alone?' All these questions were asked by different people at different times. The Director had not foreseen the resistance that would be encountered, which was heightened perhaps because of his previous association with criminological research. Nor had such difficulties as these been foreseen at the Nottingham Conference of experts arranged by the Home Office[1] to discuss plans for action research in delinquency areas, or at the Clevedon conference, which led to the undertaking of the Project.

Through the Lord Mayor, acting on behalf of a representative committee, Bristol officially had invited the Project. But how far do official invitations commit local Bristol citizens? No one at Upfield had given any such invitation.

The analogy mentioned between action research in a housing estate and the doctor-patient relationship is relevant only for certain broad similarities of method. The patient has a problem and seeks the help of a doctor, who makes a diagnosis and prescribes

---

[1] See the *Report (Sixth) on the Work of the Children's Department* (1951).

treatment. Success of the treatment depends in large measure on the collaboration of the patient. It is less relevant, however, when we reformulate the problem in terms of an area. Our problem is not that of a single patient.

The definition of a problem varies according to the person by whom it is stated. In the case of stresses and strains in the form of delinquency and the other indices selected for the initial survey, we encountered a variety of attitudes – denial by some, hostility by others, and apathy by others. It was clear that a direct approach was not feasible. There were several reasons for this. The action-research team has to win the trust and confidence of the community – it cannot assume that it will have it. Delinquency is not a popular problem with which to deal. Only if the action-research team can act like the refuse collector and remove the problem from the neighbourhood is its help welcome.

But stresses and strains of this kind do not constitute a problem which can be dealt with by removal. They are the results of a complex situation which concerns both the delinquents and their non-delinquent neighbours. Our first approach, therefore, was to the estate *as a whole* and towards gaining an understanding of its needs. By first strengthening the *growing points* we believed that we might in turn deal more effectively with the stresses and strains in the Upfield estate where our main resources were to be deployed.

The activity of the Project during the early period of Stage II is to be seen with this particular object in view, of strengthening the growing points. There were, for example, the discussions leading to the Adventure Playground, the attachment of the group worker to the Wood Grove Club, the production of a local newspaper, the *Upfield Echo*, and the planning and building of the Meeting Rooms. In the building of the Meeting Rooms the Project's main function was that of enabler or facilitator. The Director, for instance, acted as go-between between the architect and the local committee.

The simplest and most easily understable form of help was often considered to be the giving of money. Several 'leaders' of the

Upfield estate, though puzzled about our other functions, saw this as an obvious means of gaining help for a community enterprise of one kind or another. From the point of view of the Project, however, such financial help as we were able to give was as a means to an end. The end was the hope that ultimately the Project team would leave behind it a community in some measure better equipped to deal with its stresses and strains. Financial help was in fact confined to the building and initial maintenance of the Meeting Rooms.

But stresses and strains are essentially intangible. Their alleviation does not depend merely on bricks and mortar, or on money. Insight and understanding are needed. The Project team's role as enabler was clearly only one aspect of its work, and deeper insight was required. It was the demand for deeper insight which prompted us to press for the addition of a psychiatric social worker and the advice of a psychiatrist. This demand arose both from our experience with the Families Research, which the sociologist had begun in 1955, and from our awareness that more was required from our members than the role of enabler.

But the translation of the initial demand for psychiatric advice into a workable scheme was a long process – much longer certainly than the Director had foreseen. The main features are relevant to the argument at this point. The specific proposal agreed on by the Project Committee was the appointment of a psychiatric social worker to the team with the aim of working in the Upfield Clinic. Her help would thus be available to those mothers on the estate who were experiencing strain and stress in bringing up a young family. Long negotiations for a plan of this kind proved unsuccessful. They illustrate clearly the resistance on the part of the city to the introduction of this kind of help through a team of 'outsiders'. In the end we decided to use such a worker predominantly for the purpose of research in collaboration with the University Department of Child Health.

Thus Miss Cassidy's appointment as psychiatric social worker in the Project team was for the primary object of working with the sociologist in the Families Research. But her experience in a psychiatric unit as a member of a medical team working together in the rehabilitation of men and women with long-standing difficulties proved invaluable to us as we found ourselves looking afresh at the problem of stress and strain.

This process of rethinking was a gradual one and there is no clear dividing line. The development of Mrs. Andes's work with groups, but above all the commencement of her work with the Espressos as an independent group outside the Wood Grove Girls Club, brought before the Project Committee and the Upfield Community Council the contrast between the Project's earlier method of strengthening the growing points and the threatening nature of group work with disorganized adolescents. Experience with the Espressos faced all of us, both laymen and professionals, with the sternest challenge. We were compelled to look at our own attitudes towards perhaps one of the most stressful groups in the community.

In this context it was natural that strong differences of opinion in the use of authority emerged both in the Committee and in the team. The process of working through these differences was slow and time-consuming and the Executive Committee enjoyed the hospitality of one of its members in a one-day conference devoted to some of the issues raised by the turbulent non-conformity of the Espressos. It was no accident, therefore, that one of the main themes of this conference was freedom and authority.

We had returned to the initial problem of 'stresses and strains in a developing community'. The policy of strengthening the growing points and of encouraging local pride and initiative did not in itself provide a solution for the symptoms of stress and strain which were complex and deep-seated in the causes which gave rise to them. But it did something towards fostering local confidence.

Perhaps a simple analogy may serve to clarify this last point. We might see the initial problem of juvenile delinquency and the symptoms of stress and strain examined by the Director in Stage I of the Project as cracks in a ceiling. The Committee decides to call in the builders (Project team). The manager (Director) arrives and does a preliminary survey of the room and the workmen arrive on the job. At this point they discover that the occupants of neighbouring buildings are anxious that the cracks be covered over without too much dirt and noise, and that the owner of the building sees little unusual in a few cracks of that kind (Upfield disliked the publicity that focus on delinquency would bring with it). The surveyor (sociologist), introduced by the foreman to make a further examination of the building, points out that the cause of the cracks is in the total structure of the building itself. Rather reluctantly he agrees that an appropriate strut in the right place (Meeting Rooms) will certainly help. His colleague (the psychiatric social worker) sees the trouble not so much in the structure of the building as in the feelings and attitudes of the neighbourhood towards the cracks. Upfield's leaders feel worried by the news the surveyor gives them and are critical of his survey and of the workmen. But some at least feel responsible for calling in the builders and agree to help in the work. By helping in the work they come to understand not only the whole fabric of the building but some of the changes in the structure that are likely to help.

As Mack pointed out in his report, there can be no precise point of termination in action research of this kind. From the purely academic point of view, the problem-centred approach has many weaknesses, not the least of which are the theoretical difficulties created by a continual reformulation of the problem and the involvement of the social scientist in policy decisions. On the other hand, as a method of maintaining the collaboration between layman and professional which we take to be essential it is of particular value.

THE PROCESS OF FACILITATING CHANGE

Implicit in the argument of the preceding paragraphs is the continual interplay of diagnosis and action. This means that in the course of the Project our diagnosis changed as new elements in the situation emerged, or, put in another way, as the problem was reformulated. Action and research took place step by step. We may

29

contrast this method with the alternative method in which there are three distinct stages – diagnosis, action, and evaluation.[1]

Two major questions arise from a description of action research as 'a process of facilitating social change': In what sense can we say that the aim of the Project is to attempt to bring about change? How can we know what change has taken place because of the intervention of the Project? These are two extremely complex questions and we shall try to answer them. But first we must make two general points:

(a) The areas in which we worked are certainly not self-contained communities, but are related to the rest of the city surrounding them in innumerable ways. Indeed it is doubtful whether one should apply to them the label of 'community', which generally implies a measure of *common* activity and the possession of *common* standards, which the three areas do not possess. They are closely related, also, not merely to the city of Bristol but to English society in general.

The inhabitants of Upfield, Boltwood, or Mount View, for example, do not work in the areas where they live. Their work takes them all over the city. For their leisure, also, they frequently visit friends and relatives living outside the boundaries of their neighbourhood; they go to cinemas and shops in the centre of Bristol; they read Bristol and national newspapers, watch the BBC and commercial television, and listen to regional and national programmes on their wireless. Purely local activities form only a small part of their daily life.

Their leaders, too, the priest, the councillor, the Member of Parliament, and the doctor, are all closely dependent on national and city policy and its interpretation by national and municipal

---

[1] The latter method was proposed in the 'Elephant' project in New York dealing with the serious problem of drug addiction in certain areas. In the 'Elephant' project the initial diagnostic stage was the analysis and study of those areas with a high rate of addiction. The second action stage was the concentration of the resources of the project in certain areas and the selection of 'control' areas where these services were not employed. The third and final stage was that of evaluation in which an attempt was made to evaluate the effect of the project's action.

groups and associations of various kinds. The views of the neighbourhood constitute only one factor in the decisions which the
local leaders take, and they often may face conflicting opinions
according to the group with which they are working. The head
teacher, for example, in working out the disciplinary policy of his
school may encounter different attitudes to discipline on the part
of parents, the school managers, the officers of the Local Education Authority, Her Majesty's Inspectors, and the National Union
of Teachers. All of these may have an influence on any particular
decisions which he takes.

It is to this kind of situation we refer when we speak of an open
society. One of the main tasks facing an action-research project
in a community setting is that of deciding to which problems
social action is appropriate at the level of the neighbourhood, and
to which at a higher level.

Thus, action research in an open society presents problems
which are entirely different from those of the closed community
of the factory, for example, or the boarding school, or a prison
or mental hospital. The success of action research depends on
establishing relationships of confidence – in respect of both inquiry
and action – at a variety of levels in a society where few attitudes
and actions are determined either entirely by local considerations
or by general non-local factors. The research team cannot set
clearly defined boundaries to its field of work in the way in which
boundaries exist in an institution. The activities of the team in
Bristol involved relationships not only with the residents and
leaders of Upfield and Boltwood but also with other leading
citizens whose public decisions affected the life of the estates in
different ways.

(b) The second general point is that our areas, too, are continually
changing in various ways. These changes, moreover, are in part
the consequence of internal, and in part of external, factors. The
composition of the two estates, for example, alters nearly every
week as new families arrive to replace the old families who have
left. As we suggest later, the result of the freedom of choice offered

to tenants or prospective tenants by the Corporation Housing Department is the process of 'natural selection' by which families sort themselves out in streets and neighbourhoods which they feel are most appropriate to their social status. Some streets and neighbourhoods then acquire a good reputation while others are considered to be low in public esteem.

This example from the field of housing illustrates the continual process of change going on in the areas quite irrespective of any action-research programme, and also the difficulty of evaluating what precisely are the effects of social action. It would be tempting to try to relate changes in the annual rate of juvenile delinquency on the estate to the presence or absence of such social measures as the creation of an adventure playground. But such an argument could be misleading if it failed to take account also of those natural processes of change which are continually taking place. There are forces at work in the city as a whole which can certainly militate against social action directed primarily at a particular housing estate. To quote from the vicar of an estate in another part of Bristol:

> What makes my job as vicar of this parish so hard is the constant movement of the leaders of my church – Sunday School teachers, members of the parochial church council, etc. – away from this estate to other places which have higher status and where they feel their children will make better friends. So I am faced all the time with the job of helping new people to be leaders in the parish.

One might say that in this kind of estate the vicar was in fact contributing to the movement of parishioners to other higher-status parts of the city. So also with action research. Its effect in our open and dynamic society, far from helping to make Upfield 'better' in terms of the social composition of its residents may, on the contrary, be to help in perpetuating an existing state of affairs. The 'better' families move out but in their place 'worse' families move in.

These two points, that (a) our areas are only a part of a much larger society and closely dependent on it, and (b) changes are continually taking place both inside and outside their boundaries, are neither of them arguments against action research as a process of facilitating social change. They do, however, emphasize the complexity of the problem. Certain factors in social change are rapid and drastic – the physical up-rooting and setting-down of people, the economic redeployment of resources (both income and expenditure), or the arrival of television – while other changes are slow and complicated – the capacity of the human mind to perceive changes of role and attitude and to adapt accordingly.

In what sense, then, can we say that the object of the Project is to bring about change?

One of our tasks was to isolate those situations where change is both desirable and feasible. But who is to be involved and in what way? The very fact that action research is problem-centred, and that the problem was initially defined in the way it was, provides some answer. First and foremost, change will be involved in dealing with the fundamental problem of 'stresses and strains in a developing community'. These stresses and strains were at first defined as 'delinquency and other disturbances'. Nearly everyone in the Project recognized that change was demanded from the families and individuals covered by this initial definition. The delinquents needed changing because their disturbing behaviour was a nuisance to society, and one which the more respectable members were unwilling to tolerate.

Here, then, was something on which everyone concerned with the Project in the early days was agreed. Of the precise methods to be employed, however, little was said at that stage by the leading citizens of Bristol who formed the Main and Executive Committees. They were anxious that the Director should be free to work out a plan after he had had the opportunity of making his own diagnosis.

Each member of the Committee, nevertheless, had his own expectations of what the Project might achieve. There were those who approached the Project from the point of view that the

33

absence of social and public amenities so undermines the confidence of the more responsible citizens that they do not get a
chance to set a high standard for life in the neighbourhood. This
group tended to assess the value of the Project almost entirely by
its success or failure in achieving these social amenities at Upfield.

Second, there were those, not sharply distinct from the first
group, who accepted the need for a planned society in the interests
of equality of opportunity and the good life, but discovered that
this means the necessity for taking responsibility for what goes
wrong rather than placing responsibility on the villain of the
moment. For them the purpose of the Project was a means of
finding out more about the stresses and strains and doing something about them.

Third, there were people, such as magistrates, especially those
working in juvenile courts, who looked for something which
would remove from them the burden of insoluble cases and
prevent these cases from arising.

Fourth, there were those, such as the Chairman, who were
aware of the pace of change and the complexity of society and had
become uneasy about their capacity as citizens to cope with the
consequences of this change. Believing in individuality rather than
adjustment as the heart of a healthy society, they were troubled by
the stresses and strains of a neighbourhood where there was neither
adjustment nor individuality of a constructive kind.

Some people at Upfield, moreover, had other ideas primarily
focused on a general dislike of being stigmatized by the presence
of a project concerned with certain kinds of stress and strain. But
Upfield, nevertheless, *was* prepared to accept certain kinds of
change, primarily, as we said earlier, in terms of its growing
points – an Adventure Playground, the Meeting Rooms, the
Goslings Club, and the help of a group worker in the Wood
Grove Girls Club.

Thus, the statement that the function of an action-research
project is to bring about change raises the difficult question of
what is meant by change: Who, for example, is to do the changing?
Who is to decide what the nature and direction of the change

ought to be? What are the methods by which change is to be brought about?

The experience of the Project certainly suggests that both team and Committee were confused in the initial views which they held on these questions. In posing them, moreover, we do so with hindsight rather than foresight, for it was only in Stage III that the questions were clarified and the answers discussed.

There appear to us to be *three senses* in which we may speak of change in an action-research project:

CHANGE IN THE FIRST SENSE

The first kind of change is comparatively simple – change of a predominantly straightforward material kind – money, buildings, and helpers. The goals are set mainly by the people concerned themselves and are not necessarily the goals of the action-research team. They are limited goals and are the means to an end rather than ends in themselves. The means used in their achievement are rational and obvious help. In attempting to bring them about, the team acts primarily as an enabler or facilitator.

CHANGE IN THE SECOND SENSE

In the second sense of change the primary goal is an educative one. The method is that of involvement. The idea of 'education through involvement' is sometimes expressed in the well-known idea of 'learning through doing'. Unlike change in the first sense the goal is non-material and long-range. It is set by the action-research team rather than by the community with which the team works. The means used are rational. A basic assumption is the mutual interaction of team and community: each learns by being concerned together in the solution of a problem (we wrote earlier of action research as a problem-solving process), and change through common involvement is certainly not the prerogative of one party alone.

Change in the second sense takes place most effectively within an appropriate social structure. A formal or rigid social setting seriously diminishes the possibility of change in this sense. An important point of contrast between change in the first and in the second sense is that, whereas the test of success in the first sense is the achievement of the goal, in the second sense success is to be defined in greater awareness of the *process* by which the goal is attained.

CHANGE IN THE THIRD SENSE

The third sense of change is the most complex of the three. It depends on a body of theory, which we shall discuss later in this chapter when we consider the three senses of change at greater length. Like change in the second sense it is non-material and the goal is long-range. But whereas change in the second sense was predominantly rational, focused primarily on ideas, change in the third sense contains an important irrational element and is focused primarily on feelings. Our feelings towards people are rooted in the unconscious mind, which works irrationally.

Change in the third sense is concerned with relationships and learning about relationships, whereas change in the second sense is concerned mainly with learning about ideas. The achievement of goals, unlike change in the first sense, is of minor importance. The goals – if indeed this term is appropriate in this context – are those of the action-research team, in contrast to change in the first sense where the goals are those of the people themselves.

Finally, the structure through which change in the third sense is effected – even more than in the second sense where the rational element involved is greater – is of the greatest importance. For change to take place at the level of feelings and relationships, the structure of the group needs to be such that feelings can be freely and openly expressed. A formal structure inhibits the free expression of feelings and does not allow for the 'working through' of resistance to new ways of behaviour.[1]

---

[1] This was the reason for the movement towards the very free group structure of the teachers' and social workers' groups in their final phases (see Chapters 7 and 8).

The experience of the Project sheds some light on these three senses of change. In attempting to bring about change in the first sense, the Project team acted mainly in the role of enabler. In this role the members recognized that the involvement of the community was their primary task. In the words of Sir Philip Morris at the Clevedon conference: 'Any such project will have to be founded on self-help: it will go deliberately against the present decline in voluntary effort in social affairs.'

The purpose of enabling is a simple one. It is to help the individual, or group, or society, to achieve its goals. The enabler remains in the background and drops out when the particular activity which he has helped to facilitate has got under way. But although the purpose is simple to state, it may be difficult to achieve. The goal in question may sometimes be neither obvious nor generally agreed upon. The enabler must possess the skill and the knowledge to help people, in Furnivall's phrase, to 'want what they need', and he must be able to stimulate the desire for change. He requires judgement in approaching the most appropriate individuals or groups – appropriate, that is to say, for the particular goal to be achieved. This is the first stage of the enabling process.

Later on when a start has been made, the enabler can help in several ways: he may act as a go-between, easing the process by which one group gets into touch with another; he may help by encouraging; he may make clear the alternative methods available or the potential obstacles to a course of action; he may help if necessary by getting down to the job in hand himself. On several occasions, for example, members of the Project team got down to work with pick and shovel at Upfield. The enabler must be clear, however, that by using his own efforts he is not lessening the incentive of others to use theirs. In the final stage he should be ready to withdraw at the right moment.

One straightforward example from the history of the Project team's role as enabler is the building of the Meeting Rooms. Various members of the Committee and the team gave assistance, but they did not at any stage attempt to take away responsibility from the Upfield committee which had undertaken the job. They were predominantly enablers, sometimes acting as go-betweens and as helpers in several different and often quite simple ways. They withdrew when the building had been finished and was put into use.

The first sense of change of which we speak, therefore, is of a quite straightforward kind. The method rests on the assumption that men are essentially rational beings who can be helped to see what is considered to be in their best interest and who will readily accept assistance in achieving it. We need not scrutinize too closely the reasons of the individual, group, or society, for desiring change. Prestige, comfort, or economic improvement are all possible motives. An action-research project intending to bring about change will have regard for all these.

Change in the first sense is assumed to be essentially a rational process, and the various ways of achieving it are based on this assumption. The Project was certainly seen primarily in this way by the Executive and Main Committees and their early expectations were of a Project which would work on this basis. The building of the Meeting Rooms and the editing and production of the *Upfield Echo* are two examples of this simple process of change.

The basic assumption of 'education through involvement' is the mutual interaction between layman and professional. We learn through being involved together in the solution of a problem to which each has a contribution to make. This is certainly no new discovery, but it is fundamental to our idea of action research. It affects layman and professional alike, and change through common involvement is certainly not the prerogative of one party alone. To see the function of the Project in terms of change on the part of the community only would be both naïve and presumptuous.

But if change in this second sense is to be effective, we need not only willingness to change on the part of those involved, but also an appropriate social structure, that is, we need conditions in which change can take place most effectively. *Rigid conditions make change an impossibility*. In a society where standards of behaviour are strictly enforced and where everyone knows precisely what is expected of him, the problem of changing behaviour is more difficult than in a society where there are no generally understood patterns of conduct and no clearly defined methods of gaining conformity from the deviant.

The main source of contact between the community and the Project team was the group. These groups took several forms, ranging from the formally constituted committee to the informal group of friends or acquaintances. At one end there was the Project Committee, at the other the adolescent Espressos. There are certain principles which help us not only to generalize about the conditions and methods of change, but to relate two such diverse groups to one another.

The Project Committee was based very largely on representation. The leading citizens of Bristol of whom the Committee was composed played an important role in widely varying sectors of the public life of the city – religious, political, academic, administrative, and social. Each member had close ties with his or her own group and association and had an important role to play. The Project Committee was yet another activity to add to a busy life. As representatives, some members were expected to report to their organizations, whether formally or informally, on the Project's work.

The consequences of this structure of the Committee were properly understood by the Director only in the later stages. A committee formed in this way faced certain handicaps when considered from the point of view of change. On the one hand, it placed an obligation on some members of the Project Committee to give some account of current events to the body which they represented. On the other hand, it was expected that they would represent the views of their own associations on the Committee.

To facilitate change we need the conditions under which change is feasible. The fact is that by setting up a representative committee we had certainly provided the conditions through which the wide diversity of interests characteristic of a large city could be represented, but we had seriously handicapped the possibility of

39

certain kinds of change, and particularly of change in the second and third senses. Reflecting on the early years of the Project at a meeting towards its conclusion, one member emphasized the pressure exerted on her by the members of her organization to tell them precisely what was happening on the Committee: 'It was embarrassing to be unable to give a report of definite plans when asked to do so.'

Membership of a representative committee carried with it other obstacles to change. Some members of the Committee felt it hard to identify themselves with the Project, because they did not see what it was trying to do. This was particularly true of the members of the party in power in the City Council. They were faced with a conflict of roles. They felt that, as the 'government', it was they who, first and last, carried responsibility for the welfare of Bristol's citizens. As 'action research', the Project was committed to investigating inadequacies and supplying answers. In those terms the Project was a busy-body rather than a help. It was especially hard for these representatives to avoid the role of watchdog on the Project. The basic assumption of 'education through involvement' requires the readiness of both laymen and professionals to commit themselves wholeheartedly to the common enterprise.

The role of the Executive Committee was described in the following terms:

> In action research, however, the problem and the method are different from the conventional method. The assumption is that the research team, the local community, and the Executive Committee are involved together in what is happening in the action research. We are learning together and our mutual interaction is itself part of the situation we are trying to understand. In consequence of this the way in which Committee decisions are taken and later revised in an action-research project differs from the method employed in conventional social research.

This description of the role of the Executive Committee was never openly disagreed with. At the same time, the view was held that the corporate responsibility of the Executive Committee for action initiated by the staff did not extend beyond the responsibility for the expenditure of money. The fact is that there was no adequate clarification of the Executive Committee's role in the early stages. Only through experience did we gain greater understanding of the roles of both Committee and team alike.

What, then, was the difference between the Project Committee and the committee of an ordinary association? The Main Committee was, in fact, little different from an ordinary committee and its main characteristic was that it was representative of different interests. The Executive Committee, on the other hand, was smaller in number, and its involvement in the work of the team was very much closer. It is to the Executive Committee that the statement of role, mentioned above, was applied. How far was the Executive seen as the *élite* of the Main Committee? It is difficult to answer this question, but the facts of attendance suggest that it may have been so.

The difference between the Project Executive Committee and a conventional committee lay not in a vagueness or diffuseness of responsibility for the action done, but rather in the role of the members. Responsibility for action, with the exception of financial expenditure, rested with the team. The role of the Committee differed from a conventional role in that it specifically included a learning role. The team also accepted the obligation to learn, for this after all is a basic assumption of action research. For the Committee, however, the initial motive for joining was that of management; the motive of learning was marginal to this purpose. Each Committee member in the course of his own occupation was concerned with a different aspect of the Project's work – for health, for housing, for youth work, for family welfare, for juvenile delinquency, and so on. Had the Committee taken an advisory rather than a management role, many of the difficulties which arose might not have arisen.

It was natural that individual members should be most closely involved in those aspects of the Project which were nearest to their own field of interest. Nevertheless, there gradually evolved in the Executive a common framework of understanding, which was the fruit of the sharing of both achievements and disappointments. Some of the most controversial issues contributed most, for it is in moments of disagreement that our values are most openly exposed. The Director felt that less was gained from discussions leading to administrative decisions than from the exploration of fundamental questions of principle. In his presentation of problems to the Committee he was more interested in achieving involvement and learning than in decision-making. The episode of the 'Fence' is a useful illustration of this point.

The Fence was a shopkeeper on one of the estates who carried out his ordinary business and at the same time received stolen property from local residents, advanced money on Family Allowance Books, and bought up household goods on which the hire-purchase instalments had not been paid. These two rather different functions were known to different types of customers.

The Director presented to the Committee at one of its meetings a paper on the Fence written by the field worker (Bill Miller). The Committee was irritated by this paper, because the members were uncertain what they were expected to do about it. The Chairman suggested that its importance lay in the fact that alongside the attitudes of people like teachers, councillors, and clergy went the attitudes of people such as the Fence who to many residents on the estate seemed to be performing a far more useful practical purpose in the business of daily living than those who are conventionally thought of as leaders.

After the presentation of the paper the Committee began to discuss the kind of action to be taken in this situation and whether knowledge of this kind should be withheld from the police. Unable to agree on any clear line of action, the Committee ended the meeting with feelings of rather irritated frustration.

The Chairman and the Director indicated that they had not presented the paper in anticipation that action would be taken but rather as an opportunity for learning and discussion on the variety of moral standards on the estate. But the Committee expressed its exasperation at what seemed to be a waste of the members' time.

Some felt that the Chairman and the Director were merely naïve in believing that a useful discussion could follow the presentation of a paper of this kind in the context of a committee meeting.

The question arises, therefore, whether it is reasonable to expect an executive committee, formally constituted in the initial stage for taking administrative decisions, to modify its role so that the emphasis shifts to learning and to the sharing of feelings about the issues. The most obvious conflict of role is between an interest in the achievement of a *goal*, on the one hand, and in the *process* lying behind the achievement, on the other. An action-research committee, by contrast with the conventional administrative committee, is concerned with *process* as well as *goal*-seeking, or, to say the same thing in simpler terms, with the method of achieving results as well as with the results themselves. The satisfaction of the members lies less in the attainment of the *goal* towards which they have worked than in the understanding of the *process* involved in its attainment. Their criteria of success, therefore, differ from the conventional criteria. The lessons of failure, moreover, may prove of greater value *in the long run* than those of success.

This dual role for an action-research committee is difficult to understand. There are good reasons why the professional should be interested in *process*: it is the very essence of his job. For the layman, the reasons are less obvious: his satisfaction comes from participation in easily demonstrable successes. The building of the Meeting Rooms in Upfield, for example, was felt by some members of the Committee to be clear and tangible evidence of the Project's work.

A conflict of this kind is inevitable in action research. Certainly it was not confined to the Committee, as is clearly seen from the discussion on the approach of the team (see following chapter). Preoccupation with *process*, moreover, has its own peculiar risks. It is tempting, for example, to rationalize failure in a particular action by pointing to the value of the lessons learned.

In the course of five years the Executive Committee was at least partially successful in developing an emotional climate and a structure whereby the fundamental purpose of 'education through involvement' could operate. Two one-day conferences in the homes of two Committee members provided an ideal background for the growth of common understanding.

The possibility of change, using the word in this second sense of non-material and rational, varied according to the nature and the structure of the group. The Executive Committee gradually worked out a structure which facilitated the possibility of change. It did not abandon entirely the formal committee meeting, but came to rely during the latter period, particularly after the formal conclusion of the Project, on a series of informal conferences when it enjoyed the hospitality of one of its members. The Main Committee, on the other hand, maintained a quite consistent structure throughout the five years. Involvement of the members in the Project's work was less close than that of the Executive and the meetings were less frequent.

The role of the Project team, however, differed at Upfield and at Boltwood. At Upfield it was initially that of enabler – through the Meeting Rooms, the *Echo*, the Adventure Playground. It did not attempt to effect change in the second sense. The team was cast by the Community Council in the role of enabler and never succeeded in moving beyond this. At Boltwood, on the other hand, the intervention of the Director and the sociologist was confined mainly to helping in the clarification of a particular problem and also to reporting back on their observations of the Community Council's method of working. They did not act as enablers at Boltwood. Had we had an effective measuring rod it would have been useful to have compared the change effected in the two estates by two very different methods. There were also differences in the two Councils themselves, not in the formal composition of their membership, for this was basically similar, but in the personality of the members and in the general level of morale.

Finally, there are the groups with which the Project team worked in the role of leader or group worker. These groups, which are dealt with in Parts II and III, were in the main created for the purpose of achieving change. They were not structured in a formal way, as were the Community Councils or the Project

Committee, with formally elected officers, using the normal methods of committee procedure based on a formal constitution.

Here also there is a relationship between the type of group, the method employed, and the possibility of change. The general trend in the case of groups with which Miss Cassidy and Mrs. Andes worked was to move from a more formal and controlled to a more permissive and unstructured climate. Part II describes the phases through which the teachers' group and the social workers' group passed. A similar contrast between the initial and later stages may be observed in the phases of Mrs. Andes's work, first at the Wood Grove Club and later on with the Espressos.

In each of the three types of group mentioned, that is, the Project Committees, the Community Councils, and the groups in which the Project team had the role of leader, some degree of change in the sense of learning by doing was a legitimate expectation. The experience of planning and managing the Adventure Playground, for example, helped the committee members to see more closely the problems connected with the supply of play material, the selection and availability of leaders, and the play habits of children. The Project Committee, through its discussions of the social needs of the estates both among the members and with the team, gained increased understanding of the consequences of estate life for the development of the family.

Involvement in a group concerned with the achievement of certain goals contains in itself useful opportunities for learning. Change in the second sense in which we use it is primarily of this kind, but we have argued that the greater the extent to which we can structure the committee so as to focus the members' attention also on the *nature of the process* by which certain goals are either achieved or unrealized, the greater is the possibility that the experiment will prove of value to the individual members or to the group in subsequent action. The reports, for example, which the sociologist gave to the Boltwood Joint Council were aimed at directing attention to the process lying behind its work.

Change in the third sense is well illustrated by some words of

45

The Project

Sir Philip Morris at the Clevedon conference: 'The basic problem is one of getting people into different relationships with each other.' Change in relationships and in understanding about relationships was certainly one of the objectives of the Project. To establish practical means of tackling stress and strain the Project certainly had the obligation to effect change in the first two senses, i.e. as an enabler in the fulfilment of overt needs, and in helping to provide opportunities through groups whereby the lessons of working towards certain goals may be experienced and discussed. We have already argued that for the second type of change a less rigid structure than that provided by the formal committee procedure may render this task easier.

The idea of change in the third sense is based on a considerable body of theory. We start from the assumption that exhortations to improved relationships or threats of the consequences of poor relationships are of only partial value. The fundamental need is for improved understanding of the forces at work in any given situation, and the purpose of action research is to facilitate the growth of this understanding. The members of the professional team engaged in the action research do not denigrate the value of general pleas for greater charity – of the need for greater tolerance, for example, between respectable adults and adolescent hooligans or between white and coloured in areas where there has been fighting and abuse and disorder – nor do they deny the necessity of firm police action or strong penal action in particular circumstances. But their training and experience lead them to believe that greater understanding, both of people and of the society in which people live, is an essential basis for change.

The social scientist is modest in his expectations of change. In this respect, perhaps, he differs from the social reformer, whose hopes are set on the achievement of social reform. Past experience has taught the social scientist to be cautious in utilizing his knowledge of the social sciences to bring about change in the social field. Above all, we should expect this to be true of attempts to deal with the problem of stress and strain. We must be content, therefore, with modest objectives and limited achievement.

46

The framework of our thinking concerns persons and the social situations in which they are involved. Such a statement is in fact less of a platitude than it seems at first sight. Frequently we are tempted, when looking at a particular situation involving stress and strain, to say that it is the fault of one or the other members involved. We identify ourselves, for example, with the wife of an alcoholic husband or with the irate residents of a street or meeting place disturbed by the behaviour of unruly Teddy boys. We advocate stern measures, the need for more discipline, the imposition of stricter penalties. We deplore the laxity of standards and the looseness of morality of the gang. We advise a change of heart on the part of the non-conformist minority and we plead for the breaking up of the gang and the removal of the members from our neighbourhood.

This may be called a common-sense approach to stress and strain. What we *know*, however, about personality and about society through medical and social science makes us less certain that this approach is right. The individual members of the gang have a history reaching back through their childhood. Their gang, one of many different kinds of human groups, has a purpose. Of the many important factors in the history of individuals, their relationships with parents and family in their early years are now known to be of outstanding importance, and to change established ways of behaving requires both patience and skill. The purpose of the gang, too, on closer inspection is not simply to be destructive and to terrorize; it fulfils both a social and an emotional need on the part of its members.

With this example we may look more closely at the framework within which change can be attempted. Sociologists lay emphasis on the distinction between the manifest and latent functions of an organization. That is, they try to distinguish between the generally stated and accepted purposes of the organization and those purposes which are not made explicit in either a written or an unwritten form. Some of these latent purposes may be unknown to the members although they are in fact of great significance to them. In some cases the members of the organization would think

47

them too trivial to mention, while in other cases they might not recognize or might deny their existence. The latent purpose may be both social and emotional in character.

This distinction between manifest and latent purposes may be illustrated through the antisocial adolescent gang and also through some of the more formal organizations, of which a statement of purpose is included in a written constitution. For the neighbourhood the gang is frequently a nuisance. To break it up or remove its members is a commonly adopted method. Members may be sent by a court to approved school or Borstal, or forbidden to associate with one another. The gang members themselves may express their purpose in terms which show their own awareness of the nuisance value which they possess. 'No club can hold us – we're too tough for them' was the proud boast of the gang which subsequently formed the nucleus of the Barge Boys Club in Wapping (Turner, 1953).

The latent purpose, however, is less easily recognizable. To belong to a gang has a significance for its members far deeper than the words or symbols through which membership is expressed. 'Gangs represent the spontaneous efforts of boys to create a society for themselves where none adequate to their needs exists,' wrote Thrasher (1937) in his famous study. Merely to eliminate the gang is too simple an answer to the problem. Such a policy, moreover, fails to take account of the emotional security which the gang provides for its members in a confused and often hostile environment.[1]

Perhaps we can now look a little more closely at the idea of change in the *third* sense in relation to the aims and purposes of the Bristol Social Project. It was change in the *first* and *second* senses, but above all in the first, to which the expectations of the majority of the lay committee were directed when the idea of a

---

[1] Two quotations from Merton (1949) are appropriate here: 'To seek social change, without due recognition of the manifest and latent functions performed by the social organization undergoing change, is to indulge in social ritual rather than social engineering.' 'Any attempt to eliminate an existing social structure without providing an adequate alternative structure for fulfilling the functions previously fulfilled by the abolished organization is doomed to failure.'

project was first discussed. Some lay members, including those most closely involved in it, would emphasize the Project's achievement in the first sense, taking as an example the construction of the Meeting Rooms and the growth of social activity which resulted from it. Others would emphasize the Project as an educational institution, as an experiment in how knowledge in the social sciences may be communicated most effectively between professional and layman. They would see one of the chief ways of achieving this end, as we said earlier, as 'learning through involvement'.

In thinking of change in the *third* sense, we need to return continually to the original terms of reference in which emphasis was placed on 'practical means of tackling stresses and strains'. How can Upfield be helped to deal with its stresses and strains? was a question asked at the Clevedon conference, where Sir Philip Morris observed that certain institutions seemed to possess the means whereby they could deal with stresses and strains from among their own resources. Stress and strain are a function *both* of individual personality *and* of the situation, and change in this third sense must take account of each.[1] Delinquency, for example, is a symptom of a weakness in the personality of the individual. But it is also related to the social structure of the society in which the individual lives. The insight of both psychiatrist and sociologist is contributing increasingly to our understanding of stress and strain, of which delinquency is used here merely as one among other symptoms.

Stresses and strains arise in individuals not only as the result of past experience, particularly in the family during early childhood, which constitutes the very framework for personality development, but also as the consequence of present roles and the relationships arising out of them. For example, conflict between individuals and groups may be productive of stress and strain for

[1] cf. Merton (1949, p. 53): 'The concept of dysfunction which implies the concept of strain, stress and tension on the structural level, provides an analytic approach to the study of dynamics and change. How are observed dysfunctions contained within a given structure, so that they do not produce instability? Does the accumulation of stresses and strains produce pressure for change in such directions as are likely to lead to their reduction?'

49

those concerned. These conflicts may arise either through genuine sources of disagreement or through irrational factors.[1]

We need, therefore, certain concepts through which social change in the third sense may be understood. For this, the concepts of structure, role, relationship, and culture are useful (cf. Curle, 1947). At the risk of simplification we may define structure as the framework of a society through which individual needs may be satisfied. This framework may take several forms, economic, political, familial, and so on. Within this structure there is a variety of positions occupied by the members of the society. Associated with these positions are roles, by which we mean the behaviour expected of individuals in various positions. Each individual in a society occupies a multiplicity of roles, the conflicting demands of which may in some cases cause strain and stress to the individual. A common source of conflict, for example, in the family may be the conflicting demands of the roles of father and workman. Each role may make greater demands on the individual holding it than he is able to fulfil.

It is within this framework that the individual makes social relationships with other individuals. The satisfaction which he derives from these relationships depends not only on his own personality but also on the behaviour expected of the role partners. The resources which the individual has at his disposal in making relationships within this framework include not only personality factors but also the culture of his society.[2] We speak also of the culture of particular institutions of which the individual may be a member – the culture of a factory or of a school or university. By this we mean the pattern of socially determined behaviour associated with the roles within the institutions.

That culture is neither homogeneous nor universally accepted in a society is perhaps most aptly illustrated by what is often called

---

[1] cf. Coser (1956) who distinguishes between what he calls the realistic and non-realistic sources of conflict. Coser suggests that action research may be helpful in differentiating the sources of realistic conflict from the emotional energies vested in it, but can only hope to clear the ground for better insights into the grounds for contention.

[2] 'Culture may be said to work by providing the individual with a series of techniques through which he may regulate and enrich his social relationships' (Curle, 1947, p. 47).

the sub-culture of a slum or disorganized area. For there the culture of the area is in many respects at variance with the culture of a wider society.

But culture, unlike the social structure, is not something purely external to the individual. The degree of success that all of us have in making social relationships and in learning about the roles which we take up is closely related to the extent to which we have been able to internalize our culture. 'The individual has his society within him', in Meyer Fortes's words.

The process of socialization,[1] particularly through the family during early childhood, involves the internalization of culture and the learning of social roles. Our earliest attempts at role learning are made in the context of our relationships with significant people, above all with parents. But socialization, although it begins at this point (for it is the family which is the most powerful agent of socialization), does not stop here. It may continue in a lesser degree throughout our lives. The task of the secondary modern school, for example, in facilitating a process of socialization among children from underprivileged families where standards are very different from those expected by our society, and in helping them to internalize the values of a wider culture, is enormous. The work of the Teachers Group (Chapter 7) in its final phase was very largely concerned with helping a group of teachers to work through some of the tensions involved in attempting to fulfil this task.

With the use of a framework of this kind we can see the complexity of change involving not only people as they take up roles and make relationships with one another in the context of those roles, but also the structure itself. Each of us tends to work out a *modus vivendi* in relation to the situation in which we live and to rationalize those aspects of our behaviour which do not fit in with the general assumptions on which we base our ways of behaving.

Perhaps we can illustrate this from an association in one of our areas. The association was started several years before the events

---

[1] Merton, Reader & Kendall (1957, p. 290): 'In psychological and sociological usage, socialization refers to ways in which *individuals* are shaped by their culture.'

that we describe. In the early stages the role of the elected officers was that of fighting for better social amenities for the residents in the area – for roads, for bus services, for telephone call-boxes, and so on. Such a role demanded leadership of a particular kind. It appealed to characters with a need to express their fighting qualities through public activity. Internal stresses and strains within the association were projected onto the common enemy – the city officials of various kinds. The social structure of the area made such a role appropriate at a particular stage of development. The relationships between the elected officers were in the context of this particular role.

But in the course of time as the estate developed, many of the social amenities for which the association had fought were gained and the role of the officers changed. The association's building, which the members themselves had erected through their own labour, was completed and their early objectives were achieved. The officers' role changed accordingly. Whereas their former role required aggressive personalities, their new role, with many of the initial obstacles overcome, demanded personalities of a rather different kind – personalities which can work together harmoniously on a task where success is not easily seen and demands are exacting. There were no scapegoats readily available on whom their aggression could be projected. Internal stresses and strains now began to appear. There was rivalry between the officers: each felt that his own labour had not received due recognition.

And so there grew up what the Project team called a 'martyrdom complex', which on occasion seems to characterize that tiny group of officers and committee members who continue in office year after year, complaining that everyone leaves them all the work to do and no replacements for their services are available. They enjoy their martyrdom (just as some invalids 'enjoy' ill health), but the suggestion that this is in fact a vested interest which they have an inner and compelling need to maintain is naturally resisted. Dissensions appear among the officers, there are frequent threats of resignation, and sometimes the threats become a reality. But quarrels are patched up and the officers are re-elected.

A further illustration comes from the Espressos and from the neighbourhood's attitude towards them. Assumptions by such groups as the Espressos about their role in society enable them to act in the way they do with the least possible pain to themselves. They see the world as an unfriendly and hostile place in which everyone will 'do you down' if he can. Figures in authority are to be fought, not respected (an assumption based on their own personal experience of the way authority has always been exercised in their own families). Appointments and promises have no binding claim. Life is something which you just take as it comes, the good luck of the pools and the ill fortune of accidents and death. Human feelings are not involved in either case. Work is an unfortunate necessity which if properly organized can secure good money for little effort. Neither the past nor the future has real meaning. Present happiness alone is important.

It is around such values as these that the Espressos in our society take up their roles. Past mistakes of socialization in the family and present experiences of how people behave towards them both contribute to their role expectations. The neighbourhood for its part has different values and different expectations and sees its own role in relation to the Espressos in a different light. It sees Espressos as part of the Teddy-boy menace. They are thugs who beat up women, with no respect for people or property. A thrashing would do them good. They should be removed from *our* neighbourhood which they disturb and disgrace. Their parents are also to blame for them and should be punished. The juvenile courts are not strict enough and ought to deal with them severely. We must express our disapproval of their behaviour in forthright and strong terms. They are only fit for the roughest jobs. We can't run the risk of disorganizing our youth clubs with their behaviour.

The task facing an action-research project in helping to change a problem of this kind is, first, as an interpreter of the Espressos to the neighbourhood and vice versa, and next to attempt a more realistic understanding of the expectations which each has of the other's role.

The above two examples of attitudes, drawn from rather

53

different sections of the social life of our areas, illustrate not only the close connection between role and personality in the context of a particular social structure, but also the implications for change which follow from it.[1] To effect change in the stresses and strains of an area it is necessary to look both at the social structure of the area, the roles which people take within that structure, their culture and their values, and at the personalities of the individuals themselves.

To clarify a situation with the individuals and groups concerned is an important first step in effecting change, *but it does not automatically produce it*. The reasons for this lie in the resistance which all of us have to changing an established pattern of behaviour. The *modus vivendi* which we have worked out for ourselves is generally adapted to meet our own emotional needs.

The important problem is the feelings and attitudes of individuals as they take up their roles and modify them to suit their own internal needs. Intellectual understanding of the external demands of the social structure is certainly an important element in the more effective performance of the task. But even more important than intellectual understanding is the working-through of the feelings associated with the roles. Inaccurate perception of a role is a matter not only of our intellect, but also of our feelings and emotions. It is for this reason that we place strong emphasis, in the analysis of group work method, on the significance of a structure where the group can learn about its own feelings – through what we have called learning through the here-and-now situation.

Resistance to change is a characteristic of both individuals and groups. All of us have vested interests in an existing situation, whether economic or social or emotional. Some vested interests may be easily recognized and openly expressed, such as the resistance of property owners to the proposals of town planners for changes in land use, whereas others – predominantly social and

[1] cf. Jaques (1951, Ch. 9): 'In planning changes of any type it is necessary to pay attention to the requisite alterations in social structure, the likely shifts in culture, and the personal readjustments of the individuals concerned.'

emotional – are more subtle and disguised, such as the retention of positions of high status and prestige for the power which they give to the occupier. The reasons for resistance are both simple and complex. Some are amenable to rational discussion and argument, while others demand deeper understanding.

We wrote earlier of the 'martyrdom complex' of the elected officers in a voluntary association. On the face of it, there seem to be no obvious reasons why the officers should continue in office year after year, complaining continually of the apathy of members and of all the work which is left to them. They derive no economic advantage; they are frequently criticized. What makes them continue? To answer this question we need to know more about the stresses and strains to which they are subject, particularly in the family, but also in their work. We may then see that their apparently curious behaviour is based on important reasons of which they themselves are in fact unconscious. For some, community life is a retreat from responsibilities in the home or from stresses and strains which are felt to be unbearable. For others it may help to compensate for lack of prestige at work.

In his study of the Boltwood Joint Council (to appear in Volume 2) the sociologist illustrates some of the ways in which the group, when faced with a multiplicity of roles, evolves a method of working to suit its own particular needs. A community council has no single clearly defined task. It cannot easily evaluate its success or failure in terms of quite specific criteria. Its aims are phrased in vague and very general language.[1] It can use the confusion over its roles to switch from those ends which are difficult to perform to those which are easier. It has, as it were, a vested interest in the vagueness and generality of its statement of aims. By this means it can avoid a too close scrutiny of its working. To promote 'community' is more respectable than to act as a pressure group.

[1] The aims of the Boltwood Joint Council are stated in the following terms: '(a) To promote the well-being of the Community resident in the area ... by means of encouraging and providing facilities for educational, social and moral development, and any other charitable objects for the benefit of members; (b) To provide an organized means of approach to the Bristol City Council and any other authority on all matters affecting the improvement of the Estate and amenities of the dwellings.'

GROUP WORK IN THE LIGHT OF SOCIAL CHANGE

It is no accident that right from the start of the Project the method of group work was chosen as the main method through which the possibility of change could be explored. We use the word 'explore' quite deliberately, because, for the team at least, the various ways in which group work may be useful have become clearer during the past five years. In Parts II and III we describe some of the differences in approach to working with groups and the results of our own experiences and learning. What deserves emphasis here in a discussion on the idea of change through action research is the relevance of this particular method to the 'problem' of stresses and strains in a developing community as it emerged in the course of the Project.

The method is appropriate for three reasons, of which perhaps only the first was clearly understood in the initial stage of the Project. The first reason was the need to develop activities in the area in which the members themselves would take responsibility. A characteristic feature of the 'high delinquency' area, and particularly of the estate, has always been a low degree of interest in organized social activities, whether club, community centre, evening institute, or church. Leadership for these activities tends to be imported from outside. Ways of developing *local* responsibility had been a theme of the Clevedon conference. The group work method was seen as particularly important for this purpose.

Second, in growing urban areas, many of the traditional methods of social control and of resolving stresses and strains which arise in areas with a wide diversity of standards and values are absent. We can no longer assume in the highly industrialized society of the Western world that institutions will spontaneously emerge, without conscious deliberation and planning, through which the stresses and strains involved in modern urban living may be alleviated. Throughout this report we have emphasized that in the housing estate each person is in a social situation peculiar to himself alone, to a quite unparalleled extent. There is no general pattern of response to outside influences.

In the isolated and self-contained communities of the past it might have been possible to trace many expressions of behaviour to a common cause – traditional methods of bringing up children, cultural values which deviated from those of respectable society, the nature of employment, and so on. In such communities, and in the primitive community *par excellence*, the closely knit ties of kinship and common activity automatically provided some of the necessary social mechanisms by which stresses and strains in the individual could be shared and thereby lessened. In modern society, on the other hand – and it is not perhaps altogether unreasonable to take the housing estate as a prototype of a great deal of contemporary suburban living – these mechanisms are conspicuously absent.

The special aspect of this problem which was posed for the Bristol Project arose, in part at least, from the movement of population from closely knit central areas to new estates on the periphery of cities. In studying the contrast between an old central area (St. Ebbe's) and a new housing estate (Barton) at Oxford, Mogey described the emergence on the housing estate of a family-centred society in place of the neighbourhood-centred society of the old area (Mogey, 1956, Ch. 4). For us the question arises as to what is the effect of movement of this kind for the stability of the family and in particular for children growing up, and what changes are desirable which can help the family to come to terms with the new environment?

Thus, one aim of group work is to provide a means of alleviating the strains and stresses which arise through the emergence of a pattern of living in which the families involved neither possess nor can readily acquire the appropriate knowledge of how to handle their social relationships. In the terminology which we defined earlier, they are unable to use the social structure of their neighbourhood, and this inability leads to a vicious circle in which cause and effect are not clearly distinguishable. Social control by members of a society is inhibited by an anxiety that they cannot understand the forces at work among them, and in consequence they are led either to a denial of the issues to be faced, or to aggressive and hostile action in dealing with them.

The third reason for the use of group work in an action-research project became clearer only towards the end of the Project, when the experience of the group worker and the psychiatric social worker was studied and discussed. There were in fact some changes in the methods used by the Project. We have already emphasized the limitations imposed by a formal committee structure on the task of learning about *process* as contrasted with the *achievement of goals* in the case of the Executive Committee. The value of the particular method developed by the psychiatric social worker in the case of the teachers' and social workers' groups is in the opportunity which it provides for facilitating change in the third sense. It does this by deliberately creating the conditions by which the members of a group can look at the here-and-now situation in which they are involved. The worker's job is that of an interpreter to the group, and he may be seen as a kind of catalyst in effecting social change. We wrote earlier of the close interrelationship of role and personality. By refusing to accept responsibility for the control and direction of the group, the worker is able to help the members to understand better the emotional content of behaviour and the feelings associated with their own role as members. By learning through the here-and-now situation of a permissive group, they become able to apply the insight gained to clarifying their roles and the relationships involved in taking up these roles in the ordinary business of daily living. We must add, however, that group work in this sense of learning through the here-and-now situation of a permissive group is very different from group work in the sense of the scout troop or a toddlers' club.[1]

We discussed above the significance of resistance to change and some of the reasons for it, and we emphasized the fact that, for reasons of personality, we frequently adapt our role to suit our emotional needs. Through the group work method using the here-and-now situation there is an opportunity to work through

[1] A distinction which is discussed fully in Chapter 4 on group work.

some of the resistances to change. We distinguish between imposed and spontaneous change. Spontaneous changes are less likely to provoke resistances of the kind we discussed earlier than are imposed changes – changes, for example, imposed by the leader of the group. Here, also, the work group organized on the basis of a committee has an inappropriate structure for carrying through spontaneous change, since its primary task is the taking of formal decisions on policy and action. Change which occurs spontaneously within a group is more likely to meet the inner needs of its members than is change which is imposed by decisions taken outside the group.

The example of the Espressos is relevant here. The behaviour of the members is considered by the neighbourhood to be undesirable. They are said to be aggressive, destructive, and sometimes delinquent. The measures generally advocated to deal with them are to apply stronger discipline, stricter control, and firmer methods of training. Expressed in our own language, the measures proposed are based on the assumption that imposed change is not only desirable but also efficacious. But imposed change through the use of more authority, far from producing a greater sense of responsibility in the non-conformist minority, often leads to greater hostility and destructiveness. The group worker's methods with the Espressos were based on the principle that spontaneous change is possible only in situations where there is a permissive relationship between worker and group. The members have an opportunity of working through their own resistance to change in their own way and at their own pace, but within the security of their relationship with the worker.

The potential dangers in the use of the group work method are so enormous and so frightening that it may be wise at this stage to add a note on what we did not try to do and would not wish ever to attempt. We did not try to use the group as a method simply of gaining conformity or of producing a mystical sense of togetherness. The methods of Communist China (cf. Sprott, 1958, pp. 194–5) in securing a false conformity through the technique of the small group, or the self-confessional sessions of the Oxford

Group (whose methods we have been accused of spreading), are, in our view, perversions of a method which, rightly used, can serve to enlarge the opportunities for human freedom and the strengthening of personal responsibility. But it would be wrong to deny the danger involved in the adoption of these methods merely to secure conformity. It is certainly possible to conceive of situations where, as techniques for gaining assent to a particular policy, their value might seem to lie. Whyte's lively study of the *Organization Man* (1956) presents a realistic picture of the use of the group in American industry and of the perils of non-conformity in a middle-class American housing estate. *Corruptio optimi pessima* is indeed a very real possibility.

CHAPTER 3

Multi-Discipline Approach: The Project Team

AS A WORKING GROUP

THE outstanding characteristic of the Project team was its diversity. The main difference was between the practical and the academic members, the former concerned primarily with bringing about change and with practice, the latter interested in a theoretical understanding. On the one hand, there was the academic emphasis on precision of definition, the dislike of commitment to a particular course of action, the desire to relate observations to a coherent body of theory, and the responsibility to an academic discipline. On the other hand, for those workers with a practical role the primary responsibility was to people, to their feelings and their happiness. Observation and research were of secondary importance, and the pen was subservient to the act.

But in spite of the difficulties of achieving unity of purpose through two such diverse approaches, we remain convinced of the value to be derived from this opportunity of relating theory and practice to one another. In the course of the weekly team discussions we arrived at a working compromise. To be faced with the conflict between the demands of analysis and of action was itself a valuable experience, as two members of the team have described:

When not in contact with the social worker, the research worker tends to act as if nobody had ever done any work on the subject before. The social worker without any contact with the research worker tends to act as if no work need be done on the subject ever again. The experience of the Bristol Social Project has been that the social workers have been persuaded to look at their interpretations more carefully, with a more lively appreciation of the source and scientific respectability of the theories they implicitly depend on. The research workers, for their part, have moved toward the view that interpretation of the facts in the light of existing hypotheses is itself a perfectly respectable activity (Tuxford & Dennis, 1958, p. 462).

There was also diversity in the educational and social backgrounds of the eleven members of the team. Some were experienced in university teaching and research, and others in a variety of social-work settings, such as the mental hospital, the youth service, and family casework. Among both of these two groups the field worker (Miller) held a unique position. His previous employment as the salesman of a travelling hardware van had taken him to several housing estates on the periphery of Bristol. His natural perceptiveness, together with an exceptional ability to communicate with both the team and the neighbourhoods, made him a particularly valuable member.

No less important than the distinction between the claims of research and of action was the difference between the sociological and the psychiatric approach. Although the team had no permanent psychiatric member we were fortunate in our consultant help and in our discussions with the Director of the Bristol Child Guidance Clinic. In much of the work there was no conflict of opinion. The sociologist, for example, was concerned with the social structure of the neighbourhoods, their size, the nature and range of occupations, and with their social institutions. In the Family Study he concentrated primarily on the roles and standards of behaviour of the spouses as husbands and wives, as parents, and as citizens and neighbours. The psychiatric social worker, on the other hand, looked at the behaviour of the spouses in the ordinary families in terms of their personality, their feelings, and the background of their early childhood. The group worker thought primarily in terms of human relationships and especially of her own relationship with her groups.

Disagreements arose mainly in our attempts at the explanation of behaviour, but particularly in the case of the Espressos. The Espressos became a test case for our differences in understanding. To what extent were they the product of a society which had rejected them? Should we describe them in the neutral terminology of the psychiatrist as disordered personalities, or in the more popular language of the community as young hooligans? The sociologist looked first at their low status in the neighbourhood, the psychiatric social worker at the deprived relationships with their parents. In the early stages, at least, of the team's discussions on the Espressos there was strong disagreement as to the appropriate emphasis to be given to the needs of individual personality, on the one hand, and to the claims of society, on the other.

Each discipline learned from the other, and this process of mutual learning took place throughout the whole life of the team. But, clearly, more could have been achieved. Only towards the end of the Project did we learn the important lesson that real co-operation between team members with such a diversity of roles demands patient and extremely frank discussion of feelings. The earlier meetings of the team were too closely parallel to the university seminar, too organized, with papers prepared in advance.

To achieve an exchange of feelings is not easy. It requires time, mutual confidence, and a willingness to gain insight into the unacknowledged obstacles to effective team collaboration. Perhaps most of all it depends on a sense of security on the part of the members of the group themselves. As the team gained in insight and security, so it was able, particularly in the later period, to discuss some, at least, of the inevitable conflicts in feelings arising from status, from class differences, and from the appropriate emphasis on intellect and emotion in the explanation of behaviour.

Thus, the team's experiences illustrate an aspect of communication between members of a working group which is frequently overlooked. It is not enough that there is good communication at a formal level (that is, regular staff meetings and well-planned agenda) or in a purely social way. There must also be communication of a different kind, in which the feelings and values of the group lying behind the intellectual content of the discussion are not only expressed but also worked through.

An action-research team, unlike, perhaps, teams engaged in certain forms of pure research, cannot afford to be neutral over values. By committing ourselves to facilitating change in society, we have to be explicit in our assumptions over the kind of change we wish to see. To generalize on the underlying values of our work may be misleading, but it would be fair to say that each member of the team saw his role as helping in some way towards the common purpose of achieving a better understanding of stresses and strains on the estates.

But motives for action are hard to discern and many of the more powerful forces are unconscious. Although objectivity in the assessment of our own values is difficult to achieve, at least we have the obligation to be objective in our description of the community in which we worked. As Gunnar Myrdal (1953, p. 241) points out: 'Value premises should be introduced openly. They should be explicitly stated and not kept hidden as tacit assumptions. . . . This is incidentally our only protection against bias in research, for bias implies being directed by unacknowledged valuations.' During the team discussions, members sought to check their valuation of what they had seen or done against the valuation of their colleagues.

EXTERNAL ROLES AND RELATIONSHIPS

The Project team had the dual obligation of helping a community in dealing with its stresses and strains, and also of keeping records for preparation of a report to the Carnegie Trust with a view to later publication. This twofold obligation undoubtedly proved to be a major influence on the relationships between team and community and raised continually the difficult question of confidentiality. The community was frequently anxious and uncertain in its feelings towards our obligation to keep records, the more so since the situations involving the team were so varied, some formal and others informal, some were public meetings and others, meetings privately with families or individuals.

In the early days in particular, the Project was overwhelmed by publicity of various kinds. The Committee spent as much time and effort on trying to keep the subject out of the press – or at least to avoid a spectacular story – as on any other single issue. The Tavistock Institute team working on an action-research project in the Glacier Metal Company was perhaps wiser than we in making a strict rule that there would be no public comments except in consultation with Glacier (Jaques, 1951, p. 16). The Project's problem was more difficult. Our work was not confined within the boundaries of a factory, but was the responsibility of a committee representative of the public life of a large city. It was impossible to consult every group in the city likely to have an interest at stake.

In discussing the external relationships of the Project team we confine ourselves to the development of professional relationships in action research carried out in the open community. We start from certain of the basic assumptions of the Tavistock Institute team at the Glacier Metal Company.

The Tavistock team emphasized its professional role in collaborating with a client who had asked for help. The outstanding characteristic of this professional role was the need to preserve independence of judgement. To avoid being captured by any particular group in the factory, the team decided to have *no personal relationships* with individuals in the factory *either inside or outside working hours* (ibid. p. 14, italics ours). In this way it attempted to minimize the difficulties which inevitably arise when a team becomes identified with the interest of a particular group.

The relationship between layman and professional team (defined in Chapter 2 as one of the main characteristics of action research) becomes clearer through the analogy of the doctor-patient relationship. The doctor's role is to help the patient to recover from his illness. In addition to his proved medical competence he has an elaborate and well-established code of professional ethics to support him. The patient, too, as a sick person, has an expected role to play, such as exemption from certain social responsibilities, the obligation to get well, to seek technically competent help, and to co-operate with the doctor in what is a common task (Parsons, 1951, p. 436).

These obligations are not accidents which have occurred in a purely haphazard way. They are necessary elements in the relationship designed to facilitate the doctor's task of helping his patient. Their reason is best illustrated from psychotherapy, where objectivity and detachment on the part of the doctor are essential for effective treatment. The therapist cannot 'enter into' the kind of relationship which the patient, generally unconsciously, wants (ibid. p. 460). The therapist must be protected against the demands of his own emotions. To return friendship with friendship, or hostility with hostility, seriously damages the process of treatment.

Although the Tavistock principle was an ideal at which we aimed, action research in a city proved to be very different from research in a factory. There was no single and obvious common objective, such as improvement in organization and relationships for the purpose of increased factory output, and no straightforward test of success or failure. Public expectations of the objective of the Project were diverse and often conflicting. Although the Director's office was located in the university, the problem of capture by conflicting interest groups was always with us. Some critics argued that the initial decision to place administrative responsibility with the Bristol Council of Social Service was a serious mistake, since it identified the Project with voluntary social service as distinct from the public services under the control of the city.

At the Glacier Metal Company the idea of a project originated with a small group of the top management who had strong feelings in favour of the research. The Tavistock team, however, insisted that a project could be successful only if it had the support of the Works Council, and so the team gave the Works Council the opportunity of either accepting or rejecting its services.

Multi-Discipline Approach: The Project Team

In a city, authority is assumed to lie with the citizens who elect their chosen representatives to the City Council. Did the Bristol Project originate from a demand of the citizens of Bristol? One Committee member has remarked: 'The trouble with the Project was that it was wished on Bristol.' One should add, too, that it was wished on the three neighbourhoods chosen for the research, but particularly on Upfield.[1] In the case of Bristol, at least one important representative group – the Lord Mayor's Committee – had given an invitation for a project to the Carnegie Trustees. On the other hand, the three neighbourhoods had never asked for the collaboration of the Project team.

Upfield, in particular, was clearly uncertain about its being chosen as one of the three Project areas. Some of those with the highest status disliked the stigma which was attached to the alleged concentration of delinquency within the estate and suggested that the team should go elsewhere. The team, however, was doubtful as to the extent to which these views of the 'formal' leaders of Upfield were representative of the estate as a whole and felt that there was a strong case for standing by the decision.

What then was the Project team's experience in the light of these general principles?

In the first place, the team's emphasis in the early period was on its role as an enabler in bringing about what we have called change in the first sense. The focus was on assisting Upfield to achieve some of its overt needs – the Meeting Rooms, the Adventure Playground, and the estate newspaper as a method of improving communication and of helping the estate to become more articulate about its needs. The problem of stress and strain was largely neglected. The two members of the team who went to live on the estates played an active part in local associations. Whereas the Director's relationships were mainly with the leaders

[1] Dr. A. T. M. Wilson (1947, p. 23) has written perceptively of the element of resentment likely to be felt by a community when a solution of the 'problem' is ultimately provided by someone called in from outside the group, for example, by the social scientist or social worker: 'It is this same situation, too, which makes it essential for an outsider called in to help with a problem to remain, in the later phases of the work, in the role of an adviser.'

of the estate, the sociologist (George Harris) and the field worker (Bill Miller) were accepted as residents and neighbours.

Second, as the composition of the team changed with the appointment of the psychiatric social worker and the group worker, so the focus of the Project began to shift to the task of bringing about change in the second and third senses. It was during the later phase that it became evident that the initial *structure* of the Project, though appropriate for the team's role as observers and enablers, was inappropriate for the performance of a professional role in dealing with stress and strain.

The first reason for this was the ambiguity of status of those members of the team who were residents of the estates. At one time they were known as friends and neighbours to other residents on the estate; at another time they were expected to take part, as people with expert or professional knowledge, in committees at the neighbourhood and city level. The sociologist, moreover, has commented on the embarrassment which resulted when a field worker was faced with a resident who had known him in one role while he was playing another (i.e. as ordinary resident and then as house-to-house interviewer).

The second reason has been discussed in the previous chapter. We refer to the formality of the committee structure at the levels of both the housing estate and the city. It was easier to alter the structure of the team meetings than of the committees with which the team was related.

Our work with the Espressos provides a useful illustration of this point. We start from the basic assumption that it is not enough only to work with the Espressos; we must also work with the community in which they live. In practice this means working with the leaders of the community, at least in the first instance. Ideally, the function of an action-research team is to help in bringing about change among the leaders as well as in a group such as the Espressos. For a variety of reasons, including the Project team's lack of skill but also because of an inadequate structure through which team members and committees could relate to one another, less was accomplished in helping the estate leaders to work through anxiety over the Espressos than we had at first hoped to achieve.

The change in the structure of the Teachers Group, on the other hand, provides an interesting point of contrast. Here, as we show later, there was an important change from a formal to an informal structure in which it was possible for teachers to deal with their own feelings and anxieties within the security of a group.

The question as to the strictness with which a professional role on the analogy of clinical medicine should be defined in action research within the setting of city and neighbourhood must be left an open one. The Director, for his part, after the experience of five years' work, would wish to place a much greater emphasis on professional relationships than in fact he did during the Project.

PART II

Working with Groups

CHAPTER 4

Aspects of Group Work

SINCE Great Britain, unlike the United States and Canada, has no established and recognized professional training for social group workers, the Project's entry into this field was experimental. It will be clear from the following narrative that although the two group workers started from fundamental psycho-analytic principles, the methods which they adopted to put them into practice varied considerably, both from group to group and from time to time.

The choice of groups was dictated by local needs, not by theoretical considerations of research. The members of the groups came voluntarily because the experience of membership was either enjoyable or helpful, and not *primarily* because the Project required material on which to conduct research. The members were not guinea pigs at the disposal of the intellectual curiosity of the workers. In consequence of this the field material (from the research point of view) leaves much to be desired. Records were generally written up at the end of each session with all the mistakes and omissions that such a method entails. Unfortunately, there were occasions when records were left unwritten, and the narrative has suffered in consequence. The worker's intention in the keeping of any notes or records was primarily for her own understanding of the group from one meeting to the next.

There were two main reasons for using group work as a method of help. The first arose from our diagnosis of the situation. An

73

outstanding characteristic of the housing estate is the isolation of the inhabitants in an environment where social contacts are not easily formed. Our diagnosis had suggested that there were certain needs at Upfield to which priority should be given, as opportunities for social activity and interaction were more adequately provided for some members of society than for others. Also, for emotional reasons, certain people need the help of a skilled and trained worker if they are to be encouraged to engage in meaningful social activity and interaction.

The most obvious needs felt by the neighbourhood – as indeed by any neighbourhood with a similar social structure – are those which centre on the family and the bringing-up of children. Mothers with young children still under school age are limited in the distance they can travel. It is the mothers, moreover, who feel most acutely the isolation and loneliness of the estate. The needs of mothers and young children are of general importance everywhere and in particular in those areas where community and kinship ties no longer provide the traditional form of help and support.

The adolescent also claimed our attention. The adolescent is both child and adult, and the apparently conflicting elements in his behaviour are the outcome of this dual role. He is both dependent and independent, needing support and encouragement in making decisions, but needing at the same time freedom to experiment in his own way and at his own pace. Developed in physique, but emotionally still immature, he fluctuates in the intensity of feeling for his own or for the opposite sex. At one moment he may choose isolation and at another may seek to merge his identity with the gang. The social phenomenon of the Teddy boy in various forms has been a characteristic feature of post-war industrial society. It belongs to no single country, but has been observed in every Western country with a highly industrialized economy and increasingly in the Eastern world as well. In Germany, for example, the *Halbstarken* have attracted attention and concern in a similar way. Of the many factors leading to this phenomenon, confusion of the social role of the adolescent in our society is outstanding. For 70 per cent of our adolescents, the edu-

74

cational system ends at the point when the effect of psychological and biological changes is being felt and when the social pressures of the mass media are at their strongest. Unlike the primitive society with its *rites de passage*, we provide only the most rudimentary help for adolescents in making the transition from the dependent role of a child at home to the independent role of the young adult.[1]

A difficult problem, however, was the precise selection of groups. One of the tests of our achievement would be the persistence of the activity after the end of the Project's life. The choice of groups in each case was made with the primary aim of continuity, but the history of the groups suggests that we were only partially successful in our choice.

The second reason for choosing the group work method was our belief in its value as a way of providing the kind of help which our diagnosis suggested was appropriate to the fundamental needs of the community. The stresses and strains of family life in a housing estate are predominantly those of human relationships. In all societies the small group has provided man with opportunities for the exercise of satisfying and responsible relationships. It may seem strange, therefore, that what has in the past happened unselfconsciously should now be made the object of study demanding training and skill in its practitioners. For so it is, and the method we shall describe is the more difficult to understand precisely because it is both obvious and familiar and at the same time complex and controversial in many of its assumptions.

SOME BASIC PRINCIPLES

When we analyse our life experience closely, we perceive that it is through membership of the groups in which we have established formal and informal human relationships that we have come to our stature as mature and responsible persons. Through

[1] Richards (1956, p. 162): 'The chisungu is a test in the eyes of the performers. Whatever her doubts and fears the girl has jumped the faggots successfully: she has caught the ujele insect and killed the chickens. The teenager in our society has no such tangible proof that she is actually a grown-up and can safely and successfully behave like one.'

75

our relationships with others, we have felt our way into what are good or tolerable forms of agreement and disagreement, conformity or difference, obedience or initiative. We have learnt partly by unselfconscious observation, partly by trial and error, knowing that while error would lead to disapproval, it would not usually lead to rejection or expulsion from the group. Our parents, our teachers, our employers, our sports clubs, our neighbours, have been able to teach us and to criticize us explicitly or by implication, often in such subtle ways as raising an eyebrow or saying 'good morning' in a different tone of voice – without making us feel so rebellious and resentful that we have responded by becoming antisocial in our attitudes.

Until recently what lay behind this sort of spontaneous or organized aspect of the common life was taken for granted. Since the second world war, however, the significance of the relationship between group members and individual behaviour has been the subject of much study. Some of the principles which have emerged are relevant to some aspects of the issues dealt with by the Project. This is not the place to deal exhaustively with the principles of social group work; we cannot do more than state briefly some of the principles on which the Project's efforts in this field have been based.

The basic principle of social group work is that the fundamental need of the individual member is for satisfying human relationships, though this need is more often unconscious than conscious. Often the relationships are of more real importance to the individuals than the apparent outward activities of the group, whether they be educational or recreational.

These activities – the 'work task'[1] – are, as it were, the vehicle through which the relationships are sought. A 'good home' is not one in which all activity goes like clockwork, and all physical arrangements approximate to perfection: what the good home has is a quality of relationships which enables people to be themselves, to share their joys and sorrows, their perplexities, dis-

---

[1] 'Work task' is group work jargon, but as useful shorthand it is used throughout this chapter.

coveries, angers, aspirations, irritations, frustrations, and ecstasies with a reasonable measure of emotional freedom, so that what one says or does not say, does or does not do, is understood and 'accepted' by the others, even though it may not be approved of and may, indeed, lead to warm outbursts of anger or recrimination. When there is fundamental emotional security, people can risk being themselves, and in being themselves can learn to become their better selves, more able to be tolerant of the irritating behaviour of others, more able to be sensitively aware of how to understand and respond to the needs of others, more able to act differently from others without being offensive about it, and through all this becoming more at peace with themselves without in any way becoming less persons with lives to live of their own.

Most people achieve this quality of human relationship quite unselfconsciously at a level adequate for everyday purposes of social living, though it may well be somewhat superficial and break down in certain conditions of strain. But there are two kinds of situation in which people who badly need this sort of relationship may be deprived of it. On the one hand, there are those whose personal and family history and temperament are such that they have never been able to grow as persons through the experience of emotionally secure group relationships; in consequence they either sink into isolation (e.g. the Mothers Group), or tend towards personal or gang aggression (e.g. the Espressos). On the other hand, there are those engaged in singularly exacting professional work, such as teachers and social workers, whose professional responsibility *can* be discharged at a certain level of outward action, but whose emotional feelings about their work and all that it involves may well need a group-work setting for expression, consideration, and understanding.

The social group worker whose service lies with people in this sort of need has the professional responsibility of helping the individuals who are in the group to fulfil their roles, and the human relationships implied in their roles, more satisfactorily. The group worker's resources consist primarily in his ability to handle his relationship with the group and its members. Skills in organizing

77

leisure, recreational, or educational activities, though useful elements in his work, remain secondary to the primary skill. The group worker does not come to teach, but to help the members of the group with their learning, though this may not be at all obvious. Thus, the Espressos were a group of antisocial adolescents who came to 'have fun', as they expressed it. The aim of the worker, on the other hand, was to help them to achieve better interpersonal relationships through the medium of having fun. To do this, the worker must possess two skills which do not come easily. He must know himself and his own emotional attitudes, so that he may recognize and control his own responses to the group and its members, and he must be able to 'start at the level of the group'. Like many other apparently obvious statements, the latter phrase is deceptive: it presupposes not only a knowledge on the part of the worker of what is the emotional and social level of the group, but also an ability to stand up to tremendous tension. To do group work with a delinquent gang, for example, the worker has to convince the gang that while he does not share in or approve of their delinquent activity, yet he accepts it as fact. He has to convince them that, no matter how difficult they are to him or to other people, his own warm feelings for them as persons and his services to them will not be withdrawn. That is a difficult enough position to sustain in any case; it is much more difficult to sustain in an open situation, such as Upfield, where the Espressos were often seen to be a public nuisance, and where, in the public mind, it was impossible to distinguish between the worker's professional acceptance and understanding of the gang's behaviour as a fact and her detachment from the gang's values, which it was often felt she condoned or encouraged.

The role of the social group worker is, consequently, not one for the volunteer or the untrained.

THE STRUCTURE OF GROUPS

Experience in the family group leads the individual to have certain expectations of all other groups. All effective groups which give their members real satisfaction must, in addition to the achievement of the work task, provide two aspects of experience: the members must have an inner sense of assurance that they 'belong', and they must feel that what they think and feel 'counts' when the group commits itself to action, particularly as the group finds itself faced with changing circumstances which oblige it to make adjustments. The achievement of these aspects of experience becomes the 'primary function'[1] of the group if the group is to be one in which learning, both intellectual and emotional, is to be an enriching process. We can illustrate this from an aspect of family life which we often met in the Upfield and Boltwood families – for family life is, in many ways, the prototype of all group experience in its essentials. Where there is at least one child still at home in the family, dependent on the mother for attention, love, and care, the family, expressed in the actions and attitudes and leadership of mother and father, seems to be functioning adequately and happily. When, eventually, the last child goes to school, a crisis point arises in the family in relation to its primary function. All the children now belong to other groups as well as to the home. The school now shares in the upbringing of the children to such an extent that the mother must use her time differently if she is to feel needed and fully occupied. *All* the relationships in the family need to change to meet the changed needs of one of its members. The children now look outwards as well as inwards and need mother in different, less demanding, ways. In technical terms, the family group has to revaluate its goals, and find a new pattern of belonging together. This means reconsidering what its members 'do' together. So far as the family itself is concerned, the process of revaluation may be entirely unselfconscious, while it proceeds harmoniously. But the mother may resent the loss of the children, may not know what to do with her time, and may become irritable and fussy. On the other hand, she may go off to work. If she does, however, the rest of the family may come to realize that, in return for the benefits of Mum's freedom and earnings, they must

---

[1] 'Primary function' is used subsequently in this chapter as useful jargon to describe these two aspects of experience.

now take on some of what used to be her jobs around the home. They may bitterly resent the break in their comfortable dependence on her. Some family groups have such a robust sense of mutual 'belonging' and individual 'counting' that they can make adjustments of this kind by good sense, mutual understanding, and unconscious generosity; belongingness and mutual support survive through the challenge and crisis of change, and may indeed grow. The primary function may be more richly fulfilled. But some family groups cannot make the responses to close the gap, and a sense of fragmentation, diversity of purpose, and a diminishing sense of belongingness may set in. The group may fail in its primary function in the new circumstances.

In the family group what happens is largely, and in the first instance almost entirely, the result of the quality of effective leadership given by the parents. In the artificial group the same sort of function falls to the leader, helped and hampered by his own personality, self-consciousness, and knowledge of how to analyse group needs and behaviour.

Certain other experiences are also common to groups with a recognized membership, whether it is a family, a class of children, a seminar of students, the Espressos, the Goslings Club, or the Teachers Group, and must be taken into account when an attempt is made to understand the group. These common experiences stem from the attitude of: (1) the group members to the leader; (2) the group members to each other; (3) the group members towards the external world; and (4) the external world to the group. All attempts by the leader of the group to control or deal with these four experiences, together with the achievement of the work task, will affect the 'structure of the group'.

In all groups there is a manifest acceptance of the work task. The primary function may be of paramount importance to the members of the group, but it is never made as explicit as the achievement of the work task. A student seminar can accept the fact that its members come together to study, for example, the history of Western philosophy – they may be little aware, however, that if the primary function is not achieved, their learning may be to some extent impaired.

All groups tend to be structured so that the work task can be achieved without undue interference from one or all of the four experiences. In some groups the structure is rigid and attitudes towards the leader are ritualized. Feelings of criticism, approval, affection, and dislike are couched in prescribed ways. Discontentment about the structure of the group, or the leadership, may arise if all the members are not clear about the nature of the work task or how it should be achieved.

An example of this problem was often mentioned in the Teachers Group. The teachers felt that the organization and structure of schools, and of classrooms in particular, should not be uniform throughout the education system as a whole. In grammar schools the structure of the class as a group is well suited to academic learning and the passing of examinations. In secondary modern schools the same structure is not appropriate to the needs of the pupils where the work task of the classroom group is as much the development of character as the process of learning.

A leader who is sensitive to the changing work task of the group will be aware that at times of change the fulfilment of the primary function is most important, and, by satisfying it, the group will be better able to redefine the work task and modify the structure accordingly. This is far easier said than done, for the four common experiences continually affect the situation and make definite planning impossible.

In most situations where the work task is known and acceptable the structure can be created accordingly. When the work task is achieved the group will cease to function. Problems of structure, organization, and leadership occur when the work task is ill-defined, as in the Espressos or the Mothers Group. It is at this point that a skilled group worker will use the imprecision to help the members of the group to become involved in its structuring and to become aware of their part in the whole. Often this is achieved by the leader's helping the members to be aware of their relationships to each other, to the group as a whole, and to the leader. In this way the individual member of the group may become more aware of himself and his effect upon the others, and by their effect on him he may learn to modify or change his behaviour in a way which is more appropriate in his everyday social or professional life.

This is what started to happen in the Espressos. The work task, apart from having fun, was ill-defined. The worker helped to create an atmosphere of belonging and acceptance where the members could share and discuss their values. In doing this we believe that they were beginning to learn the need to discipline or modify the manifestation of these values (their behaviour) in a way which was acceptable to the others, to the leader, and in time, it was hoped, to the community. This way of becoming involved helped them to have a little more awareness of their own and other people's behaviour and its effect upon the community.

The Espressos were uncertain as to the precise nature of the work task. This could not be said about the groups of teachers and social workers. Their professional skills as teachers or social workers were to a large extent dependent upon their understanding of the effects of their own behaviour on others. They also needed to know the effect of interaction between people and, for the teachers especially, the effects of certain kinds of leadership and group structure. It is debatable how best to teach people to understand and know these things which need to be understood and appreciated emotionally as well as intellectually.

The Teachers Group, and to some extent the Social Workers Group, tried several methods, which we describe in some detail later on. The last method which was employed in both groups made them in essence like the Espressos. Because the Espressos were imprecise about their work task, a certain method was adopted so that they could be helped to become aware of the effect of their behaviour upon each other and upon society and to modify this behaviour in the execution of a work task which, though often changing, was decided upon by them all. In the Teachers and Social Workers Groups it was hoped that by making the work task imprecise the same opportunity to learn about the

82

effects of behaviour would occur. In this way the teachers, health visitors, church workers, probation officers, and other social workers would learn about the effects of their own behaviour on others. They would also have an opportunity to experience the effects of different kinds of leadership and group structure in the achievement of the work task.

These general observations about group work will, it is hoped, become clearer from the narrative of each of the five groups in action which follows in the next chapters.

CHAPTER 5

The Mothers Group

THE small group of Upfield mothers who met together with the group worker, Mrs. Andes, week by week for some fifteen months illustrates the help and support that mothers whose stresses and strains are unusually difficult can derive from a skilled and sensitive worker.

The group was an extension of a group in existence – the Home Advice Group, the aims of which had been predominantly educational in the broad sense. It was already clear from what had been learned about the mothers from the Family Study that some of them had family problems of very considerable difficulty, and it was to the needs of this particular minority that we decided to devote the resources of the new worker. For this minority, a less formal and less activity-centred group than the Home Advice Group appeared to be the most suitable method of helping.

Through her diagnosis of the mothers' needs, the group worker quickly recognized that what was necessary above all else was a group from which they could gain support for the strains and stresses of family life. Her method was not to make plans for talks from visitors, or to arrange outings, or to fix up accommodation in the Meeting Rooms. The planning and organization she left to the members themselves. But her method certainly was to encourage and to facilitate activity and to make it easier for the mothers to do the kinds of things which they secretly hoped for, but had not the energy or initiative to do without encouragement,

84

such as the planning of a party or an outing with their families. Above all, it was to help them to be more understanding and tolerant of one another and to make relationships which would be a source of support. When invited – and this happened on several occasions – Mrs. Andes joined the mothers and their families on special occasions, such as a visit to an approved school to see one of the children, or a grammar school commemoration service in the cathedral.

The choice of twelve mothers for membership of the new group was made partly on their own relationships with one another and partly on the caseworker's assessment of their emotional needs and the stresses which seemed to be troubling them. At this point we should explain that five of the mothers were known to the Child Guidance Clinic and in several cases either they themselves or their husbands had been patients in a mental hospital. This fact emerged only in the course of the group's life, but it serves to emphasize the absolute necessity of looking behind the symptoms of social and family disorganization to the underlying psychological causes.

Four facts, above all others, characterized the members of this group of mothers:

1. *The tragedies of their early upbringing.* All of the mothers appear to have had unhappy childhoods; most of them came from broken homes. Yet their families, in spite of the rows and the quarrels (in one case, at least, of considerable violence), stuck together. Whenever there was an outing the mothers always wanted the husbands and children with them. Their immaturity is well illustrated by their dependence on their toddlers. They enjoyed this dependency and the feeling of security which it gave them. For them – unlike the mature and secure mother – the departure of their toddlers to school was a traumatic experience, the end of an episode.

2. *The consequences of living on a small and fluctuating budget.* All the homes represented by these mothers suffered periods of unemployment, debt, rent arrears, etc. The diary of the worker in the

Family Study contains many references to the stresses involved for the mothers in this way of living: the daily bottle of milk for two adults and four children in one home; the wistful recollection by one of how she had enjoyed a meal four years ago at a neighbour's just because she didn't have to cook it; the joy at getting a rent rebate, etc.

3. *The poverty of their social relationships.* None of the mothers was able to maintain warm and friendly relationships with neighbours or with the social organizations, such as clubs or churches, in their neighbourhood. They were a lonely and isolated group, who felt conscious of their own inadequacies and unhappy over the criticisms they had incurred from welfare workers in the various services on account of their household management or the care of their children. Though appreciative of the vicar and the church worker, they were angry at the snobbishness of some of the church congregations.

4. *The continual illness of some member of their families and their dependence on the doctor.* A fourth characteristic of this group of mothers was the continual round of illness in their families – the mothers themselves, their husbands, and their children. This illness, however, was not always the common round of epidemics, of colds and flu, and mumps and measles. For a layman to label it 'psychosomatic' would be presumptuous, and in any case labels not infrequently lead to greater confusion. But what we know of these families from psychiatric sources does in fact emphasize the physical consequences of stresses and strains which are deeply rooted in the personality. Several of the children were bed-wetters, and there are continual references in the diary to migraine among the mothers. In certain families, moreover, there was evidence of specific mental illness for which mental hospital treatment was necessary.

The mothers spoke with gratitude of the help they had got from doctors. But the doctor, in addition to being a source of support for them, was also an important channel of advice. Although it was the general practitioner who was closest to them, this good feeling for doctors included the clinic and the hospital. It embodied also an aura of respect.

The value of the Mothers Group lay in the support which it provided for women whose stresses were serious enough to have won the attention of those who recommended them for group membership. This was its main function, for it was support rather than therapy, on the one hand, or informal home advice, on the other hand, that these mothers, with their particular background and in their present circumstances, most needed. The group was able to provide them with support in dealing with their fluctuating needs and the stresses of daily living.

Two mothers themselves put it this way, on the arrival of a new member, Mrs. D:[1]

Mrs. M and Mrs. T took to Mrs. D at once. They talked with her and told her how much it mattered to have friends. *Mrs. D*: I thought there would be something like twenty women here and I was scared. *Mrs. M*: We are not many, but we talk, and many a problem has been sorted out that way.

The group worker noted in her diary: 'It was the first time that anyone in the group had mentioned that talking had helped them,[2] as I had never stressed the meaning of our meetings.'

The role adopted by the group worker in the Mothers Group was similar to her role in Phase IV of her work with the adolescents – the Espressos. She welcomed and accepted the mothers as they were, encouraging and helping them to do the kind of things over which they felt most comfortable and to talk about some of the stresses they felt in themselves and in their families. Her aim was to stimulate independence slowly as they grew in confidence, but not to do things for them. In the early stages of the group she had introduced herself to the members individually at their homes, explaining how she had heard about them from doctors and social workers and asking them if they would like to

[1] This and similar extracts are taken from the diary kept by the group worker.
[2] The group had then been running for six months.

87

meet together; and later on, she would from time to time drop in for a chat at their homes.

She herself emphasized the permissiveness and passivity of her role. But these two qualities are not to be taken as an indication of neutrality of values or of inactivity on the part of the worker: she had very clear values and standards. Rather, they are a reflection of her interpretation of her *professional* role. This means that she certainly avoided talking too much about herself and making it difficult for the members to make their own interpretation of her role. The worker acts professionally by allowing the members to cast her in the role most suited to their own emotional needs. Her skill consists in recognizing this diversity of needs and in acting, not necessarily in the expected way, but in the way best suited to meet these needs.

The mothers certainly had a stereotyped picture of Mrs. Andes, which was that of the voluntary social worker whose sewing group they had once attended – and enjoyed. They saw her as a person from a different world: 'I suppose it makes a nice change in your work for you to come out here,' said Mrs. T on one occasion. On another occasion, however, they talked about the sadness of her job in seeing so much of other people's troubles: 'You see so much misery.'

Towards the end of the meetings of the group, when Mrs. Andes had insisted on paying her share towards the cost of an outing, Mrs. M giggled and said: 'You'd think she wasn't one of us, the way she goes on.' There was, nevertheless, a definite aura of respect and a feeling that she wasn't quite one of them, though they would very much have liked her to make herself one of them. So dependent were the mothers on the worker that at times it was hard for her to avoid the patronizing role of 'Lady Bountiful'.

In the later meetings (but not the earlier ones) Mrs. Andes came to be given the best cup and the best chair. She was introduced by Mrs. B to her neighbours as 'My friend Mrs. Andes', and by Mrs. T to the clergyman at her husband's funeral as 'This is a friend of mine'.

During the group meetings Mrs. Andes saw her role as that of steering the group away from irrelevancies. But she did *not* make any direct interpretations, believing that the group comes to see the meaning of its behaviour in the course of time. She maintained a balance of power in the group, supporting the leadership of Mrs. M. She was able, too, to assist their understanding of outside agencies – the Child Guidance Clinic, for example, over which two or three of the mothers felt puzzled and sometimes angry, particularly when treatment did not conform to their expectations. As one mother put it when asked by Mrs. Andes whether the Child Guidance Clinic had helped her Jenny: 'They don't seem to give her any treatment. No tablets, nothing. They just talk to her rather like I talk to you now. Still, she certainly seems to have improved.' When Mrs. Andes said, 'I suppose talking sometimes helps,' the mother replied, 'It must do something to her.'

The work did not involve merely the meetings of the group. There were the visits to the mothers' homes, the jumble sales, the outings to Bath and to Longleat, the celebration of birthdays and festivals, the invitations to street parties, and the family visits to children away from home. Towards Christmas the group started a savings club together.

In the first six months the group met together in the Meeting Rooms, although several of the mothers were overawed by the 'poshness', as they put it, of the rooms. After three months the worker began to drop hints about meeting in their own homes. Gradually they picked up the significance of this idea and after six months the new custom began, continuing until the end of the group. The worker supported it warmly. During these meetings the mothers felt that they had the worker more to themselves. Several of them brought children to the group, and although in the Meeting Rooms a second room was set aside for the children to play in, in fact they did not keep to this but played in the same room where the group was meeting. During the meetings in the homes, the children played mostly in the kitchen and in the street outside.

There is continual evidence in the diary kept by the worker of the way in which the group helped the members to divest themselves of their egocentricity and to take an interest in the others and their troubles. But it also helped some of the mothers, who were afraid of going out, to meet people in a safe and secure environment. The diary records a visit of Mrs. N and her girl with the worker to an Ideal Home Exhibition:

> We went to the Exhibition and Mrs. N enjoyed it very much. She had told me she was sometimes terrified of people. There were weeks when she did not feel like facing the shops. Only the other day she had gone to buy some apples and just managed to grab up her parcel and run out of the shop. She told me that she thought it made a lot of difference that the mothers went to have tea at each other's houses. 'If one of your neighbours was ill, you wouldn't feel worried about going in, but I never have much to do with anyone. The other day I was running to work and wouldn't have stopped for anyone, but I met Mrs. T and she seemed to have so many troubles. I listened to her and realized how much better off I was. Yes, we are all in the same boat more or less and got to cope.'

Although the total list of members contains twelve names, the regulars were in fact five in number. Three mothers found the demands of the group too great to bear and failed to keep up their attendance. For them, in particular, a combined casework/group work approach might have been particularly helpful. The stresses in their families were such that the group was too difficult for them. It is well to remind ourselves that there are situations where this is so, because it is all too easy to take for granted the normal ability of people to participate in groups, characteristic for example of the ordinary members of Women's Institutes and Townswomen's Guilds.

New members, at first sight, were welcome. But the established members were happiest if the newcomers remained as visitors, when the members could demonstrate to them the fact that they had a group. It was the worker's purpose gradually to try to remove the dependence of the group on her and to encourage the group to take greater responsibility for helping new members. She was continually aware of the need to avoid the dangers of a dependency situation. She had made a practice of reminding the members from time to time that her stay with them was for a definite period. The preparation for her forthcoming visit to Israel in April–May 1957 was a useful tryout for the group. Could they stand on their own feet during her absence? Would they collaborate together in the forthcoming jumble sale?

During the worker's absence in Israel the group did not in fact meet regularly. On her return she made a date for tea in the Meeting Rooms with all the members, but no one turned up. She then wrote, saying she hoped they would meet. Mrs. M, the group's letter-writer, answered in three weeks' time excusing the delay and saying that she had been busy at home, a chatty and friendly letter, but added: 'No one seems to bother to keep up the club. I see Mrs. G and Mrs. T as you know, as we are all friends.'

The worker was present at a meeting of the group some weeks later. In general their attitude was ambivalent towards her with signs of depression at the prospect of the termination of her work.

The meetings of the group during the autumn and winter were at longer intervals, generally about a month. They were usually cheerful and friendly in spite of the continual round of problems and accidents which had occurred in the members' families. But there was less interaction between the women. They mainly talked to the worker and were very keen that she should listen to what they had to say.

During these occasional winter meetings the worker had an opportunity of assessing the meaning of the group in relation to the mothers' needs and their feelings towards herself. What stands out from her reflections is the *continuing* need of mothers with severe stresses and strains for work of this kind and their own inability to plan and organize such meetings without skilled and sensitive guidance. This is certainly not a job for the student, the immature, or the inexperienced worker.

After one of these meetings the worker wrote:

> When I left I thought how difficult a job it really was to leave on a cheerful and good note with these women, particularly a cheerful one, and that though I felt fairly confident I could achieve it, it wasn't all that easy. Because I really feel that they could do with somebody just coming round from time to time and giving them that little push they so badly need.
>
> Though their lives are very set and there isn't much that could be altered, I think as regards the way they affect their children they could be helped a great deal.

One is tempted to ask at this point whether these mothers were in fact a group, or a collection of individuals with their own friendships and hostilities among themselves. There is no simple answer to this question; the evidence is conflicting.

The way of life of these mothers was such that, apart from Mrs. M and Mrs. G, they did not see much of one another outside the group itself. Yet their own evidence on the precise amount of interaction outside the group is conflicting and determined more by their own needs than by the facts. Mrs. T, for example, said that she never saw Mrs. N. Mrs. N, on the other hand, said that she saw a lot of Mrs. T. Both were truthful witnesses. Mrs. T, however, was less busy than Mrs. N and had a greater need of social relationships. Although they live opposite one another, Mrs. T learned that Mrs. N was expecting a baby only through neighbours with whom Mrs. B and Mrs. M were friendly. Nor did any of the group know that Mrs. N's father had won nearly £50,000 in the football pools, in spite of all the press publicity.

A final outing to the Bristol Hippodrome was planned, part of the cost to be defrayed by the sale of the cups and saucers (a legacy from an earlier social club). Mrs. B had kept the accounts and was keen to get the tickets. Mrs. G, on the other hand, strongly preferred an outing to the cinema. Each member was keen to give the worker a good time before she left. But there was a muddle over the tickets and, as things turned out, there were two separate

Hippodrome parties, the worker going with Mrs. B, while Mrs. M and Mrs. G went with a neighbour. Of the meeting following the theatre visits, the worker wrote:

> What most struck me during the meeting was that they really were a group, and that they were fighting like mad for leadership now that I was going. They somehow had managed to scapegoat Mrs. B, and Mrs. N wasn't really taking much part in the struggle. Mrs. T tagged on to Mrs. M, as did Mrs. G. Mrs. B had got the money from the cups, which by chance had been stored in her house – I think because she had a larger hall – and this had upset the balance of power.

It is always difficult to assess results, but the effects of the Mothers Group, though hard to disentangle from the fluctuations in mood and circumstance of the members, certainly did constitute a positive achievement. Although the members were not able to continue the group after the worker left, they gained in security during the two years when the worker was in contact with them. There are several references to this in the diary, and the statement is supported by change in their appearance and by their ability to handle the daily problems of looking after a family. Of one member, for example, the worker wrote, 'She herself looked much calmer and quieter and seemed much more secure and sure of herself.' There was improvement, too, in the general tidiness and cleanliness of the homes in which the meetings took place. But the main justification for the work must lie not in better house management but in greater security to meet stress and strain. This is the function of the supportive group.

In spite of these positive gains, the main lesson of this group is the continuing need for support which these mothers have. For them the Mothers Group was no more than the end of a chapter. It would be pleasant to record that the group had done all that was necessary to provide a transitional phase, at the end of which no further help from outside was necessary. We cannot in fairness say this. The worker had planned at an early stage for the process of weaning away the group from dependence on her in readiness for her eventual departure. What she learned, however, from the events during her absence in Israel and from the closing stages of the group was the mothers' inability to organize their own group. Much as Mrs. M enjoyed the role of organizer and letter-writer for the group, the task of handling the relationships between the mothers was too difficult for her without outside help.

What stands out in fact is the *continuing need* of these mothers – and others with a similar degree of stress – for a small accepting and supportive group. Here is certainly one of the unmet needs of modern society.

CHAPTER 6

The Goslings Club

THE observations of the team on the needs of Upfield emphasized again and again the importance of the young family, and
in particular of mothers with children at the toddler stage, three
to five years. This was in part because on the housing estate, and
especially the new estate, young families predominate, and in part
because of the absence of those traditional patterns of mutual aid
provided by grandmothers and relations and a closely knit old-
established area. It was not easy for mothers to get an afternoon
away from their toddlers. The choice of Friday afternoon – a
popular time with Upfield women for shopping – as the time for
the Club was made because the mothers enjoyed the opportunity
of getting away from the estate to do their shopping in the centre
of Bristol, where the facilities were better and things were
cheaper.

The aims of the Goslings Club at Upfield were seen as fourfold:

1. To enable mothers to have a free afternoon each week to
   do shopping, etc.
2. To help the toddlers to play in a group with adult supervision.
3. To provide the mothers with an opportunity for informal
   discussion about their own and their children's experiences.
4. To help the local community to take part in an activity
   which would meet a practical need of the estate.

The Goslings Club was neither a Child Guidance Clinic in miniature nor a nursery school in the conventional sense. It should be assessed rather as a neighbourhood activity and as an opportunity for better social relationships on the part of children and their mothers. These are legitimate and important aims, but they require very different skills and methods. The kind of skill required, moreover, was different from that needed in the Espressos and the Mothers Group. In the group worker's opinion the Goslings Club was the least useful of these three group activities, though in the eyes of the neighbourhood it appeared to be adjudged the most useful. Indeed, there seems to have been a conflict of local opinion as to how anyone, such as the group worker, could at the same time be associated with so disreputable a group as the Espressos and so useful an enterprise as the Goslings Club.

Mrs. Andes, the worker, herself compared the ease with which she started the Espressos and the difficulty which she experienced in the work, with the difficulty of starting the Goslings Club and the ease with which the Club was in fact organized. Whereas the Espressos consisted of the non-conformist minority at the adolescent stage, the Goslings Club was eminently respectable; it catered largely for the conformers.

It contrasts very noticeably with the Mothers Group, which served the needs of that minority of mothers whose stresses prevented them from taking part in the ordinary social activities of Upfield. The same is certainly *not* true of the Goslings Club: the children of the poorer and underprivileged families, such as those from which the Bums and the Espressos came, were conspicuously absent. There was one exception, however. Richard, the one noticeably neglected child who used the Club, did so by reason of the relationship formed between his mother and Mrs. Andes in the Mothers Group. Without her intervention it is unlikely that he would have been selected by the Club committee.

The members of the Club committee were among the most active mothers in the various women's associations at Upfield. This was the reason why, at least in the early stages of the Club, they were nominated as members. It was important, in the Director's view, in establishing the Club to have the interest and support of women who had the confidence of the associations which they represented.

The idea of a toddlers' club was borrowed from Boltwood, where the experience gained from three years' work provided a useful starting-point as well as evidence that the Club could fulfil a need on the part of the estate. The Meeting Rooms building, situated in the centre of Upfield, provided with a storeroom for toys and equipment, and an enclosed courtyard for play in the open air on summer afternoons, was convenient and well designed for the purpose of the Club. A maximum of twenty children was fixed in view of the size of the rooms available, although the group worker advised the committee to maintain a maximum of fifteen.

The Goslings Club was at no time in its history well supplied with toys and equipment. It failed to obtain, in spite of two applications, a loan for equipment from the Local Education Authority (Boltwood had obtained £60 for this purpose some years previously). But this very shortage of toys was not without compensation. The committee members very quickly busied themselves with collecting and making simple toys, and above all with getting together the materials for play. Sand from a building contractor, for example, came through the good offices of a committee member whose husband was foreman; a large tin bath for water play came from the home of a member; bricks came from a third, and so on. Through the Inspector of Schools (responsible for nursery schools) one infants' school at least contributed generously to the Club's store of paper, chalks, paints, bricks; also a blackboard and simple games for counting. The committee also made mackintosh pinafores to protect the children at play with the water and the sand, and brought old blankets for the polished floor of the Meeting Rooms, the pride of the caretaker.

The initial list of thirteen families whom Mrs. Andes subsequently visited to tell them about the Club was derived from three sources. Some names were suggested by the committee itself, some by an infants' school head-teacher from her waiting list, and one by the Anglican Church worker. It was after these visits that Mrs. Andes drew attention to the first lesson about the role of the Club – the obstacles to using it which faced the poorer mothers. Friday afternoon (the time fixed for the Club) was a luxury which they could not afford, and there was the trouble of dressing up the child in clean clothes and bringing him to the Meeting Rooms. Few of them saw the point of it, though they would have welcomed a daily club to have enabled them to go out to work.

Most of the names suggested were of quite ordinary and stable families, but a few were characterized by stresses and strains generally labelled as 'nerves' by the committee in their discussion with Mrs. Andes. For the opening meeting in January 1957 she sent an invitation to eight mothers, with one exception the more stable mothers on the list. She also gave an invitation to Mrs. G from the Mothers Group. These invitations were accepted, and with two exceptions the children continued with the Club until going on to school at the age of five. Of these two, one family left Bristol when the father moved to another job, the other – one of the most unstable mothers – ceased coming to the Club when Mrs. Andes was away in Israel.

Subsequently, however, there was no selection for membership by the worker. Names were suggested by head-teachers, the committee, and the mothers themselves, and placed on the waiting list. When a vacancy occurred the name at the top of the queue was admitted. The role of committee member did not carry with it the privilege of introducing friends to the Club out of turn.

Numbers varied according to the season of the year and in January–February 1958 dropped to six or seven, but in general were maintained at between twelve and fourteen, with one or two places reserved for mothers in an emergency. Children left when their turn came to go to school, but there were few breaks in membership for other reasons.

The routine of the Club which gradually developed conformed in many respects to the initial plans, but by no means in all. Mothers brought their toddlers at 1.30 p.m. and returned to collect them about 3.30 p.m., staying for a cup of tea and a chat together. This rule of the mothers' bringing and collecting children was a strict one, but it added to the difficulties of some mothers whose circumstances at home did not easily allow them to leave the house. The plan, however, of fairly formal discussion with the worker and the mothers in a group over tea, in a room set apart from the children, preceded on occasions by a short film on child care, was not entirely successful. Informality in the meeting was the more popular approach, and the mothers seemed happiest when in the same room with the children, though the noise was too great for talk as a group. It was, therefore, a wise move to shift the mothers' discussion from the small room apart from the children to the more informal setting of the large room in which the children played. This method of discussion they found easier to take.

In the committee meetings, too, the members were most at home in planning the social events to be run as an adjunct to the Club rather than in the organization of the Club itself. For the latter they relied gladly on the worker, who had the role of an outsider. They felt comfortable in the organization of the regular whist drives in each other's homes and of the Easter and Christmas parties. Liaison with outside bodies, the local authority, for example, they preferred to entrust to the Director of the Project, who was a member of the Club committee.

The significance of informality in approach and of opportunities for predominantly social activities emerges as one of the chief characteristics of the Club as a community responsibility. Related to this is the change in the composition of the committee which occurred during the period under review. Broadly speaking, the committee lost its representative character and became instead a 'users'' committee. By the end of fifteen months, only three of the original committee, selected by the various women's groups of Upfield as their representatives, remained. Of these three, two were Chairman and Treasurer. The turnover in membership also emphasized the significance of informality in committee relationships; the new members were drawn from mothers who were using the Club, and the Director's idea of a committee representative of the estate was quietly buried.

The same contrast between formality and informality relates also to the roles of the helpers. The blending of the right demands made by Mrs. Andes on helpers contributed to the success of the Club. Experience had taught her how to make wise use of the helpers' interests and abilities and to relate the demands made upon them to their capacities. At one point, for example, in the early history of the Club she believed that the falling-off in helpers among Upfield mothers was because too much was expected of them.

It is useful to distinguish between skill required in handling children, particularly the more difficult children, which is best fulfilled by people with training and experience, and the more straightforward tasks of putting out the equipment or making the tea. The professional worker may find the greatest difficulty over those helpers – sometimes without children of their own – who are anxious to play with the children and to gain the children's affection so as to meet their own inner needs, and who find it hard to understand new ideas about children's play. Such helpers are not content with the simpler tasks. Their own need makes them seek out a role which gives them closer contact with children. Every club has had experience of the helper whose enthusiasm for doing everything leads to inactivity and apathy among the remainder. In the deployment and use of helpers the group worker's ability is finely tested.

The Goslings Club certainly illustrates a general point in the Project's argument – the absolute necessity of training and experience in the organization of a club of this kind and the need to draw on help from outside the estate for certain functions. The outsider has the additional role of taking the blame in situations where conflict arises and where hostility is likely to disrupt relationships within the group.[1] The Club also illustrates the value to the student helper of a period of work with a children's group

[1] For an interesting and penetrating anthropological study of the function of the outsider in a Welsh village, see Frankenberg (1957).

under the guidance of a trained worker as practical experience during a university course in education for social work.

In the Goslings Club, the group worker was in effect concerned with not one group but three groups – children, mothers, and committee. Most of the helpers did not form a fourth group, but were drawn from the committee. There were, in addition, three helpers at different times in the history of the Club from outside Upfield. Mrs. Andes's role in each of the three groups naturally differed according to the nature of the group, but it was at all times a professional role. She was seen as a paid and skilled worker whose methods were valued and respected even though they turned out to be different from original expectations. Initially, at least, both the committee and the mothers had expected a much more active role, that is, someone who would organize the children into games and so forth.

The methods of the group worker in the Goslings Club were basically similar to her methods with the other groups. She placed emphasis on the strengthening of relationships, not on the development of activities. Her professional role she interpreted as providing the framework within which this could take place. At one point she defined this skill as 'withstanding the juggling of the clients into positions advantageous to them'.

The atmosphere of the Club was free and permissive. The demands made on the group, both of children and of mothers, were in terms of the group's own capacity and level of maturity and understanding.

The early meetings of the Club provided a settling-down period for the children. Most of them came and left happily, and as they got to know one another the early jealousy over the possession of particular toys or equipment lessened. The girls were noticeably less active in their play than were the boys. There was, however, the tiny minority of more difficult children, making heavy demands on the time and attention of the worker and the helper, either clinging continually to them or creating havoc among the others. With the small number of children who would not be left by their mothers, Mrs. Andes encouraged the mothers not to hurry their departure but to stay with their children until they were happy to be left on their own.

This process took time. It was only at the end of the third month, for example, that Robert settled down happily without his mother. By this time, however, a new member had arrived, Alan, whose anxiety over separation was just as intense. This is how one of the helpers (trained as a nurse and married to a doctor) described Alan's second visit:

> I can't give any detailed account of this afternoon. Alan's rage, tears, and continual clinging rather blocked my view of the other children, and claimed all my attention. David often came up to Alan offering obscure bits of information and comfort, but Alan would have nothing to do with him. By the end of the afternoon he was calm and quiet and happy, sitting on the floor beside me, reading one book after another, making many comments on them. He would notice the moment my attention wandered from him, and if it were for long, would try to climb on to my lap. I am told he is just as tyrannical with his mother, sleeping between his parents in their bed, and has always done so. But this is hearsay. One of the committee coped with the other children and all was well. (This was during Mrs. Andes's holiday.)

Only one child, David, came with a reputation for trouble-making in the neighbourhood. His mother was anxious to explain how difficult he was at home and the need for discipline in the Club:

> Mrs. W thought there would be discipline. David needed discipline, anyway he didn't love her (I am afraid I couldn't quite see the connection). The Child Guidance Clinic was a waste of time. They did nothing there for the children. The nursery was a good place, because children had a lot of organized activities. She had often shaken David 'until his teeth rattle' but somehow it did no good.

David's mother asked whether his father could fetch him after the third meeting he attended, as she had to go to see some relations:

I said it would be nice if she could make arrangements to fetch him herself in future but I would, of course, be very pleased to see David's father.

Father is a lorry-driver and obviously at his wits' end with David. He shouted at him and then made the child kiss him. We had quite a lengthy chat, he obviously wanted a recipe as to what to do with David. When I told him there was no way of changing David from today to tomorrow, he said he knew this; and when I said he might drop in from time to time for a chat, he verbally agreed and didn't think it a waste of time. Though I felt he didn't see much value in talking, he was anxious to do everything he could so that his conscience could be clear, that he hadn't neglected the child. He said he knew the fault was the parents. I quickly tried to reassure him, but he yelled for David, dressed him roughly, demanded a kiss, and forced him to wave and say good-bye. 'He has no feeling, that child,' said Mr. W.

To follow David's vicissitudes through the Goslings Club would take a paper on its own. At first he played alone, isolated and subdued, demanding attention from the worker in language hard to understand. Gradually his behaviour changed to aggression towards the other children and gave rise to anxiety from some mothers and a strong demand for firmer control from one of the helpers. Mrs. Andes persevered and encouraged Mrs. W to maintain contact with the Children's Hospital.

Through concern about David's behaviour and the viewing of a few simple documentary films on children at play, the mothers gradually came to see a little of the function of the group as a method of helping children to grow more secure and independent. David, for example, was a constant user of the sand and water which was available for play, and for which the courtyard in the summer months was particularly useful. Mrs. Andes was able to explain to the mothers the help which he derived from this kind of opportunity, and through seeing improvement in him they came to understand the value of the social experience gained in the Club.

In August David's younger sister (the favoured child) began to come to the Club. Though David was very jealous of her, he was pleased to have an opportunity of showing off his sister. Mrs. Andes writes in her diary:

> Evidently at home these two children are continually fighting, but not a cross word or action passed between them at the Club the whole afternoon. David acted as 'host' to his little sister and generally looked after her quite well. At milk time he was quite delightful when he asked her 'Nice?' while she was drinking. Once or twice during the afternoon David threw water about rather wildly but there were no big scenes or crises.

By the middle of September the head-teacher of an infants' school admitted David to her nursery class, and David, we learned, settled down quite happily. His sister continued at the Club. Though given disproportionate emphasis here, David's story suggests the help that a warm and understanding worker can provide through a play group, at least as a background to Clinic treatment and as a prelude to school. In a toddlers' club sponsored by the local community the number of such children that the club can carry is strictly limited – not more, perhaps, than two or three.

After David's departure there were other children whose first break with 'Mum' was eased and softened by joining the Club, but the general trend in the committee's selection policy, as children gradually left the Club for school and new members took their places, was towards the choice of fewer children with difficulties.

The mothers evolved their own tradition in the course of the first nine months. Their meetings were certainly of a much more informal pattern than the Director had proposed in his initial plans to the committee. This perhaps is an important lesson learned. The idea of a group of mothers meeting over tea with the worker in a small room slightly apart from the children's main play room gave way to a much noisier and less controlled pattern in which tea was taken in the big room with the children. Mothers approached the worker when there were difficulties, but in general were liveliest when there was no opportunity for controlled discussion.

There were exceptions. On three occasions short films on child care were shown and general talk about the subject of the films followed. For these showings, the mothers came slightly earlier, but this arrangement shortened their own private plans for the afternoon. There were two parties at Christmas and Easter which the committee planned. The teacher of a local nursery class gave a talk on the methods used in the school. It was a helpful talk, and the mothers sat round in a circle. In the discussion which followed, on the system of priorities for admission to the class, strong views were expressed and some criticism. Mrs. Andes comments in her diary:

> I thought that the talk obviously had done a great deal of good – it had made them move into a group and they were able to raise all their doubts and questions.

The mothers, too, played their part in the running of the Club. Some of them joined the committee; all took their turn in helping with the tea; some suggested new members. They were in the main a high-status group and rather intolerant of the few mothers whose standards were much lower than their own.

Of the change in the structure of the committee from one representative of Upfield groups to a committee of users, we have already written. It was a lively group with a genuine interest in the Club. Morale was highest in the group when the parties and social events – whist drives in particular – were in full swing. The whist drives were held in the homes of committee members in turn and produced a sum of £16 in October for the funds. But their function was as much a social as a money-raising one. In the organization of these social activities their chairman was quite exceptionally gifted. The responsibility for the handling of the children she left to Mrs. Andes.

Unlike the Mothers Group and the Espressos, the Goslings Club has continued successfully after the termination of the Project. The Save the Children Fund give advice and some financial help. The services of a trained and experienced worker as successor to Mrs. Andes were fortunately available and the Club has grown in numbers. The contribution of the mothers to the cost of the Club is now 6*d*. per day.

The Goslings Club serves several useful purposes. First, it provides an opportunity for children at the pre-school stage to play together in a group and to gain that kind of social experience which proves so helpful to them when they move on to the infants' school. Second, it enables the mothers to get away from their toddlers for a free afternoon for their shopping and their household chores. Third, it makes possible the kind of informal discussion about their children from which the mothers can learn about their care and upbringing. Finally, it acts as a useful opportunity for social activity in a neighbourhood group on the part of the committee and the mothers. Even after their children had left, the mothers still kept occasional contacts with the Club.

But it is equally important to be clear about what it does *not* do. On the one hand, it does not meet the need of those mothers who would find it useful to have a place where their children could be looked after much more frequently. It is certainly not an alternative to the nursery class or the day nursery for mothers who have to go out to work. On the other hand, in terms of offering a means whereby a neighbourhood such as Upfield could itself absorb and deal with disturbed stresses and strains, the Goslings Club provided further evidence of the unreasonableness of such hopes. The mothers and the committee members clearly had qualities of responsibility and public-spiritedness, but it was only by pressure from a skilled professional worker that they accepted a few difficult children, and they never really saw their activity as something that could be remedial.

CHAPTER 7

Upfield Teachers Group

THE nature of the experience and of the relationships in this group make it inappropriate to present the happenings in diary form. Instead, an attempt has been made to describe in a summarized form the historical development of the group, and to show how the structure and method of leadership changed and the reasons why this was done.

The group arose directly out of a meeting held at the Royal Fort (University Department of Education) in June 1954, when the Vice-Chancellor and the Director spoke to the leaders and professional workers of Upfield and Boltwood about the aims of the Project.

In addressing the meeing, the Vice-Chancellor said, 'The only way in which social progress towards a better society in a housing estate can be achieved is from within the estate itself.' He added that the Project did not intend to do things for people in the direct sense but aimed to *encourage, inspire, and assist* the development of social activity.

In the course of the discussion which followed, the Director invited the help and co-operation of the leaders of the community who had attended the meeting. It was in response to this invitation that the Upfield Teachers Group was formed. The Director explained that the reason for his invitation for help was that teachers constituted one of the most important professional groups on the estate; they were in daily contact with the schoolchildren and their help and goodwill were absolutely essential for the implementation of the Project.

At this point it may be useful to say something about the schools at Upfield. In 1954, when the group commenced, there were eight schools serving both the estate and a small area of privately owned houses on its eastern boundary. Of these eight schools, three were for infants, three for juniors, and two were secondary schools, one for boys and the other for girls. A fourth primary school was opened in 1956. Two of the infants' schools had nursery classes. These schools were situated evenly in all parts of the estate. Prior to 1955 the boundaries of the areas for each of the schools had been clearly defined, but after that date parents were at liberty to send their children to the school of their own choice. In practice the infants' and junior schools drew on the families in the immediate locality, while the two secondary schools covered the whole estate.

Thus the intention of the Director in forming a Teachers Group was to draw an important section of professional workers at Upfield into the life of the Project. By doing so it was hoped they would become more conscious of the needs of the estate and better able to fulfil those needs. The teachers were encouraged to look more closely at the social and family life of the children in their schools.

These were the initial aims. In retrospect it is easy to confuse the early issues and to interpolate ideas which emerged only in the course of time. The form and methods which characterized the third and final phase of the Teachers Group were not the result of deliberate and conscious planning from the beginning. The method of work during the first three years was conventional in character and is to be regarded mainly as a prelude to the group worker's own analysis of the experience in the final years.

The four years' work, from the opening meeting in September 1954 until the final meeting in June 1958, can be divided into three phases:

In the first phase the Director was leader. In the second phase leadership was shared with Professor Wallace,[1] and in the third phase with Miss Cassidy, the group worker. The group experience provided the teachers with an opportunity for expressing feelings about their own work and particularly about the stresses and strains involved in it.

During the first phase there were two groups running parallel to one another, one consisting of primary and the other of secondary teachers. They devoted their attention to a specific job of work – the work task –which was the collection of information about the family and social background of a random sample of children in their own classes. Their primary intention was to help the Project, and the Project's aim, as the Vice-Chancellor had pointed out, was to help Upfield.

In the second phase there was only one group. The emphasis shifted, first to the discussion of other professional workers' experiences at Upfield, and then to the presentation of material drawn from the teachers' own observations of children as members of groups at work and play. The method used in the first and second phases was similar to that used in the seminar. In the third phase the group began to look at itself.

The feelings expressed by the group about schools and their function may give rise to strong criticism from some quarters. It is, however, important to distinguish between facts and feelings. Both deserve serious attention, since our understanding of facts is often influenced by our feelings about them. In the third phase of the group we were primarily concerned with these feelings, and Miss Cassidy, by virtue of her training and experience, was well qualified to help the group to gain a better understanding of them. There is a sharp contrast between the first and the third phases of the group. In the first phase the teachers were concerned primarily with facts: the questionnaire which evolved in the course of the first five meetings was designed to elicit certain facts about their children's families, their size, their jobs, their contacts with relations, and so on. In the third phase the group was encouraged to

[1] Professor Wallace, visiting Fulbright lecturer, was consultant on group work to the Project.

develop a flexible structure, so that feelings about the teacher's job could be freely expressed, considered, and understood.

During these three phases the work task changed. So, too, did the attendance of the teachers. It was highest in the first two phases. During the third phase the size of the group remained constant at seven or eight members, excluding the Director and Miss Cassidy. What deserves emphasis, however, is not the fact that attendance gradually diminished but that in our view the method employed in the third phase could be developed only in a small group.

Of the seven members who remained to the end, six had attended regularly from the beginning. Most of them were secondary school teachers, and the only teacher who had not belonged from the beginning did not come to the estate until 1956. All of them were teachers of at least three years' experience, but the majority had taught for very much longer. During Phases I and II approximately one-third of the group consisted of younger teachers who had only recently completed their training. This suggests, perhaps, that the method of Phase III is most acceptable to the more experienced. It may also underline the fact that many of the sharpest problems of present-day education are centred in the secondary modern school, and that teachers in these schools are anxious to find ways of solving them.

The proportion of men and women who attended the group reflects the proportion of men and women teachers on the estate as a whole and deserves little comment. What is of interest is the analysis of membership according to type of school. By the second phase, the attendance of junior teachers had dropped very considerably. In retrospect, the initial division into primary and secondary groups may have been most useful to the junior school teachers and its discontinuation in Phase II a disappointment. On the other hand, the majority of members who attended in the second phase were insistent on the value of learning about teaching children in different age-groups and were sorry to lose the experience of the other teachers.

The presence of head-teachers also gave rise to disagreement.

Some members felt that freedom of expression would be difficult if head-teachers were also members of the group. Others felt that the greater experience and knowledge of such teachers would be a real help in discussion. Here also there is a contrast between the first two phases and the third phase. In the search for facts centred upon the discussion of children, those heads who came made a valuable contribution. During the third phase, on the other hand, only one head remained, and none of the other members of the group taught in that school. As the Project team itself came to learn, it is not an easy experience for members of an institution who are related hierarchically to one another to take part in a group in which feelings of liking and disliking may be openly expressed.

As compared with the hierarchical structure of the school, the group had little formal structure. There was no claim of authority, and the leader wielded little power. Relationships were friendly and intimate. Some members of the group were close friends, and several members came because they had friends in the group whose company they enjoyed. But this was by no means universally true. Others came because they enjoyed the experience and felt it useful for themselves or for the Project.

PHASE I

Initially the teachers decided to work in two groups, one for primary and the other for secondary school teachers. A small number of teachers expressed the wish that primary and secondary teachers might work together, and accordingly it was suggested that in the new year there should be an amalgamation of the two groups.

'In fact,' wrote the Director, in an earlier report on the Teachers Group, 'our discussions moved slower than we had anticipated and the division into two groups remained unaltered throughout the whole academic year.' To some this was a disappointment and an experience of autocratic leadership, the effects of which, as we shall see, were present in Phase III.

These two groups met consistently each month throughout the year 1954–55. Attendance varied, and the original number of fifteen primary teachers fell to about eight.

The purpose of the group during its first phase was twofold. It was decided by the Director, who became the leader in each group, that they should together:

1. work out a questionnaire which would, when completed, provide information relating to the performance of a random sample (10 per cent of the school population) of Upfield schoolchildren in relation to their family and social background;
2. present case histories or pen-portraits of children in whom members of the two groups were particularly interested, thus illustrating the ways in which home background and behaviour as stated in the questionnaire were related.

During this year the groups adopted a seminar structure and discussed many topics concerning their work. The group of primary school teachers discussed such topics as: social status on the housing estate; mothers at work; the effect of the home on children; immaturity of parents; the function of the head-teacher; and friendships among children. The group of secondary school teachers met concurrently with the group of primary school teachers and discussed such topics as: the role of the school welfare officer; the behaviour of Teddy boys; methods of studying the home; and some studies in the development of individual children in their own class.

Both groups had been given the specific task of providing information about the home background of a ten per cent sample of the schoolchildren. Although there were many gaps in the sample, and the analysis of the results was handicapped for this reason, the exercise did provide the groups with an opportunity of talking about their particular problems in a relatively unstructured way. These problems were seen as centring upon the child. Time was usefully spent in learning more about him and his problems and how better to understand, teach, and help him. The groups were encouraged to concentrate upon their work task. During this phase their need to defer to the leader for guidance appears quite obvious, culminating in the decision by both groups that in the following session they should have a formal pro- gramme, more structure in the group, and stronger leadership. At this point amalgamation of the two groups was not discussed with them although on several occasions the primary school teachers had mentioned it.

PHASE II

The second phase, which began in November 1955 and lasted until May 1956, can be divided into two stages. During the inter- val between Phases I and II the Director had decided upon amalga- mation without specific reference to either of the groups. At the beginning of Phase II the attendance of the primary school teachers fell off rapidly and this decline continued until the end of 1956, when only one member of a primary school attended regu- larly. In the course of this period membership fluctuated between ten and twenty members with an average attendance of seventeen. Throughout the entire history of the group there was a faithful band of people who came regularly. The Director had invited Professor Wallace to the group, and it is noticeable that during Phase II decisions were taken for the group by the Director and Professor Wallace without the participation of the group in decision-making.

Stage one of the second phase was devoted to talks from outside workers on family casework, probation, and 'problem families', followed by discussion.

Stage two. At the fourth meeting it was decided that outside workers should no longer be invited and that the members of the group should present case studies. Over the next five meetings between February and May 1956 participation by the group in- creased, as did average attendance. Discussion was informed and lively.

During this stage Professor Wallace assumed the leadership of the group, and meetings were organized in such a way that the individual members could take as large a part as possible, not only in the presentation of case material but in the discussion which followed. Professor Wallace's role was that of the teacher helping the individual members of the group to see more clearly the reasons why children might behave in the way they did. He would endeavour to help the group to understand this behaviour in terms of the knowledge gained from the study of child psychology. Thus the focus of the teachers' group at this stage was the *subject-matter* under discussion, and the members tended to learn formally and efficiently about it. The feelings and attitudes of individual members of the group, which were often aroused by the discussion of the case material, were not discussed. The work task remained the focus of attention.

This can be seen *in the first meeting* of Phase II, stage two. After the description of a difficult gang at school, the group looked at the gang in detail and questions were asked about the children. The teachers raised the matter of confidentiality and repeatedly returned to this point. Some members wondered whether or not the presence of this difficult gang in school reflected upon the teaching. Others began to look at themselves and the effects of their attitude to this gang on the class, but they quickly turned to the task in hand, that of looking closely at the children. At this stage both the leader and the group avoided looking at the attitudes of individual members of the group which were present in the group itself, and were also affecting the behaviour of the gang and the class.

During the next four meetings the group discussed the talks by individual teachers on deprived and rejected children whose problem behaviour seriously disturbed their classes. Professor Wallace directed the group's attention to the ways in which teachers and other workers might help to meet these children's needs. But the group did not seek to learn about rejection and acceptance by looking at its own ways of accepting and making its members feel accepted and wanted.

At a later meeting the group discussed what had been achieved in the group, as the result of discussion. The teachers felt that discussions had enabled them to see the problem child more clearly and to clarify their role in relation to him. They saw the importance of the home background and the work of the social worker in relation to it. They were, however, anxious to get answers about how specifically to deal with these problems and wanted to hear much more about what was being done to provide these answers. It was decided at the end of this period that these questions should be explored further during the next session.

Throughout this phase the group had experienced a degree of formal structuring, together with a certain type of leadership, which in turn affected its behaviour. Professor Wallace, who had assumed leadership, had decided that it would be appropriate for this group to learn about the problem child in relation to the teacher. Professor Wallace behaved as a teacher. He helped to give the members a greater knowledge about and understanding of the problems they brought to the group. The structure of the group was set by the leader. Within this structure the group functioned efficiently. Members were able to go away after each meeting and at the end of the session saying that they had learnt certain things about certain problems, although they were still anxious for answers. During this phase the group could be described as dependent for its learning upon a leader who could teach members about matters of which they had no knowledge.

In making recommendations for the following session they had shown their need to continue this dependency by demanding answers from experts who would be invited to talk to the group. Their approach to their work was in terms of problems and appropriate technical answers. During this time members were not encouraged to learn about personal relationships and about relationships in groups by looking at what was happening in their own group in particular. Nor were they helped to relate their feelings as they met in the group, and an understanding of these feelings, to the problem under discussion.

PHASE III

Phase III began in November 1956 and lasted until July 1958. During this time the group met on twenty-two occasions. For the first four meetings membership was high but fluctuating. Some junior school members attended but they were in the minority. From the fifth meeting onwards the group stabilized itself and its composition remained stable from then until meetings ceased in 1958. The group was made up of secondary modern school teachers with the exception of one teacher who was head of a junior school. There was one member of the group who had kept loose and intermittent contact with its activities from the beginning and he continued in the same way during Phase III. He was, however, well known to all the members of the group and was never treated as an outsider or an interloper. If members were not able to come, reasons for their non-attendance together with apologies were always sent to the group in person or by a letter. On two occasions members brought strangers to the group but the visits were not repeated.

Phase III can be divided into three stages. The first stage, covering the first five meetings, was concerned primarily with the group's desire to find a strong leader. Members showed some disapproval when the Director would not fill this role, and looked for a substitute. They wished to have the guidance of a strong leader who would increase their self-confidence by telling them what would work and why (cf. Professor Wallace's leadership).

As a consequence of Miss Cassidy's membership of the group and her advice as to its future development, the Director began to steer the group away from a formal programme of talks towards the growth of an informal structure. The emphasis was to be on the group's reliance on its own leadership and on looking at *its own* behaviour and feelings. This change was resisted and progress was very slow. Throughout these five meetings of Phase III each member of the group was able to try out the extent to which he or she could take over the leadership of the group and to discover how far the Director would himself tolerate criticism. This struggle was epitomized in the extent to which the group kept to the planned programme and in the varying capacity of its members to look more closely at themselves individually and collectively.

The second stage began to develop with the sixth meeting, when Miss Cassidy spoke for four minutes on the family as a group and the effect of this experience on individuals with regard to their actions within, and expectations of, any groups of which they subsequently became members. The members of the group then began to talk about their own families, as both children and parents, and turned to talk about themselves as a group. They compared the present and past running of the group, and discussed the Director's leadership. They felt that without a programme it became very difficult to tell outsiders about the group and to explain what happened in it. They talked a little of the different kinds of leadership in the schools in relation to the headmaster, and decided that much of value was gained when they did not keep to a programme.

Gradually during this second stage the Director abdicated from the 'old idea' of the strong leader who was supposed to know all the answers. Though at first bewildered by this change in role, the members began to explore the meaning of this new pattern of leadership in terms of the Project team and then in relation to themselves.

The tenth meeting saw the beginning of the third stage in Phase III. On this, and on all subsequent occasions, the group meeting had *no* specific beginning or end. On this occasion the group began talking about two young children who had been murdered in Bristol. Members criticized the attitude of parents who allowed children to roam about alone. This led to the presentation of personal experience regarding the different ways in which men and women express grief. Then discussion centred on the expression of other feelings, especially aggression, and they brought case material on how children expressed aggression at school. It was seen by the group to be important to understand the reasons for behaviour and the feelings that lay behind it. Several members of the group spoke a little about their own reactions to the behaviour they often met with in the classroom and how they sometimes had little understanding of their own feelings in relation to it. It was generally agreed that to talk about these feelings to somebody was helpful, but that in many situations there was no opportunity for this. The group talked about the different ways in which people reacted to difficult situations and recognized the value of having a safety-valve. Some members of the group put forward the opinion that sickness could be an outlet for unexpressed feelings. Finally, as this was the last meeting before the summer recess, they discussed the future of the group during the next session and decided that there was particular value in free discussions and that they would not go back to the formal programme of topics for discussion.

The eleventh meeting took place after a break of two months. Discussion centred upon other social clubs and groups like the teachers' group, and mention was made of how people came to be included in groups, and how cliques within the group were used to exclude some people. From here the group discussed the ways in which new staff members were made to feel part of the school. The group also discussed itself and other groups with regard to conformity in behaviour and stressed how important it was for an individual within a group to have the approval of the other members.

From this period till the group terminated in 1958 the Director and Miss Cassidy played an extremely passive role. They interrupted only when they felt that learning might be increased if the group were to look at its own functioning. At this time the morale of the group and a sense of individual belongingness increased, and the group found it easier to express feelings and personal experiences as well as to discuss topics of professional interest.

During the next ten meetings the group discussed the following topics: the ways by which we assess children and adults; the sources of our standards of behaviour and the reasons why teachers impose standards on children; the relationship between clothes, conformity, and discipline; the differences between justice, punishment, and discipline; rivalry in the school; and the delinquency of children and themselves (i.e. the group members).

During the last four or five meetings there was an increasing number of opportunities for the group and its individual members to see the attitudes they were adopting in relation to a problem or to each other. The group at this stage in its development was ready to look much more realistically at itself, both collectively and individually. If the group had continued for another year it would, no doubt, have become more possible to help members by encouraging them to look at their behaviour 'here-and-now' in the group and to relate this experience to other experiences outside the group.

It is difficult to say exactly what was achieved during this period. The Director could not say he had taught the group certain things. It was impossible to assess whether the group had learned to relate differently to other people. It is doubtful whether the group members could have said what if anything it was they had learnt.

At the Clevedon conference in 1951 Sir Philip Morris said that the basic problem was one of getting people into different relationships with each other. Perhaps the members of the group had increased both their intellectual awareness of and insight into people's behaviour in relation to others.

What did this experience of group work amount to for those who joined in all its phases and stages? The exercise had begun by their having a closer look at the way children behaved in and out of school, and proceeded, by way of tutorial guidance, to an analysis of the psychological and sociological reasons for difficult behaviour. These phases were useful in helping the participating teachers to observe more sensitively and accurately, and in introducing them, through an analysis of their own case studies, to principles in terms of which much difficult behaviour can be understood.

The third phase took a much smaller group a step further. Members came to see that part of the difficulties of the children lay in their (the teachers') own difficulties: not the difficulties of inadequate technique or time or equipment or staff, but difficulties rooted in the teachers' own feelings about their work and relationships, feelings they did not know they had or would not have thought mattered until they found themselves talking about their feelings in the last stage of Phase III.

From a vague awareness that somehow they were not doing a good job as teachers with a significant number of their children, and that the real fault lay with the badness of parents, they looked at their own feelings more and more closely and came to see how they themselves might be contributing to the difficulties of the children. Then, by applying reason to interpret their feelings, this picture emerged: Almost all qualified teachers have been successful pupils in grammar schools. Their own most recent experience of school is of an institution in which the basic assumption is, quite rightly, that pupils can and do learn academically, and that the success or failure of the school is, in a large measure, assessed in terms of apparently straightforward and easily understood examination results. In the minds of many thoughtful people examination results are by no means the sole criterion by which to assess the quality of a school. But parents, employers, and work-a-day teachers all tend to look for a simple criterion and this tends to turn on the quantity of knowledge absorbed by the pupils. As former grammar-school pupils themselves, most teachers in schools other than grammar schools start with grammar-school presuppositions, which become more or less modified, though against the teachers' inclinations, by what arises in practice.

But the secondary modern members of the Teachers Group found that they had become increasingly aware that a considerable number of their children were apparently untouched by any desire for academic knowledge; and they had come to feel that they were failing their pupils if they stressed teaching, in even a modified academic sense, as the *main* link in the relationship between pupil and teacher. They were worried that, in place of performing what looked like the simple function of teacher, they seemed to be taking over many of the functions traditionally ascribed to parents; and this they could not avoid as they were faced day by day in the classroom with the problems of rewards and punishments, discipline, personal relationships, and the teaching of morality. This was something quite different from what they had, in their picture of teaching as they remembered it from their own schooldays, expected teaching to be.

Confused by the problem of what they ought to be doing – purveying knowledge or improving character – the teachers felt, rather than understood, that their work in their classrooms was purposeless and yet they could not see at what goals they ought to be aiming. What was the criterion of success with such children? In the matter of discipline, for instance, the aim, symbolized by the pattern of rewards and punishments, could differ widely in one class of the school as compared with another. And this was felt to be confusing for the child. Yet it was a factor in the child's life for which the teachers, not the child, were responsible.

This situation did not, the teachers felt, arise in this form in the setting of the grammar school, for there the school values, held in common by all concerned as a group, were also held by each individual as a person, and in these circumstances the purpose of the school was clearly perceived and reasonably easily and contentedly fulfilled. There was a coherence of aspiration and expectation among staff and pupils which gave corresponding definiteness to attitudes and organization. But so far as secondary modern schools were concerned, the teachers felt that, though the set-up within which they worked was geared to the values and attitudes appropriate to the grammar school, these did not correspond to the attitudes of many of their pupils, nor to what teachers actually found themselves doing, as they responded, positively or negatively, to the attitudes of the children. The pattern of organization and personal relationship in schools did not allow time and opportunity for staff to express their perplexities and to work through to a mutual understanding of their different personal attitudes to the problems of character-building. The tensions were there, but were not made tolerable and constructive by understanding; they remained as elements of conflict.[1] And the children

[1] For a penetrating study of the teacher's role and the problem of conflict, see Wilson (1962, pp. 15-32).

- especially the insecure ones – suffered in consequence of this conflict. Time and again in the Teachers Group someone would express the wish that there might be in schools opportunities for teachers to discuss problems of this sort freely among themselves with the help of a group leader.

CHAPTER 8

Upfield Social Workers Group

UNLIKE the Teachers Group, which was begun by the Bristol Social Project, the Social Workers Group was in existence before the Project became active in Upfield.

In the tradition of voluntary associations engaged in social work, the Bristol Council of Social Service was anxious to engage colleagues and interested laymen in certain aspects of the work undertaken by the Council, and had therefore started the Social Workers Group.

Various social workers in Upfield, both statutory and voluntary, had been asked to become members of this group to help the worker of the Bristol Council of Social Service with her work, which was concerned with certain families living in the area who were in difficulties. At this time the group was known as the 'Upfield Case Committee'.

The Director of the Bristol Social Project at the beginning of his contact with the Case Committee was interested in the way in which it could provide useful background material for the Project. Only later did it become one of the groups in which the Project, through its members, became actively engaged. First the Director, then the social worker employed jointly by the Bristol Council of Social Service and the Project, and lastly the psychiatric social worker employed primarily for the research into family functioning, all took a lively interest and participated in the group's activities.

123

Unfortunately, the activities of this group are incompletely recorded, and on a few occasions records are missing. As the group was never considered to be a major sphere of activity, no detailed records were kept, although there is a minuted account of the proceedings kept by the Secretary of the Case Committee itself. Experience with the group showed that the problems of the group and the methods used to resolve them have some bearing upon the life of an estate such as Upfield, and reflect problems currently facing social workers in the community today.

The last fifty years have seen a rapid growth in the social services, accompanied by an increase in the number of social workers. The social worker today has many colleagues who can help her in her job, but at the same time the number of social workers active in an area such as Upfield increases the need for adequate communication between them. Often a considerable amount of time has to be found to facilitate understanding between people with different trainings, spheres of activity, and responsibility.

The history of the Social Workers Group at Upfield is an account of how a number of people concerned both with helping people to improve their personal relationships and with helping the community to improve its conditions, came together in an attempt to solve these problems more adequately. Social workers' luncheon clubs and co-ordination committees are two familiar ways of making time and finding a way of communication which makes for greater co-operation. The problem of communication is likely to become more acute with the increase in the number of social workers, and unless the problem of adequate communication is solved, the work of the individual social worker will be hampered to a considerable extent.

For three and a half years the Project was connected with the Social Workers Group, and during this period the group members used their time together in different ways. By looking in some detail at these various methods, it may be possible to assess their efficiency in helping people to share and understand the problems that beset them in their everyday work.

The Project had definite ideas about the ways in which group discussion could be facilitated, and it was possible to implement these ideas in those groups which the Project had itself started. This was not so easily achieved in the Social Workers Group, which team members of the Project joined after the group's inception. At some time the two Project field workers who were involved with the group were asked to take the chair, and this provided them with an opportunity to change the patterns of leadership.

The history of the Upfield Social Workers Group falls roughly into three phases:

PHASE I

The first phase extended from February 1955 to March 1956. Attendance during this period was always high, with membership increasing. The school welfare officer, workers from the Children's Department, the probation officers, a British Legion worker, workers from the Family Service Unit, the Church of England vicar (who joined towards the end of this phase), the health visitors, members of the Bristol Council of Social Service and the Bristol Social Project all attended regularly, and the minutes show a lively interest in the problems which were discussed – problems relating to all aspects of social work.

During this period the group concentrated upon the discussion of cases or on a variety of related subjects which were often introduced by outside speakers, such as the consequences of hire-purchase and the handling of hostility. The minutes at this time make several references to the function of the group itself, but this subject was never really discussed. Concern was often expressed about how to encourage a high attendance and how to use the time in a way most useful to members of the group. There appears to have been some confusion about the precise function of the group. It was seen variously as an advisory panel, as a forum for case discussion, and as an educational group when a visiting speaker came.

PHASE II

The second phase extended from March 1956 to June 1957. The earlier high attendance was maintained during this period, although in the actual figures there is an indication of future trends, when staff from the Children's Department, the probation officers, and the health visitors became less active and regular in their support of the group. During this time too the local Co-ordinating Committee[1] was formed, and the pressures to discuss cases, as had been done previously, became less acute.

During the second phase the speakers included a general practitioner from the estate, the vicar, a visiting marriage guidance counsellor, and members of the group itself. The topics included various aspects of marriage breakdown; problems of collaboration between workers with the family; and the life of the estate.

Emphasis was placed upon talks of an informative or educational nature, and the group's formal structure of a chairman, secretary, and treasurer was rigidly maintained. Only one session was given over to the discussion of a case. Six of the talks were given by guest speakers, and as in the first phase some concern was expressed about the attendance at the meetings and the precise nature of the group's function.

PHASE III

The third phase extended from July 1957 to September 1958 but, owing to an experience in the spring of 1958, the character of the group work changed a good deal over the last few months. During this third phase attendance fell off substantially from the peak reached during the end of the first phase and the beginning of the second. By April 1958, attendance by members of the Children's Department, the probation service, and the health

[1] The local Co-ordinating Committee was one of a number of committees set up by the local authority to provide an opportunity for all the social workers in the area to discuss families which were giving them much concern.

visiting service had pretty well ceased; on the other hand, a local headmistress had become active in the group.

The fall in membership coincided with a change in the group's method of working. All the talks except one were given by members of the group. The outside expert imparting authoritative knowledge no longer provided the programme. Instead, the members found themselves sharing the difficulties and perplexities experienced by them individually as they went about their jobs in Upfield. This was of particular importance to those of the group who were working alone and not as members of a team, and who had therefore to carry their cases and the anxieties arising out of them without the support of colleagues. For these workers the intimate and unportentous discussions in the group provided a means of encouragement and support as well as an exchange of ideas. Those who continued to come were troubled by the non-attendance of the statutory workers who were members of teams, for the former wanted the support and encouragement of the latter. Yet the latter, members of departments in which this sense of group support was available, may have felt that the local group had nothing to offer them and that they could use their time better than by attending.

The topics discussed during this period covered the following: the probation service; the municipal housing department; the school welfare service; the work of the health visitor and of the parish worker; and the giving of financial aid to families in need.

Quite without intention, a discussion on co-operation between statutory and voluntary bodies precipitated a situation which had a profound effect on the members of the group, about eight in number, who continued to meet. So far as the group was concerned, this situation was charged with strong feelings, and the present account is written from the point of view of the chairman and the secretary of the group. Their interpretation of events would certainly differ from the interpretation which would be made by the city officials concerned, but the picture is painted in these terms because it illustrates how easy it is for tension to arise between people of quite considerable experience and of equally intelligent compassion, simply because of the difficulty of establishing effective communication.

It had been the custom of the group to circulate after each meeting a duplicated record of the discussion, known as 'minutes'. On hindsight, it is clear that this circulation was no longer appropriate in Phase III; but group routine persisted while group experience had changed. The minutes of the discussion on the statutory and voluntary services recorded the fact that some members of the group had expressed criticism of the relationships between statutory and voluntary workers, and had even referred to some social workers as 'problems'.

It was these minutes which came, in the course of routine, to the notice of senior city officers, and as a result the chairman and the secretary of the Social Workers Group were approached by a representative of the Town Clerk's Department. From this point on, the two representatives of the Social Workers Group felt that they were treated as miscreants, or as children, or both. A suggestion from their side that they should have an informal talk in one of their own offices was turned down in favour of what they felt was a summons to attend a very formal meeting in a committee room of the Council House. The city officers concerned seemed to the social workers to be disturbed and angry, and the meeting began with several stormy passages, after which the participants settled down amicably to a discussion of the difficulties facing people not only in the voluntary, but also in the statutory, settings. The social workers tried to explain the purpose and value of the free expression of group members' feelings about their work, but they felt that this was met with superior amusement and a failure to realize that official communication at the level of co-ordinating committees does not reach to the roots of the sort of co-operation which is essential to the effectiveness of the social services in an area like Upfield. In short, the two social workers who attended this meeting left feeling angry and futile.

When they reported back to the group, the members were, on the one hand, bothered by what had seemed to be the angry reaction of the officials and the summary way in which the meeting had been called; on the other hand, they were in a measure amused that for the first time in its existence the group had been treated as if it were, in some sense, important. But the dominant feeling was of annoyance and upset.

The incident has been related as it looked at the time to one set of participants. It is, of course, clear that there was another side to the events. But we have told the story in this way simply because it illustrates the immensely important part that feelings can play, even in the outlook of those who are well aware of this fact. A reasonably rational group of social workers on a housing estate were so bothered by what they thought was the way they were being treated that they ceased for a time to talk in rational terms. City officials became positive villains. This may do no particular credit to the social workers, but the other aspect of the matter is the degree to which city officials can appear to be intimidating even when this is not their intention. Both of these aspects are important for our general thesis – that what people feel or do not feel about a situation can be far more decisive in how they interpret it than a rational examination of the facts. Once a housing estate drifts out of touch with those who personify authority, misunderstanding based on feeling may become very deep-rooted. Those with authority, especially if they are unselfconscious and warm-hearted, can very easily forget that what they intend to be persuasion may, at the other end, feel like compulsion. If this is so among professional people, the gap can be even greater where the language and values of the parties are poles apart.

This shared experience of being in the doghouse had a considerable effect on the last few months of the life of the Social Workers Group. On the one hand, the members developed a greater sense of dependency on each other and increasingly felt the importance of the group in fostering collaboration between people engaged in a difficult job of work. On the other hand, the experience was a challenge to members to look at themselves, and to discuss how they felt threatened by their work and how they could give each other mutual support. To some extent the individuals in the group were encouraged to translate the feelings they experienced through this event into other spheres of their professional work and to consider what effect their own attitudes and behaviour might have on their clients.

The history of this Social Workers Group is, in many ways, parallel to that of the Teachers Group. During the first two phases, the members examined their work and sought greater knowledge, in the hope that greater knowledge would give them answers to their problems. These discussions helped considerably to increase the workers' knowledge and to deepen their insights into the techniques they were employing. The discussions also provided an opportunity for the individuals to consider the effects of their own feelings and behaviour upon each other and gave them some insight into the way in which they went about their jobs. In the third phase, the members of the group moved hesitatingly towards an exploration of these problems and began to learn how a greater understanding of the effects of their own behaviour on others might free them for greater involvement with their clients in a meaningful and helpful way.

The history of both the Teachers Group and the Social Workers Group has been described in some detail to underline the difficulties which are to be encountered, and the problems to be resolved, in the teaching and learning processes involved in the greater understanding of interpersonal relationships.

Everyone learns about relationships in the natural, unselfconscious, and spontaneous process of living together in a family. This process only begins in the family. Learning continues at school, at work, and in leisure activities; it is in turn translated into the relationships formed in the family of one's own making and thence to one's children. Our knowledge of and ability to make relationships are to some extent always imperfect and open to improvement. If the family group is an unsatisfactory one, this knowledge about relationships may be incompletely begun or seriously impaired. Then, in the process of growing up there is a real need for an opportunity to learn or relearn how to relate to people successfully. Schools, youth clubs, and work provide some spontaneous groups where this learning can take place. Clubs such as the Espressos also provide an opportunity in which the learning process can occur.

Besides those who need to learn how to make adequate relationships in the process of growing up, because of their imperfect learning within the family at an early age, another group of people who need to know about relationships are professional workers – teachers, social workers, doctors – whose jobs take them into close relationships with people and for whom the kind of relationship they make in the course of their work may be all-important in the helping process which characterizes their work.

The groups which have been described were designed to help both these groups of people towards a greater understanding and awareness of themselves in relation to other people.

PART III

Working with Groups
(The Adolescents)

CHAPTER 9

Toffs, Bums, and Espressos

GROUP WORK with adolescents was unquestionably the Project's biggest challenge, not only to the worker's skill, but also to the understanding of the team and Committee and their own neighbourhood. The Director had decided, after consultation with some members of the Committee, that continuation of group work with adolescents after the termination of the Project would be most successful if the group worker worked within the framework of an established club. As events subsequently showed, this decision was a mistaken one. The intention was that Mrs. Andes should join the Wood Grove Girls Club at Upfield as a group worker with responsibility, under the general administration of the warden, for one or two groups of girls inside the Club.

An essential feature of the group work method within a club is the breaking down of the total membership into small and identifiable groups in relationship to the worker. In the course of two years' work at the Wood Grove Club, the group worker became aware of the serious difficulties arising from the attempt to incorporate the group work method into the framework of an existing club. The problem became more acute when she found it necessary to concentrate her attention on the low-status girls in the Club, whose stresses demanded a more permissive approach than the warden was able to tolerate. At this point the difference in approach between group worker and club leader emerged quite clearly. It was, in effect, a conflict between the group worker's concern for relationships in the groups and the club leader's emphasis on activities. Behind this conflict, however, there was also a difference in viewpoint on the nature of control to be exercised in the groups and in the Club.

The Wood Grove Girls Club first started during the war under the auspices of the Bristol Association of Girls Clubs. It was run by a full-time leader on the premises of a local school and after two years moved to a hut on the eastern boundary of the estate on the edge of some playing fields. For most of its subsequent history it had a full-time leader.

In 1953 the two managements of the Girls Club and of the Upfield Boys Club were united under a single committee. The Boys Club had a much longer history. It still meets in a hut erected by the Juvenile Organizations Committee in 1931 shortly after the estate was built, and subsequently used in the years before the second world war for a boys' club.

For a while after the union of the two clubs a married couple occupied jointly the positions of club leaders. But when Mrs. Andes began work at the Wood Grove Girls Club in December 1955 the girls had a part-time leader. The full-time warden of the Boys Club had overall responsibility for the organization of the two clubs.

Throughout the history of the two clubs, inadequate premises have proved to be a continual handicap. They are situated about six minutes' walk from one another and both have suffered from the limitations of a wooden hut unsuited to the needs of the club. When we attempted to break down the total club population into smaller groups and to use group work methods in the Wood Grove Club, the need for suitably planned premises emerged more strongly perhaps than before. Privacy and independence for individual groups are well-nigh impossible in the wooden hut.

From the past records of the Club we gained certain impressions of club activities and the girls' responses to them which are probably typical of girls' clubs in neighbourhoods similar to Upfield. In the course of a survey of the Bristol Youth Service for the

136

Bristol Youth Leaders School carried out in 1950, the full-time leader describes a membership in the Club of 106 girls with an age-range of 9–18 years. There were no members over 18 though the upper age-limit was technically 21. Two-thirds of the membership were juniors and one-third seniors. The weekly programme organized for twelve months by the leader alone covered six nights each week, with juniors on two nights between 5.00 and 7.00 o'clock and seniors on five nights between 7.00 and 9.30, and one evening in which there was mixed activity for senior boys and senior girls. This mixed evening attracted about forty-five members, the biggest attendance of the week.

The leader observed that 'table-tennis and ball-room dancing, which were very popular, were the only energetic activities which the girls over 15 years of age supported. Most of the girls worked in factories or were shop assistants.' A youth organizer added: 'The Wood Grove Youth Centre always appeared to resist team games.' The leader commented that 'a change in the girls' attitude is needed. It is largely a mental attitude. After tea when girls come home from work they dress up for the evening and they usually spend the whole of Saturday afternoon in getting ready for going out in the evening.' She herself was a qualified PT and dancing instructor, but was unable to persuade the girls to take part in physical exercise.

The Youth Leaders School in their findings emphasized the high proportion of members of the organizations who were under 15, or, if over 15, were still attending school, e.g. virtually all Girl Guides in Bristol (4,000–5,000) and 80 per cent of Boy Scouts (about 6,000), while of the eight youth clubs represented in the survey, over 40 per cent of the members were still in full-time attendance at school and approximately one-third were under 15. They spoke also of the 'large unsatisfied demand for junior clubs and play centres, particularly on the housing estates, where there are many young families'.

The survey of the Youth Leaders School poses clearly the problem of the Youth Service in the light of contemporary adolescent needs. Certainly the pressure of what we may call a youth culture on the older adolescent girls still militates strongly against the kind of physical and organized activities which youth workers have thought desirable. The group worker, on the other hand, starts from different assumptions. He recognizes the force of these cultural pressures about what is considered appropriate behaviour by young people and plans his work *within* the culture, accepting the adolescents' attitudes *as they are*. Girls at school and girls at work have very different needs and interests. The group worker attempts to work within the framework of these differences of culture and interest. But above all he emphasizes the importance of personal relationships among adolescents. He uses these relationships as his starting-point, that is, he looks for the adolescents' own natural groups, their friendships and their hostilities, and he tries to facilitate their healthy growth and development.

Mrs. Andes's work with the adolescents at Upfield may be divided for convenience of analysis into four phases:

PHASE I represents her initial experiences in the Wood Grove Club.

PHASE II covers the planning of the division into Toffs and Bums in the Wood Grove Club under the guidance of Professor Wallace.[1]

PHASE III constitutes the later experiences following the division.

PHASE IV is the period between May 1957 and April 1958 when the group was re-formed independently of the Wood Grove Club. This is the phase of the Espressos.

The main point of contrast is between Phases I to III and Phase IV. It was in Phase IV that the group was able to develop an identity and a morale of its own unrestricted by the handicaps of belonging to a larger organization whose code of behaviour was

[1] See footnote on p. 109.

138

too difficult for the group to accept. Phases I to III, therefore, describe a group work experiment within an organized and well-established club. Phase IV tells the story of the group on its own. In this last phase the worker made only such demands on the members with regard to their behaviour as she considered they were able to accept, but she did not insist on their conforming to the standards of an ordinary youth club. They were not yet ready for the demands of an orthodox club.

In Phases I to III, however, there is a further point of contrast which we attempt to illustrate through this history – the contrast between what may be called activity-centred and relationship-centred work. Here, clearly, we must disclose our own bias in favour of group work as a relationship-centred activity in which help from the professional worker over the understanding of social relationships is the first consideration. The organization of activities takes second place. Thus the problem facing Mrs. Andes and Professor Wallace at the beginning of Phase II was how to introduce group work methods into an ordinary youth club.

PHASE I

When Mrs. Andes first joined the Wood Grove Club at the beginning of December 1955, the weekly programme consisted of three evenings spent by the senior girls alone in their hut and three evenings with the boys at the Lads Club. There was a part-time leader, Miss Fox, working mainly with the junior girls on two evenings. The worker noted in her diary:

> The atmosphere was quiet and the girls friendly – a contrast, Miss Fox explained, to the previous week when the girls had been terrible and she had called in the police. But this had frightened them and they were now much better. The girls explained that the Club was 'somewhere to go on a dark night' but that not many big girls came to the Club as they mostly went out with boys. A few, however, did come to the 9.00–10.00 p.m. dancing at the boys' club.

By Christmas it had already become apparent that there were in the Club considerable differences in levels of social behaviour and of emotional development, which showed themselves most particularly in the attitudes of the girls towards a firmly organized club. Some found it easy and natural to belong to a club in which there was a rather strict system of rules of behaviour. Others were unable to conform to this pattern in their leisure time and found the restriction irksome. Inside the Club it was clear that there were two main divisions: the girls to whom the structure of the Club in the terms understood by leader and Management Committee was both congenial and expected; and those to whom it was irksome and meaningless. Because of the Project's emphasis on the stresses and strains of Upfield, it was with the latter group that our main interest lay. According to our understanding of the group work method, moreover, there was no virtue to be gained from forcing a particular type of club programme on an unwilling audience. Some might be seriously handicapped in gaining what ought to be a living experience by the imposition of uncongenial methods.

The most noticeable feature of the Wood Grove Club at this time was the diversity of standards among the senior girls. These differences constituted a serious handicap to the kind of group relationships which it was the group worker's task to develop. On Professor Wallace's advice we had begun to discuss the advantages of separating the girls into two groups so as to make it possible for girls of a similar social background to gain a greater sense of security within the group.

PHASE II

We had submitted certain plans to the Management Committee of the Club, and Mrs. Andes together with Professor Wallace appeared before the Committee to explain the ideas which lay behind them. With one dissentient voice the Management Committee agreed to accept our help. The basis of the proposals for Mrs. Andes's work was the limitation of numbers to one group, or, if necessary, two groups, of not more than twenty girls, thus placing a maximum on the size of the groups, as is essential for close personal contact and control between worker and girls. Each group would have the girls' club for two evenings, and for the last part of the evening, between 9.00 and 10.00 p.m., would join the boys in mixed activities in the boys' club.

These plans, however, were not immediately put into operation. Meanwhile the evidence as to some of the girls' own stresses and strains and the form in which they were expressed at the Club accumulated steadily. Mrs. Andes explained to the girls the idea of splitting the Club into two smaller groups and some of the reasons for it. Although this would mean that they would come for two instead of four evenings each week, there would be greater opportunity to do things with their friends. The method would be to vote by ballot for the ones to be in each group. The girls accepted the idea but by no means all were in favour of it:

Hazel Q: 'All this splitting up of people is darn daft.'
Jill L thought the same: 'They should be split up if they want to do drama, and things like that.'
Mrs. Andes: 'I had thought that going according to friends might be best in the beginning, but I am quite prepared to reconsider it.'
Hazel: 'No, I think it's all right. I see what you mean – to be with your friends.'
Mrs. Andes: 'What puzzled you about it before?'
Hazel: 'It's a new idea.'

It was decided to open the voting slips for the groups on Monday. Two of the girls stayed behind on the evening of the voting to sort out the votes for the groups. 'These go with the goodie-goodies; these go with us' was their decision in certain disputed cases. The voting resulted in two groups, to which the girls gave the names of 'Toffs' and 'Bums'. These names speak for themselves and reflect, as they are intended to do, the status of the members. Toffs were the high-status, and Bums the low-status group. The members of each group lived near one another in different parts of the estate. Toffs came from the better organized homes and found the ordinary regulations of the youth club congenial and reasonable, though they, too, were full of the problems of adolescence. The Bums, by contrast, were scornful of the goodie-goodies, preferring freedom in the use of language and dirty stories. Their homes were disorganized in many ways: materially through irregular employment and lack of any routine, emotionally through the presence of marital tensions and conflicts, and morally through the absence of a clear and coherent set of standards. The Bums lived in those streets in Upfield stigmatized as rough and they were sensitive to this low reputation.

The Bums had a leader who set the standard for the others. There was a close inner circle, with the other members in various positions outside the circle. Occasionally the girls would pair off in twos and threes. Later they formed themselves into small friendship groups. Although friendships among the Bums would change rapidly, they seemed to be confined to members of the group and did not extend to outsiders.

One reason for the splitting into two groups deserves further explanation. It was *not* a deliberate attempt to foster feelings of rivalry and inequality among groups of girls and to encourage those distinctions of behaviour and status beyond the limits which already obtained. Nothing could have been further from the minds of the Project team in accepting the advice of Professor Wallace and recommending his plan to the Wood Grove Club Committee than to create a form of 'apartheid'. Some members of the Project Committee certainly criticized the plan on the grounds that it encouraged social inequality among the girls. On the contrary, the intention was to make possible a friendly and secure atmosphere within which good human relationships could develop among the members themselves and between the worker and the group. Her diary illustrates the diversity of standards among these girls and the rivalry between the rough members of low social status and the well-behaved girls of high status who conformed to the standards of the Club. One of the basic principles of group work is 'to start working at the level of the group'. The object of splitting, therefore, was to enable Mrs. Andes to work more closely at the particular social and emotional level at which the girls were at the time, so that they could develop in maturity and responsibility. It was a starting-point, not an ultimate goal.

One disadvantage of the large club, which the use of this group work method seeks to break down, is the anonymity of relationships. Some children, particularly the insecure and the disturbed – and the diary indicates that there were many such in the Club – find that meetings where they cannot remain anonymous, and where demands are made on their capacity to form friendships and to take a constructive part in the life of the group, are too difficult to face. We expected some resentment from the girls that the opportunities for anonymity would be fewer (that is, it would be harder for them to fade into the background in a smaller group). We did not, however, anticipate that the method of splitting the girls into two groups would present so strange a threat as in fact it did to the more insecure members of the Club. No longer were they able to hide beneath a cloak of anonymity. Some of them, no doubt, would have preferred to have done so. But the essence of working with groups is that it aims at strengthening the weaker members. In the process of getting better and of growing up, however, they may from time to time revert to more primitive and immature ways of behaving.

PHASE III

After the division into the two groups had been made, each group was allotted two evenings at the Wood Grove Club – Monday and Wednesday for the Bums, and Tuesday and Thursday for the Toffs.

The girls' initial reaction to the new plan was, 'What shall we do on the nights we can't come?' Mrs. Andes explained that on an average they didn't come more than twice a week anyway, so that possibly it meant only reorganizing their different activities:

Someone: 'It won't work.' *I*: 'We'll have to try and see.'
Jill W: 'It's all right dividing up, only coming less often, that's the trouble.' The atmosphere was generally one of mild uncertainty about the value of the new arrangement.

It was difficult for the girls to foresee the full implications of the division into two groups in spite of explanations given beforehand. It meant to them meeting less frequently, and only on specific days. For them this involved a reorganization of their weekly programmes and such arrangements as baby-sitting. Inevitably there were feelings of resentment at seeing Mrs. Andes working with another group when it was not their own night. By good fortune, however, we had the services of a senior Fulbright student from America, Miss Mary Brandon, who took responsibility for the Toffs from March until June 1956. The presence of a second worker certainly lessened considerably the feelings of rivalry between the two groups, and this enabled Mrs. Andes to devote her attention to the Bums.

It has not been easy to assess accurately the precise effects of splitting into two groups. Some of the advantages became quickly obvious. Mrs. Andes was able to move into the group more closely as a friend to whom troubles could be told without fear of authority or punishment. Previously there had been a rather 'anonymous mass' with so great an influx of girls. As one girl said after being a member of a crowded club for three years, 'I only know two people here; some I know by sight.' By contrast there is the remark from another girl about a month after the splitting of the group: 'It's fewer girls since we split up, but everyone speaks to you now and you know everyone. It is much friendlier. You get more friends that way.' This girl had gone through a severe emotional experience at home and it was through the support that she gained from her friends, in other words the group, that she was able to bear it more easily.

As the diary of the group worker for the next few months shows, more intensive work with individual girls became possible. Mrs. Andes came to learn about the problems which troubled them, and the fact that there was an understanding listener to whom their problems mattered was a source of help. In some cases the worker took active steps to find some special teaching or to help with decisions which the girls were unable to make without support. Two voluntary helpers provided help either of a special or of a more general kind.

The measurement of attendance is at least a useful method of assessing the value placed on a club by the members. In spite of the usual seasonal drop the group increased from about six or seven when the split first took place (at this time, however, there was the rival attraction of a local fair) to about fifteen. Visits from those outside the particular group made a total attendance of between twenty and thirty-five, according to the night.

It would be dishonest, however, to give the impression that this splitting of the groups was entirely successful. During the autumn and winter of 1956–57 after the return to America of the second worker, Miss Brandon, it became increasingly difficult for Mrs. Andes alone to maintain quite separate evenings for the two groups, and the advantages of preserving the identity of the two groups were no longer possible.

During the winter of 1956–57 Mrs. Andes herself found considerable difficulty in combining the role of group worker and club leader at the Wood Grove Girls Club. The initial advantages of the separation of Toffs and Bums were clearly dependent on an adequate staff. However, with the appointment in January 1957 of a new full-time woman leader, it was clearly unwise to propose any immediate change of plans. We agreed, therefore, to wait until the leader had spent sufficient time in her new job to have an opportunity of getting to know the principles on which Mrs. Andes was working.

PHASE IV

The final phase of Mrs. Andes's work with Upfield adolescents was with the 'Espressos'. In May 1957 Mrs. Andes returned to Upfield from her visit to Israel to learn that the woman leader of

145

the Wood Grove Club who had been appointed in January had resigned. The girls meanwhile had dispersed, and Mrs. Andes came back to an empty Club.

The winter's experience suggested to us that this might be an appropriate moment for a change of plans. Two alternative proposals were possible. The first was for Mrs. Andes to continue her role as group worker in the Club; the second was to build up a new group 'outside' the Club on the basis of past relationships with the Bums. The first alternative would have helped the Club by putting the services of Mrs. Andes at its disposal at a time when there was no woman leader. It carried with it, however, the very serious handicap which the winter's work had made clear to her, that it was virtually impossible to be both a club leader and a group worker at the same time. Assuming that this would have been only a temporary measure, there was still a serious underlying difficulty.

The difficulty arises in any area where there are wide differences in the standards of adolescent behaviour, as symbolized at Upfield, for instance, by the Toffs and the Bums. The Toffs are the orthodox, lively, peaceable youngsters who profit by the well-organized activities of a good club, whose committee is concerned for the promotion of sound moral standards through the experience of healthy, active club life. The Bums, on the other hand, are the youngsters who hanker after some sort of club association, but who, in personality, are too unreliable, too aggressive, too lacking in capacity or willingness to participate effectively in organized activities even when they cross the club threshold. If they do come into the club, they tend to disrupt its useful normal life and finally run the risk of the negative experience of getting thrown out. If they do not come into the club at all, they miss the opportunity of the informal education which may come through association with other adolescents under the leadership of a sympathetic adult. If, therefore, the orthodox club committee makes an effort to recruit considerable numbers of the Bum type, it runs a real risk, if successful, of disrupting its useful normal work. But to exclude the Bums from consideration is to turn away from the most difficult aspect of adolescent need.

In this fourth phase, however, the Director and Mrs. Andes discussed with the Chairman of the Wood Grove Club Management Committee an alternative plan of work. We agreed that Mrs. Andes would maintain contact with the club leader of the Management Committee but would no longer work in the club building as she had done during the earlier phases. In this way, we hoped, she would be free to help the Bum kind of girls to meet in the sort of group more appropriate to their own needs and standards.

The worker's first task, therefore, was to re-establish her contact with the Bums. Since the Club was empty she made her way around the streets in which they lived. She met one of the leaders of the Bums, Janet J, talking with some friends in the street and asked them if they would like to have a group. She offered them the use of the Project's small office in the Upfield Meeting Rooms.

The Upfield Meeting Rooms are by no means ideal for this purpose. Though conveniently placed in the middle of the estate, just opposite the main shopping centre and only some few minutes' walk from the girls' homes, they cannot contain both youths and adults together. But suitable buildings were impossible to find and we felt we must make do with rooms which were available to us.

By seeking out the Bums in the streets Mrs. Andes was following the well-established precedents of the New York Youth Board.[1] It was a method which Mrs. Andes used on several occasions throughout the months that followed. The familiar haunts of fish-and-chip shop and street corner provided the usual meeting place for them, and it was on their own ground that they felt happiest with visitors.

In offering Janet J the invitation to form a group, Mrs. Andes's intention was to bring together a small group of Bums in an atmosphere of friendship and acceptance. The response at the time was doubtful and we had certainly reckoned – as the diary of

---

[1] See, for example, New York City Youth Board (1952) and (1960); and Crawford, Malamud & Dumpson (1950).

subsequent events shows – without their boy-friends. We had reckoned too without the Toffs.

They liked this idea though I was doubtful how many would in fact turn up. On Tuesday, 14 May, about seventeen girls arrived at the Meeting Rooms.[1] What name should we give ourselves? There were many suggestions but 'Espressos' finally won the day. They would have subs and a list of members. The next evening twelve girls arrived still clutching the book of members. We made plans for an outing the following Monday. But Monday evening came and nobody turned up. I waited from 8.00 until 9.30. On Tuesday no one appeared, so I walked down Fore Street and met Pauline P, who said that everyone was broke but that they would all turn up for tea tomorrow. Wednesday came but no one except Pauline arrived. The rest had gone to a fair which was running near the estate. I explained that I was available if they wanted a group. If I made a date with them, then I would always be there to keep it.

We made a date for a cinema visit on Saturday, but again no one put in an appearance. Perhaps they didn't really want a group? At this time I met Elizabeth F, one of the leaders of the Toffs, sitting with some others near the Meeting Rooms and complaining that they had nowhere to go. I promised to try to arrange a group for them. Later I met Pauline's brother, who said that some of the boys very much wanted to join the group, and afterwards Derek G, who said everyone would be sure to turn up at the Meeting Rooms on Tuesday.

Tuesday evening came but no one appeared. I waited an hour, then went down the street where I met Pauline and Tessa A. They told me that Gladys K was 'not O.K.' 'She says she is the leader.' I explained I was sorry about this but hers was the only address I had known.

Four girls met me in the Meeting Rooms on the following

[1] Most of these had not been members of the original Bums, but were friends of some who had been.

night and we made plans for a party and a visit to the Tommy
Steele show at the weekend. They phoned on Saturday to say
there were no more tickets. This was the first time that I had
been notified that they couldn't keep an appointment.

When I arrived at the Meeting Rooms for the party at 8.00 I
was met by an angry delegation from a whist drive being held
in another room. There were complaints of noise and fighting.
The Toffs, it appeared, had heard of our hot-dog party and had
taken over the room set aside for the Espressos, with their own
gramophone. It was a very small room and there were about
thirty young people in it. Outside the building there was a third
group, still unidentified, also with a gramophone, wanting to
have a rock-and-roll session. The Espressos, unable to gain
access to the room, had gone home in a huff.

The Toffs wouldn't tell who had invited them, though I
afterwards learned it was Gladys. After pacifying the whist
drive delegation, I sent a message to the Espressos asking them
to return, but received an angry message in reply. Later they all
appeared, to tell me they were not coming. The two rival
groups began to pour abuse at each other and a fight broke out.
I supported the Espressos, explaining that the party was held by
invitation and they had booked the room. The Toffs took no
notice until the Espressos finally dislodged their gramophone
and replaced it by another. A gramophone was the symbol of
each group, and possession of the electric light plug for the
gramophone was the sign of possession of the room. The
Espressos stayed on, blaming Gladys for inviting the others –
'She had better not show her face.'

The evening ended happily with the arrival of some boy-
friends whom they brought along later.

Meanwhile, Mrs. Harper, a member of the Management
Committee, whose front room gave her a distant view of the
Meeting Rooms, telephoned to the Project Director about the
evening's affairs. We arranged to talk with her on the following
day.

Working with Groups (*The Adolescents*)

Our meeting was a friendly and helpful one. The Espressos had not been easy occupants of the Meeting Rooms during the preceding weeks and Mrs. Harper complained about behaviour and the troubles of cleaning the building, which she had taken on in the absence of the caretaker. In particular, she was troubled about the outbreak of rock-and-roll the previous evening in the entirely inappropriate Project office while an adult whist drive was going on in the main rooms. We listened to her wholly reasonable point of view and explained the reason for the collection of the Espressos into a group and the unpredictability which made it impossible to plan but which must be expected.

Mrs. Harper told us of her own work with young people in the area, and the importance of adult help for young people. She told us about Harry O who had helped with the organization of Labour Party socials. On the previous evening Harry had been the owner of a record player and the happy leader of one of the competing groups for the lamp plug. In dress and manner he fits the part of a Bum, works for short spells, and would gladly have taken over Derek's role as leader of the Espressos.

Next Monday the large room in the Meeting Rooms was available for dancing. The girls disapproved of the presence of four boys who had appeared. These four had been found guilty recently of breaking and entering. I said that it was entirely up to them who was to be in the group. Then there was quarrelling among them as to who was 'all right' and who was 'not all right'.

Beryl B was making tea. By this time she was very moody and was abrupt with me and everyone else. She wanted to rock-and-roll with me, but as soon as we started she immediately switched to a different partner. She complained that she had to spend all her time making tea. At that moment Mrs. Harper arrived together with Mrs. Brown, the caretaker. They explained that the group ought not to use the Meeting Rooms. We had a long talk aside, of which the group must have heard some part.

After the two visitors had left I returned to the group and must have looked rather worried. The atmosphere immediately was one of helpfulness towards me. When the group left the Meeting Rooms that evening there wasn't a piece of furniture out of place and the kitchen was spotless. As we were leaving, we passed Gladys standing in the street. Pauline said to me: 'Don't go up to her and ask how she is as you usually do and be friendly to her.' I said nothing but went to catch my bus. I felt at that moment it would have been more than Pauline could have borne if I had spoken to Gladys.

The gramophone which we had been using, brought by Susan, unfortunately broke down. Susan went off with her gramophone saying that she wouldn't be able to come for the next week. Her mother had refused permission for her to go out in the evening. I asked the others if they wanted to meet without a gramophone, and they said they did. I reminded them that they would have only the small room, but they said it didn't matter.

The meeting on the following night (17 June) without the gramophone was a very interesting one. We sat round in the small room – there were about thirty of them – and they told very dirty jokes and tried to play games and throw things about the room. It was a very hot evening, and as we were so crowded I suggested that we might go over to the Club to dance. They said they didn't want to go because it was too hot, and asked, 'Are you trying to get rid of us?' I reassured them. They went on telling their dirty jokes in their efforts to provoke me.

When it was time to leave, they didn't feel much like going. They left slowly, saying that I always threw them out every night. But their goodnights were friendly and they said they would be waiting for me tomorrow.

I arrived early the next evening and poured out some orange juice for them as they arrived. They were all most appreciative. They kept saying how wonderful I was. One girl came with a boy who had brought a gramophone. It was a pleasant atmosphere, they had all brought their boy-friends, and they started to rock-and-roll. They collected some money – 1*d.* per head – 'for subs' though some thought it was for the orange juice.

As we were leaving, Gladys was standing at the street corner. I was with some of the girls. I said 'Hello' to Gladys and asked her why she hadn't come to the meeting. She did not reply but just looked at the ground. I then asked the others, 'Any reason why she shouldn't come?' and they said, 'No.' I told Gladys that we should be glad to see her, and she went home together with the other girls.

These activities, reported in the diary from the Espressos' point of view, had become increasingly irritating to the local adults who used the Meeting Rooms, and in spite of our earlier talks with Mrs. Harper, the existence of the Espressos, and what went on when they were about, began to provoke local anxiety and hostility. We had been unable to foresee the success – from the Espressos' point of view – that had followed Mrs. Andes's invitation to the girls whom she had met six weeks before to use the small Project room in the Meeting Rooms. Some members of the Meeting Rooms Management Committee took the view that this was an unjustifiable use of their own community building, although Mr. Philipps made the point when Mrs. Andes and the Director came to talk over the problem with him: 'If it hadn't been for the Project, we would have had no Meeting Rooms.' We rejected this argument and explained that we had always worked on the assumption that the building was the responsibility of the neighbourhood. The leaders were perfectly free to reject our work with the group if they chose to do so.

We had, by this time, become well aware that the most difficult aspect of the work was the rejection of the Espresso group by adult society, and Mrs. Andes's diary tells of several experiences which illustrate the difficulties confronting any group worker who engages seriously in the task of helping girls and boys of the Bum type. The law-abiding, socially respectable, and community-concerned local residents expect a social worker to bring about good order, discipline, and conformity; the worker knows that the girls and boys whom she has got are far too insecure and emotionally disturbed to be able, for a long time to come, to sustain good and considerate behaviour. Indeed, the group worker knows that the outward behaviour of the group may well get worse before it becomes overtly better.

In this instance, the local tension was the greater since the Meeting Rooms were clearly inappropriate for adolescent needs. In these general circumstances, we underestimated the time and skill which were required if we were to be able to convey to the local community leaders our understanding of why the conventional answer of 'strict discipline and training', so generally recommended as appropriate, was based on a mistaken assessment of the needs of this kind of wayward youth.

Our talk with Mrs. Harper had proved less successful than we had at first supposed. Subsequent events proved that she was by no means convinced of the value of the group. She indicated to Mrs. Brown, the caretaker, on her return from a holiday that the keys of the Meeting Rooms should not be given to Mrs. Andes for a meeting of the group. Mrs. Brown was worried over the difficult decision which faced her and threatened to give up the job if blame for the group were placed on her. Mr. Philipps was more philosophical about the dispute. Complaints from committee members, he explained to us when we talked over the problem with him, were forgotten by him as soon as they were made.

We asked the Chairman of the Management Committee for an early discussion of the situation which had arisen. Meanwhile the dispute over the keys to one of the two main rooms suitable for dancing and to the kitchen which was required for tea-making had clear repercussions on the behaviour of the group. The locked main room and kitchen had a marked effect on the group's behaviour. Mrs. Andes writes in her diary for 24 June:

We had the usual rock-and-roll session after a little difficulty with Mrs. Brown over the keys to the rooms. Because they couldn't get in through the doors, the children[1] were tearing round the building, climbing in at the windows, dancing on the roof. The Director came and managed to persuade Mrs. Brown to let us have the key, but by this time about half of the children had drifted off, and the atmosphere was more charged than I have seen it since I have been working with the group. Up to Monday they always cleared up, and they had even suggested paying for the room they use. But on Monday they were tearing at the curtains, which normally they don't do. They were much noisier, much more themselves, which in a way is a good thing, but they didn't take turns to go into the kitchen to make tea – everybody took it upon himself to go into the kitchen, and they locked the door from the inside.

After they got access to the big room they danced, but some still complained that I was letting in too many. I said it was their own affair whom they allowed in. Some sat down and made a list of the regular Espressos. 'Only the booked ones can come in,' I was told. I again told them it was up to them. They left quite happily at 10.15 p.m. and tidied up before they went.

The worker's method of placing responsibility on the group for the admission and selection of members was one of her main ways of developing a sense of responsibility among them. To the local observer, all was disorder and chaos. To the members, on the other hand, the events of the first six weeks had provided an opportunity for at least the rudimentary growth of corporate responsibility. Most significant of all, perhaps, was the fact that at the height of summer, when most youth clubs see the disappearance of their members for outdoor activities, the Espressos were busy and active. Their activities were, nevertheless, far removed from conventional and respectable ideas, and the quiet moments in the group in this early period were usually short-lived.

[1] Mrs. Andes often uses the term 'children' in her diary when referring to the members of the group.

Already by the middle of June a new problem had arisen and one which proved hard to deal with effectively – the distinction between 'regulars' and 'visitors'. Ideally the worker's task would have been much simpler had there been no visitors to the Espressos. The group itself at this time numbered about eighteen, already more than Mrs. Andes had envisaged when she issued her original invitation to some of the Bums (at a later stage it increased to about thirty). The behaviour of the visitors proved to be the greatest handicap. They had no obligation to conform to the standards of the group and felt little responsibility for any disturbance which they created. Above all their relationship with Mrs. Andes tended to be casual and often tenuous.

The obvious argument is to say that the visitors should have been excluded by the worker. But this would have been contrary to the responsibility which Mrs. Andes was trying to help the Espressos to learn. The responsibility of excluding visitors and deciding on the membership of the group was one which could *not* be taken over by the worker. Group work means nothing if it is not a method of helping the members to take responsibility themselves for decisions which are of real significance to them.

Also, there were the wishes of the 'regulars'. They wavered in their choices. Personal animosities were strong; friendships flickered and burned out; associations changed from day to day. This instability in relationship was one of the most outstanding characteristics of the Espresso personalities. Indeed, the primary justification for group work of this kind lies in helping the members to make better relationships. In group work, unlike club work, in which the selection of members is usually on the basis of 'first come, first served' until a reasonable maximum is reached, the membership of the group is a matter for decision by the members.

In her diary for 25 June Mrs. Andes describes the tensions arising from the anxiety over membership at this time:

A girl, Jill, whom the 'regulars' apparently didn't like, arrived. This brought matters to a head. Janet (one of the leading Espressos) came to me and told me that she wouldn't stay if Jill did; why didn't I keep her out, she was not one of them. I said it was no good coming to me and grumbling every five minutes; they had better tell those they didn't want that they didn't want them. I would support them, but they would have to do it themselves. A verbal fight started between Jill and Janet and automatically the 'regulars' and the 'visitors' took sides. In the end the regulars told the others to clear out, which they did, taking the gramophone, which had that evening been brought by a visitor. While the visitors were still leaving and there would have been time to call them back I said to the regulars, 'Is this what you want?' They said that it was 'and anyone who is yellow can go with them'. Then they all sat round in great silence for some time, and the shock seemed to be very great. I asked if they would have a gramophone tomorrow. I was told that it seemed I could think of nothing else but gramophones. Of course they would have a gramophone; they could produce a gramophone every night. Suddenly Janet urgently asked me to go outside. I went. *Janet*: 'You are not coming tomorrow, are you?' I asked why ever not. She thought that I couldn't possibly want to come with all these happenings. I reassured her. Some of the girls went home to get tea and the others sat round a table playing snap. There were now fourteen girls and ten boys. They started to brew tea.

But at this point the 'visitors' who had been thrown out reappeared with a number of other boys and girls. They started a lot of swearing and abuse, and one of the people from the estate who sits on the Meetings Room Management Committee came and told me that this could go on no longer. He dispersed the 'visitors' and came to talk to the group. He himself looked very frightened, as obviously this behaviour had disturbed him very much. He told the girls and boys that this could not go on and that the matter would have to be discussed by the Management Committee. There was a great outcry. They told him how much they needed a place like this; that clubs as a rule threw them out sooner or later 'because some of us have got records'; that if he wanted to help them, he should see that they had a place where I and they could meet. He suggested a club which might accept them if he sent a letter. But they said they wanted one of their own 'with Mary'.[1] They cleaned the place up beautifully and came to ask if I would be there the next day. I said I would. 'Don't be late,' they shouted. I said, 'I'll be on time.'

But while the Espressos could at times of shock and crisis be charming, the internal rows, the troubles with visitors, the tensions with adult groups in the Meeting Rooms, were the regular pattern of outward happenings, and it became clear that the days of the Espressos in the Meeting Rooms were numbered. On the other hand, Mrs. Andes's diary shows that meanwhile there was steady growth in the establishment of firm relationships between her and the youngsters. Her acceptance of them as persons was consistent and unwavering and this, for all of them, was a new experience with an adult. No matter how they tested her, she made it her business never to reject them.[2]

Recognizing that the position of the Meeting Rooms would soon become impossible, Mrs. Andes encouraged the Espressos to look for another place, putting on them the responsibility for making arrangements which she could then follow up herself. This was in the middle of July. The Espressos appeared to take the position rationally and consolidated their existence by suggesting new efforts to secure the payment of subs. But when, a few days later, the Meeting Rooms Management Committee took the firm decision that they must go, the Espressos were resistant:

They told me that they would like to send a deputation of their members to a meeting if I would just fix the hour and the place. They would come any time of day or night and they would love to tell everybody what they felt about it. 'Who do these people think they are, being able to take a club away from us?'

---

[1] They called Mrs. Andes by her first name, Mary.
[2] This, of course, is the essence of professional group work relationships, as it is one aspect of good parenthood. The parable of the Prodigal Son offers appropriate reflection.

But the problem of premises was not the one uppermost in their minds at this crucial moment, even though Mrs. Andes had arranged a meeting for them with the Secretary of the Bristol Youth Committee and the Project Director to consider what could be done. For it was on this evening that there was a report in the paper describing the commotion at quarter sessions when Geoff M, one of their close friends and an early Espresso member, started to fight his way out of the dock after receiving a Borstal sentence:[1]

> It took five prison warders and three policemen to remove him from the dock as he struggled furiously with the officers.

The Espressos were indignant that eight men should restrain one lad. They read into the incident another rebuff to themselves from adult society.

It was the vicar of the Anglican Church who so generously helped the Espressos with premises by explaining their case to his parochial Church Council. He offered the use of the old Church Hall on the fringe of Upfield, and after a fortnight, with nowhere except the street and the cinema in which to meet, the Espressos moved to the hall on 30 July.

The first evening was marked by particularly destructive behaviour. The consequences of rejection by the committee of the Meeting Rooms had certainly taken effect. The Espressos lived up to their reputation – indeed exceeded it. The caretaker of the Church Hall was horrified at the new tenants: the worker had no control over them and what they needed was the stick; he had been in the Navy and knew what the whip could do; of course they didn't have it, and this was the result. As he put it some weeks later: 'This is not a club; this is a meeting place for thugs.'

The next few evenings were not much better, but by the end of the first fortnight the Espressos had begun to settle down in their new environment. Anne began to collect subs again and a fresh

---

[1] The offence for which he was sentenced was committed before the Espresso group was formed.

list of 'members' was prepared. Those who hadn't paid were the more regular attenders. The dancing continued happily: as Dopey said, 'Some difference to when we came, couldn't dance a step; now they teach me different ones each time.'

The worker talked to the Espressos about writing a letter to Geoff in Borstal:

> It is interesting how in a way they'd like to write, but putting pen to paper is just too much. Derek P said, 'Don't worry, he'll have friends there; half Upfield is there.' But in the same breath he said he'd visit Geoff and could I come too? When I said I wasn't sure whether it was allowed, he said he'd find out and, if not, would give Geoff my good wishes. I agreed.

On 13 August Rosemary W brought five other girls, known to the worker through the Wood Grove Club. A hoard of boys arrived and wanted to come in too. The members were divided as to policy towards visitors and an explosion seemed imminent. The worker asked that the gramophone be stopped, and with shouts at the back from Derek G – 'Give her a fair chance, let her speak' – there was silence:

> I told them that I had this evening been asked a lot of questions. One was, was this a club like any other? I said I didn't think so. As far as I knew, the group of girls sitting over there (pointing to the members) were the ones I had met first and we had suggested the idea of forming a group which would meet three times a week. It was for these girls and their friends. I had nothing against the visitors (murmurs of approval from the visitors); in fact I liked them very much, but as far as I knew, the boys and girls of the group had decided that one evening, Monday, was visitors' night. But not Tuesday or Wednesday. 'Now should we just show that we had no hard feelings towards the visitors and let them stay tonight?' I asked the group. They warmly agreed and Janet C embraced me. Two weeks ago it would have been impossible to do this. At the end of the evening, for the first time the hall was clear in a minute.

From this episode it would appear that the public explanation which the worker gave in such unusually strong terms was generally approved of and that it had some demonstrable effect that evening. But the swings of mood and feeling of the Espressos were infinitely varied and their behaviour unpredictable. Immediate and overt responses were frequently misleading and it was impossible to be sure of their effects.

In spite of these internal tensions, towards the end of August the meetings of the group seemed to be more peaceful and the members more settled in their policy towards visitors. The ejection from the Meeting Rooms was apparently forgotten. During the peaceful evenings there was time for conversation on many things. They began, for example, to ask about the worker and her family, not out of idle curiosity but rather from a genuine interest. Plans were made for an outing to Weston.

For reasons which are obscure this new rather peaceful mood changed in early September to one of dispiritedness and defeat. 'It's a yellow evening,' as Dopey said on one occasion. The worker had two student workers with her – one in training for medicine, the other for social work. She felt that their presence had in some way or other affected the mood of the group. But again towards the end of September a more positive atmosphere developed. Anne J, who had been in arrears with the rent of the hall, which was paid for out of subs, was absent for a while. She excused herself on the grounds of illness. On her return she owed 12s. 6d. for the rent. It was at this time, too, that Linda Y's house was burned down. Through the worker's suggestion the members took particular care that Linda was accepted and kept busy in the group. But disaster among the Espressos was seen as something very different from disaster in conventional middle-class culture. It was accepted as an everyday happening, to be met with a shrug of the shoulders. Special demonstrations of sympathy and help were felt to be out of place.

Another piece of evidence indicating the improvement of relationships among the members was to be seen in the fact that no longer were they thrown out of the Wood Grove Club on those occasions when they visited it. The worker felt that they had grown more accepting, and less ready to make trouble on any visit to a club.

While it was true to say that there was a strengthening of internal relationships within the group – and this does not by any means imply that all was peace and respectability – by the middle of October new difficulties of unprecedented virulence began to arise, again from the attention of visitors.

It is possible that the very existence of an embryonically stable group of hitherto 'antisocial' youngsters catches the attention of others like them who belong to less stable but unconsciously envious gangs. At any rate, by the middle of October, two other groups began to impinge on the Espressos, 'visiting' the hall when the Espressos were there, heightening the internal tensions, and precipitating new outbreaks of aggression, destruction, and violence. One of the groups, led by a boy known locally as 'Mugsy', was of adolescents; the other group, led by Joe, was smaller but composed of older, tougher young men, wearing ear-rings and long hair.

The members of both these gangs were known to the Espressos through acquaintanceships formed at school and on the neighbourhood street corners. What the visiting gangs got out of their visits – on Mondays, which were official visiting nights, but on other nights as well – is not clear; but the attraction was disturbingly persistent. The Espressos, for their part, had very mixed attitudes. On the one hand, they were plainly frightened by the damage they knew the visitors could do or actually did; on the other, they enjoyed the excitement of attracting new and provocative attention. And the shifting internal rivalries and associations were heightened by the use that could be made of the visitors.

In consequence the behaviour in the hall tended to remain as disturbing as ever. (It is worth noting that the Espressos always dispersed quickly in the road after the hall closed and that none of them was charged with delinquency during the existence of the club.) The caretaker, who lived next door, was increasingly troubled, and his sudden death in November strengthened local hostility. The vicar, who had so generously made the premises available, was sympathetic but puzzled and felt that there would be a limit to the patience of his Council, who had agreed only to temporary use of the hall in any event. It became clear that the Espressos would have to move again by the end of the year.

The evidence of the concluding meetings in November and December, and particularly of the Christmas party, shows that there was no good reason, beyond the shortage of money, premises, and manpower, for discontinuing the work at this particular time. The Espressos were not ready to be left without a group worker to support them. Derek P, in particular, was a young man who badly needed the help of a worker. But a search for new premises was not successful. We had been offered a room by the National Association of Girls Clubs and Mixed Clubs. The Espressos, however, were unwilling to meet so far afield. A local firm generously offered to allow a pre-fabricated hut to be erected on a piece of its land on the fringe of Upfield, and this might have been a good solution to the next stage had money been available for hut and leadership. But efforts to acquire the necessary grant in the spring of 1958 were not successful and, with the pending termination of the Project, the Espressos had to be disbanded. Mrs. Andes was able to keep in touch informally during January and February of 1958, and she gradually discontinued her relationships with the members individually as the end of the Project drew nearer and it became necessary to terminate the field work. It would be dishonest to pretend that any of the team – least of all Mrs. Andes herself – felt comfortable about ending the work with the Espressos at this particular stage.

Had the group continued in being in new conditions, there is no reason to suppose that the strong criticism of any worker would have diminished in the neighbourhood, except in so far as geographically the work would have been less obtrusive. Group work among adolescents as disturbed as the Espressos, and with personal histories like theirs, must always be frightening and perplexing to any neighbourhood, particularly a somewhat insecure new estate. It is easier to let the individuals drift and to let the social services and the police pick up the consequences in personal and family breakdown and delinquency at once or later.

It is probable that the neighbourhood was relieved by the dispersal of the Espressos. But the Espressos themselves felt let down. Some of them made sporadic visits to other clubs in areas adjoining Upfield, to the worry of their leaders, but so far as we know they did not establish any permanent ties. During the eight months following the end of the Espressos, five of the members were charged and found guilty of offences in the courts.

At Christmas, ten months later, Pauline P wrote to Mrs. Andes in Israel:

Dear Mary
Thanks for us all for your card. We sure miss you round here. We don't have a club no more. Well, Mary, how's things with you. What are chances of you coming back. I go around with Rosemary now. She sends her love, also all the boys and girls. Well we had some happy times didn't we, Mary? We still talk about the party. Ha. Ha. Please write back when you can with love
                                                          Pauline

ASSESSMENT OF SUCCESS

We have no method of making any precise assessment of the change which took place in the Espressos as a direct result of this experience. Positive results of group work with adolescents are inevitably long-term, and the growth in social relationships for which we strive may show itself only in their adult life at a much later stage. We hope, for example, that they as parents will be better able to provide for their children the essential background of a happy home. But we have no means of knowing to what extent they will succeed.

The Project team was frequently criticized for bringing the Espressos together at all: 'They were perfectly happy in the Wood Grove Club in the first instance,' said one critic, 'why then take them out of this and segregate them together?' 'They could have joined a *good* youth club where their bad behaviour would have been controlled and absorbed into the general life of the club,' said another. Instead of encouraging this, the critics said, the Project recognized them as a group, and so focused the attention of the neighbourhood on them and increased the understandable resentment of the majority.

The most valid point of criticism hinges around the use of the very centrally placed Meeting Rooms as the first base for the Espressos to meet. This precipitated the existence of the group and its offensive, destructive behaviour right into the public eye where it was most conspicuous, and it brought them straight into head-on conflict with the people who used and managed the Meeting Rooms, a group of people of goodwill who had plenty of difficulties of their own in order to establish the Meeting Rooms as a useful instrument of community life. As it was, the public misbehaviour of the Espressos aroused local hostility, and this they met with heightened aggression on their own side.

Undoubtedly, life would have been easier for all concerned if, when Mrs. Andes began her work with the Espressos, she had known of an inconspicuous place for their meetings.

But apart from this point, the criticisms arise from wishful thinking. It is true, as the sociologist's analysis (see below pp. 179–89) suggests, they were not a closely knit and well-organized gang on the American metropolitan pattern – of *West Side Story*, for instance. On the other hand, their friendships, with their continual intermittent quarrels, were long-standing, based on street play-group and on school. Irrespective of the Project's intervention, therefore, there was among them a good deal of common activity, whether at work, or at Upfield, or in other parts of Bristol.

But to argue that a good club could have absorbed them is sheer fantasy. Nor is it true to say that they were in fact regular members of the Wood Grove Club before Mrs. Andes began to work intensively with them outside the Club. Only one girl, Rosemary W, could be labelled a regular Club member. But she was so disturbed, as Mrs. Andes writes, that it was quite a step for her to join a group where, even though on the fringe, she was accepted. She had been very lonely at Wood Grove. Three girls and one boy went to the Club off and on, but the remainder did little more than visit the Club for a 'bopping' session, paying subs from time to time and getting their names on the books.

Thus the alternative of segregation or dispersal is in fact a false dichotomy. The method of social group work with the near-delinquent and non-conformist minority is certainly not based on principles of apartheid. To believe this is to misconceive the principles of the work. In fact it is the very opposite – to help individuals through group experience to make *wider* and more positive social relationships than they are at present able to achieve. But in the process of getting to this desirable end, it is essential for the worker to accept them at their own level of understanding and to work with them in a group where they feel comfortable and reasonably secure.

In such a group they are able to test the worker's confidence in them through various methods, such as dirty talk and swearing, sexual behaviour, and so on. If they still feel her confidence in them unshakable, then their trust in humanity can begin to grow again. When this happens, and only then, are they ready to take their place in the ordinary social groups and clubs of their community. As in child guidance treatment, where the process of therapy is accompanied by difficult and aggressive behaviour which the parents have to learn to tolerate for a while, so also in group work with these adolescents, the community has to learn to 'take it' in the interest of greater conformity later on.

Judging by the diary which Mrs. Andes has provided, we have no right to claim any more than a slight measure of success with the Espressos. Perhaps the most significant feature of their story is the absence of convictions for delinquency – with one exception[1] – during the period of Mrs. Andes's work with them. After her work ended, however, we have news of convictions for delinquency on the part of five members. Such evidence, of course,

---

[1] Geoff M's court appearance in the summer of 1957, it will be recalled, was for an offence committed before Mrs. Andes started working with the Espressos.

tells us only about detected offences and not about offences which remain undiscovered. It would be surprising if this in fact were the total: from reports received from club leaders in the neighbouring districts there is certainly evidence to support the assumption that the number was greater.

We may not unfairly conclude that the group fulfilled a very real need for social experience in an understanding atmosphere through a relationship with an adult who accepted them as they were. We cannot, however, be satisfied that circumstances made it necessary to discontinue this work at this particular stage. The ending of the Project in 1958 and Mrs. Andes's own plans for work in Israel were among the reasons which made it necessary to finish working with the Espressos at the end of 1957. It would be dishonest, however, not to make clear the other circumstances which were likely to handicap the future of the group. The Church Hall in which the group had been meeting since leaving the Meeting Rooms in August was no longer made available by the Church Council in the New Year. An extensive search for other premises sufficiently close to the members' homes to continue the group was unsuccessful. The only alternative, therefore, was the erection of some form of pre-fabricated building on the outskirts of the estate. But this was feasible only if there was a certainty of financial backing after the end of the Project. The necessary funds could not be found.

CHAPTER 10

The Espressos in a Sociological Perspective

ALTHOUGH there was no survey of the behaviour of a cross-section of the adolescent population, the Project team was able, through the written and verbal records of the group worker, to get close to some of the young people who give rise to particular concern in respectable society. How do they behave? Why do they behave like that? What can or ought to be done about their behaviour? These are the central questions here, as they are in the study of other people and groups elsewhere in this report.

We have already written something of the worker's experience with the Espressos during the eight months of strenuous activity in the Meeting Rooms and later at the old Church Hall. We turn now to a discussion of some aspects of their behaviour which the records describe. In all there are 167 foolscap pages of single-spaced typing relating to 92 occasions between May 1957 and January 1958. Most of these were the regular group meetings, normally held three times each week, but some of the occasions recorded are visits to dance halls, the roller-skating rink, their homes, as well as conversations at the street corner. Once again we emphasize the dangers of reading too much into records which were kept by the worker for the purpose of gaining a better under-standing of the meaning of her work as seen through the eyes of colleagues and advisers. It is not unnatural to forget the common-place and to record the unusual.

The thirty members of the Espressos (twenty girls, ten boys), ranging in age from 14 to 20, though most of them were 16 or 17, are not at all typical of young people in Upfield, much less of young people in the working class. The account itself makes that quite clear. They are the children of the small 'slum' working class, and these thirty alone probably represent a very high proportion of the most troublesome people of their age in the city, as the figures on the concentration of punishable behaviour in the city show.

But they are important for three reasons. First, because there is unusually detailed inside information from the worker about them; second, because their problems and the origins of them are not so atypical of other adolescents as to render useless the application of some of the insights gained here; and, third, because they illustrate very realistically the way in which the neighbourhood influences social behaviour, both by giving support to destructive and aggressive behaviour and also by being to some extent the basis of opposition to this behaviour.

THE WAY THEY BEHAVE
IN THE OUTSIDE WORLD

Let us go to the pictures with them:

I arrived at the cinema and was met by Anne and Rosemary. I asked about the others, and Anne said that they were probably in the cinema already. In the cinema were Desirée, Jane, and Harry, but no others from the club. I was greeted by terrific cries of 'Mary!', which soon calmed down when I sat quietly and didn't react. We were watching a Bob Hope film, which was really quite funny, but none of them seemed to take a great interest in it. They changed seats from time to time and said 'Hello' to various friends. About 5.50 Pauline and Janet came in and said that they had been waiting outside, where the boys were still waiting because they were barred. I went out and the boys clamoured round: 'Get us in!' I said I was sorry, I didn't think I could do anything about it. The girls said, 'Just say you will be responsible for them.'

While we were talking the manager came up and asked us to stop walking in and out of the cinema. I told him that, if necessary, I would pay to re-enter. He then became friendly, and took me aside for a talk. He said the young people I was with were a nuisance; he had trouble with them every day; they were not frightened of him, or of the police – they just laughed in their faces. All those I had been talking to were 'well-known characters who were always in trouble'. The only thing he could do was to keep them out altogether – once they were in, it was extremely difficult to get them out because of the way it disturbed the other patrons. I said I would like to see whether they would keep their promise if they promised me to behave. He smiled and said, 'All right – we'll see.'

When they got inside there was a terrific commotion and others came to greet them like long-lost brothers. Boys crowded round saying, 'How did you get in – through the back door?' After that they started changing seats again. Janet and Patsy discovered a girl they disliked and started sitting on her lap to annoy her. During the performance they asked me from time to time if I was enjoying myself; then they would walk off and leave me and sit next to a boy- or girl-friend – changing partners frequently. I think they themselves felt that the film was just a background to their activities. The doorkeeper and an attendant suddenly appeared and shone torches at us. I wondered what the trouble was, as they were all sitting quietly at the moment. When we got out we saw that the glass door to the entrance had been broken. The doorkeeper and attendant went down to Upfield with the boy who was explaining about the door, bidding me a rather cool goodnight.

They like to think that at certain performances they 'take over', and on Saturday and Sunday in particular they are rowdy in the two local cinemas – shouting, swearing, constantly moving from one seat to another, with three or four of the boys perhaps taking a flamboyant walk round the auditorium during the interval: they are saying, 'Look, we are here!'

Among the girls, Janet and Beryl are the keenest picture-goers; they go together at least five times a week. They pick up a few unknown boys at the cinema, and these follow them about for a week or so.

> They certainly have cuddling and kissing from sets of boys who are changed about two or three times a month. Gladys is not quite in that line, although for her, too, 'the pictures' really means 'going out with boys' – being pawed. None of the girls seems to go out much except on these sorts of adventures. Desirée was saying that she had picked up some 'squares' at the Embassy (one of the large central cinemas); one of them was Chinese, and he had kissed her in a most horrible way – she said she had the teeth marks on her neck at that moment. The ambition of all the girls is to have a 'Teddy', not a 'square'. When Desirée describes new boy-friends the question always is 'What are his trousers like – narrow at the bottom? That's all right, he's a Ted.' On the other hand, Pauline is a much quieter type in this respect; and they were saying that Jessie was too shy and too frightened to go out much with boys – by which they meant strange boys.

The self-image which this develops can be seen in the following response of the girls when the group worker told some interlopers at a meeting of the Espressos who had asked her for a date that there were plenty of nice girls without her:

> Gladys opened her blouse just towards me, and said, 'Oh yes, we're *nice* girls!' The girls then started to suggest all sorts of lewd questions I could ask the boys, and also made coarse gestures, half of which I did not really understand.

We can meet the Espressos in the open air, on Guy Fawkes night:

> I came to the café near the *Green Dragon* where already the smell of smoke and fireworks filled the air, and there was the

shouting of crowds going to the bonfire. Extra police were on duty, and the place seemed full of young people, who were on the whole behaving in a rather abandoned way. I hadn't stood there very long when about seven of the girls came up towards the café. There had been a whole crowd of them on the bus, but all the males in the company had been turned off because they had behaved badly. The girls were dressed in jeans and plastic jackets. I was told later that they had put on their jeans 'for safety'. They greeted me very effusively. They looked longingly at the café, but said they did not have the money for any tea. I said I would stand them one, and we went in. Their behaviour in the café was rather noisy and boisterous. They said the tea was 'like piss water'. On the whole, though, I think they were happy there.

After we had had the tea we went out. The bonfires were lit, and great crowds were milling round. I remember last year, when I was with some of the Bums, they tried to push me into the crowd and they themselves endeavoured to be touched and pawed as much as possible. This time it was somewhat different. Janet said, 'We'll call Mary "mother" and that'll protect us.' Anne said, 'You've got to be careful: this is the night the boys have. They look forward to it all the year. Last year some tarts got raped.' On the whole they kept close to me, but once or twice some boys chased them. Desirée came running back and collapsed near me in tears, and in absolute terror cried, 'They're chasing me! They're chasing me!' Then Janet J came and showed me a bruise on her cheek: 'They got me down on the ground.' They decided then that they all wanted to go home, though it was quite early – ten o'clock or so. I must say I was surprised by the way they kept talking about being raped, about having to be careful, and so on. They were very frightened indeed.

Later – they still had not left, though by this time it was nearing eleven – they said, 'We're going to have fun at Upfield – come on – you coming with us?' I said that I was sorry, but I would not be able to get a bus back home if I went. 'Oh, you're a spoilsport – you're spoiling everything' – they genuinely felt that I was part of the party. When I saw them to the bus and they were safely on it, nobody turned round to wave goodbye; they just went on top as if I didn't exist.

Meanwhile the male Espressos who had been put off the bus because of their hooliganism had walked the rest of the way to the festivities; their evening was rounded off with a bout of policeman-baiting.

The girls will sometimes be abusive to complete strangers in the street – girls of their own age who will not retaliate:

I met Rosemary, Anne, and Janet on the way home. Anne was cursing passing girls, using swear words that were certainly new to me. She is always using 'f......' and 'b......' at the club, but she apparently thinks of that as ordinary everyday language, and for 'real swearing' like this she needs quite different words again.

They were also observed while engaging in apple-stealing expeditions – an activity which, of course, is not always seriously condemned in children and young people:

About 9.15 the club suddenly cleared. People – especially the girls – had brought enormous shopping bags and grips, and they went out to steal apples from the hospital orchard. It obviously was not an ordinary expedition – were they sent from home? They came back with their spoils about half an hour later. I said to some of them, 'Don't eat them in here; you'll get me into trouble.' But they came around like little Eves, offering me a bite.

Not all of the Espresso girls, however, were lighthearted about it:

As I passed the hospital Gladys K was standing outside. She said the others were in stealing apples, but that her Dad would kill her if she did so.

That is an important point: not all the girls will engage in a delinquency like stealing apples, though they nearly all swear lustily. In the same way, not all the boys, even in this atypically antisocial selection, commit crimes, though they nearly all are nuisances in conventional youth clubs.

Many of the Espresso boys were, at one time or another, in fact expelled from or refused entrance to most of the youth clubs in the district and even farther afield. They may be described, as a youth leader did in fact describe them, as immediately recognizable as troublemakers – they look 'as if they had bombs in their pockets' – and refused admission. They may succeed in ingratiating themselves for a time either in a new club or in a club from which they have been at one time excluded:

> While we were walking along Tom E and Dopey T were telling us of the various reasons why they had been chucked out of most of the clubs. Dopey said that while he was doing weight-lifting at the club (a local one) the leader upset him, so he threw a crowbar at him. Tom E told me that one expulsion followed when they had tied a boy up under a pile of chairs, then put a bucket of water so that it would spill over the captive, when someone opened the door. Unfortunately the 'someone' was 'that old woman at the Social Club', who came in, so that he has never been allowed in since then.

Some months after Mrs. Andes, the group worker, had finished working with the Espressos, the Director talked with two leaders of a well-established Church Club in a neighbourhood adjoining Upfield:

> They complained of serious trouble in the club, of fighting and rough treatment. The leaders showed the Director a list of names of the offending members which contained some of the Espressos. The initial approach to the club by the adolescents had been made as individuals who appeared friendly, polite, and well behaved. No trouble was anticipated. Soon, however, the trouble started – attacks on regular club members, rocking and rolling, banging doors, and general disturbance. The Up-

173

field group always rallied to the defence of one of its members. Though mainly boys, on the night when they brought three girls with them thefts of some of the members' property also occurred.

Though anxious not to exclude the new arrivals because they felt a responsibility for them, the two club leaders were forced in desperation to call in the police to deal with the situation. They foresaw the likelihood that the permanent members of their club would no longer attend. The complaint of the visitors that nobody wanted them and there was nowhere to go was thus reinforced on yet another occasion.

These boys are also the core of the serious law-breakers. They will move out of this phase as they grow older, to be replaced by their juniors, who will react in their turn to the same problems in identical ways – solving the problem of being despised, powerless, poor, and unloved, by hooliganism, bravado, theft, and promiscuity – just as elsewhere today's delinquent boys facing these problems will be replaced by their juniors among the disadvantaged.

The Robin Hood of the Espressos was Geoff. He was convicted of housebreaking and sentenced to Borstal training, as was related earlier (see p. 158).

A nineteen-year-old factory hand caused nearly a minute's commotion at Bristol Quarter Sessions yesterday when the Recorder sentenced him to Borstal training. It took five prison warders and three policemen to remove him from the dock.

Later he escaped with some others by scaling the wall of Reading prison:

Pauline said, 'Have you heard about Geoff?' 'What about him?' 'He's escaped from prison.' Dopey came over and said, 'Isn't it good?' Derek said, 'He told me before he went to prison that he'd try to escape about Christmas and go to France.'

Derek also had been with Geoff at the time of the housebreaking. Dopey also managed to get into one or two scrapes on his own account:

> I went down to the corner where some of the long-haired boys were standing with Derek G. Derek said, 'Oh, hello Mary,' in a fairly friendly way. Then I was patted on the shoulder. I turned, and there was Dopey, who said, 'I've got a job – sewing mailbags!' I said, 'Really?' not quite realizing the implication of his remark. 'Yes, I'm on twenty-four hours' bail; it cost me twenty-five bob. I'm being fetched at 8 o'clock tomorrow to go to Whiteleaf.' I said, 'Whatever for? You only ran a van up a wall, as far as I know.' 'I did – but I pinched the van!' He sounded so cheerful that I thought he was pulling my leg, but he wasn't. He joked and laughed and didn't seem to care at all. 'We had a bit to drink and we didn't really care what was happening.' He was speaking now with the jollity of a drunkard, though he had not been drinking. He rode off. I said to the crowd, 'It seems too incredible. Is he really off to prison tomorrow?' They said, 'Well, we don't know, but we suppose so – yes.'

Dopey was, in fact, exaggerating on this occasion – a policeman had merely called in connection with the fine for the offence he refers to, which he had left unpaid; there was no immediate threat of his being taken away.

Other youths in the same locality indulge in the same kind of bravado; versions of the following account of the court appearance of two eighteen-year-olds from a nearby street appeared in the national press, thus securing for the offenders the notice for which they craved:

> Bristol magistrates heard today how two youths in Edwardian clothing stood in the middle of Dundas Road, near the *Green Dragon*, late one night, deliberately obstructing traffic by playing a game called 'Za-Za' ... To play it, two men stood in the middle of the road facing the hazards until one of them became a little alarmed and gave up. 'Then he used the words "Za-Za"

and the other man was the winner,' said the inspector. . . . They were standing in the way of the traffic so that vehicles . . . were obliged to slow down and make their way round the men, who ignored the traffic. One car had been unable to deviate, and the driver was sounding his horn and flashing his headlights . . .

Showing off in front of the outside world, swearing at it, disrupting it, destroying it – this is the behaviour of these youths that angers and frightens ordinary people. Several causes of this behaviour have been put forward. One is the personality of the individuals, and the individual profiles[1] that we have tried to sketch in from all available sources certainly support this view. Another explanation suggested is in terms of the standards of behaviour of the neighbourhood and the group to which they belong. They conform to these standards – the argument runs – because they feel rejected by society and seek security and a feeling of 'belonging' in the gangs in which they are accepted.[2] They are members of a delinquent 'sub-culture' which gives them a status denied them by the wider society.

How far indeed does the evidence of the Espressos suggest that there is a 'gang' and a 'culture' at all? How far is the presence of others, who are similarly placed in the social scale and have similar problems of personality, more correctly seen as a kind of catalyst which sets off an explosion among materials already lying there, powerful and dangerous? Some of the group worker's records throw light on the answers to these questions.

IN THE GROUP

Perhaps the most obvious characteristic emerging from the diary is the undependability of the Espressos. Appointments were continually made by the worker with the members, but frequently

[1] Appendix XI of Report to Carnegie Trust.
[2] cf. Cohen (1956, p. 12): 'Certain children are denied status in the respectable society because they cannot meet the criteria of the respectable status system. The delinquent sub-culture deals with these problems by providing criteria of status which these children can meet.'

broken. This is particularly noticeable for the two periods at the commencement of the group at the Meeting Rooms in May and during the search for new premises in January after they had been rejected by the Church Hall just before Christmas. The Espressos were similarly undependable when promising to provide anything by way of action, food, or money, to improve the future working of the club:

> They said they would very much like to have a party; they would round up people for it. They made a list of what everybody was to bring. I said I would bring the most expensive item – the sausages – as I think they could not have managed that. The day of the hot-dog party I arrived to find nobody there. A few minutes later Pauline came with a host of other girls, saying they had all been there earlier. They had not brought any food; they were impressed by the fact that I had brought the sausages. They decided to have a party the next day instead.

That incident was recorded in the early days of the Espressos. A considerable improvement can be seen in their behaviour at the last meeting they held together as a club – a Christmas party – but the same undependability is still strongly present. The worker had asked them to bring food for the party:

> I got a few tables out but on the whole made few preparations – Derek P had said he would be there at 6 o'clock sharp to help me. About 6.30 Gladys and Rosemary came all dressed up for the party and with little bags of decorations and cakes. Derek P came then, with his little brother and Dopey. None of them had brought any food. Both Dopey and Derek are out of work, but I do not think that is the reason for their not bringing anything – they definitely could have brought a token of some sort. I found this reaction to my demand that they should bring some food for the party extremely interesting – it obviously had some symbolic meaning for them. Pauline and Heather came in and said, 'We're not eating anything' – they had brought no

food. I said, 'Why ever not?' 'Our Derek's out of work.' Heather has no one out of work at her home, and Pauline herself is working at Woolworths. I think they could have managed something. They said that they had been told by Gladys K that those who brought nothing must eat nothing. The same thing applied to Janet C: she came and said, 'I won't eat anything here' – and she was the only one who stuck to it. Beryl and Janet, who had promised to bring a Dundee cake, did not bring one; they brought bottles of lemonade instead.

Undertakings to bring money to pay the normal weekly subscriptions or to pay for damage inflicted on the club room were rarely kept.

As would be expected, the central feature of the club was the dancing – and the only form of music and dancing tolerated was rock-and-roll. At the normal thrice-weekly meetings, both in the Meeting Rooms and later at the Church Hall, it was almost invariably the main interest of those attending, the only exceptions being those evenings when for one reason or another no gramophone was available. When the club was first formed some of the prominent male participants were unable to dance. Encouraged by the group worker the more proficient young women taught the others – and also taught the group worker. Acquisition of this skill enabled some of the most troublesome of the boys – for instance, Dopey T and Derek G – to attend the ordinary youth club in the vicinity without behaving so as to invite expulsion, and also led them to venture out with more confidence into the outside world – to the local dance hall. Derek P bought a gramophone on hire-purchase especially for the use of the club, though he retained full possession of it and used it as a bargaining counter in one way or another.

Rock-and-roll was undoubtedly the occupation taking up most of the time of most of the young people attending the club. The most conspicuous of the activities recorded by the group worker, however, was that which can be classified as destructive behaviour, 'shocking' behaviour, and general milling about. The same qualification applies here as was mentioned earlier: there is a tendency for these items to appear in the record, rather than evidence of ordinary, conventional behaviour. But it remains true that in the course of half a year this set of young people did all the things attributed to them by the group worker. The examples quoted below are not selections of glaringly unusual delinquencies, but their normal night-by-night behaviour in the club:

> They started to brew tea in the kitchen; this caused a great deal of commotion. Some wanted to come in and some wanted to go out. The kitchen door, however, was locked by someone. There was a terrific amount of banging.

After they had been rejected by the Meeting Rooms, when alternative accommodation was made available by the Parochial Church Council of the Anglican Church, this is part of the account of the first meeting in the Church Hall:

> The girls looked round the hall, and then in great numbers went apple-stealing. They came back with apples in their pockets, half eating them and scattering the cores on the floor. They tore up the notebook I had brought and broke the pencil. Janet, Pauline, and Beryl sat on a cupboard and started to throw furniture about. I stopped them but they went at it again as soon as my back was turned. A few others locked themselves in the kitchen and chalked the walls, ceiling, cupboard, and windows with 'We love Mary'. When I went in and with a sigh started to wipe things off, they came to 'help', but their help was destructive too. They smudged the walls and spilled water in the hall.

ARE THEY A 'GANG'?

The young people the group worker had to deal with, especially the thirty or so who were entered on the book of members, were not strangers to one another. They were roughly the same age, had been to school together, lived in neighbouring streets, were in similar jobs, and were equally low in the estimation of most people they met in their everyday life outside their own circle. Thus, six months before the group worker attempted to organize the group which became the Espressos, four of the young men, whose names the above descriptions have made familiar – Geoff M, Dopey T, Derek P, and Johnny A – were together accused of housebreaking. A cursory exploration of the closest contacts of these four soon results in a web being formed which includes many of the central characters in the Espressos: Anne J, one of the leading girls, was reputed to be Geoff M's girl-friend, and her sister Janet was also a conspicuous participant in Espresso activities. Dopey became, with Derek G, the nucleus of a group which was opposed to Derek P and his friend, Ken H, and Derek P's two sisters were also leading members of the Espresso club; Tessa and Jane A were Johnny A's sisters. Elsewhere we describe how Anne became the club organizer, Derek P and Jack V the suppliers of its gramophone and records, and above all, how these unclubbables came to the club week after week for months.

What is of greater interest and relevance in this discussion of the neighbourhood, however, is the fact that there were present very strong disruptive modes of behaviour which can be interpreted as their normal behaviour. The group worker's records certainly suggest that neither the picture of the isolated individual nor that of the solitary gang member is likely to be a very useful aid to the understanding of this kind of problem youth. We must see them also in the context of the gang.

The sexes regarded one another as indispensable, but, it appears, this fact was an unfortunate one. The great feature of the Espressos' evenings was the opportunity they gave for the young men and women to mix in an atmosphere of comparative freedom, in a situation which gave them a wide choice of contacts with eligible people of the opposite sex – 'eligible' not only in age but, even more important, in way of life also. It was dull when there were no boys present and the girls made explicit their desire to include boys in the club; the boys, for their part, were eager to have more and more girls attend. The sexes did not, however, regard each other as equals and friends. The males were dominant.

For example, though Derek P brought his gramophone regularly for the use of the Espressos, he would, if he were out of sorts, forcefully express the opinion that supplying such things was the job of the girls, and they ought to see to it. The girls, the group worker notes, were expected to carry the gramophone and records through the streets. Apparently the girls were much more assiduous in contributing to club funds and club feasts than were the boys.

Courting techniques, at least in the presence of the group worker, tended to resemble the forcible abduction of the girls by the boys. On one occasion the character of the attitude of the sexes to one another was strikingly revealed: a deputation of the Espressos had secured an interview with the Secretary of the city Youth Committee and the Director of the Project; after the interview the group worker saw some of the girls who had been on the deputation and asked how things had gone:

> They thought that the Director and the Secretary were not bad, but the boys had shown them up – the boys had been dreadful.

Shortly afterwards she saw some of the boys:

> They talked about meeting the Director and the Secretary, and said that the girls had shown them up something dreadful – Johnny R was very much down on the girls.

Age differences between those who attended the club were not marked (if the older visitors are excluded). As would be the case in most young people's clubs, the attenders who were even slightly older tended to look down on those who were younger as unreliable and unworthy of the responsibility of, for instance, getting the keys of the door from the caretaker.

Functional differentiation within the club was to be found at only a rudimentary level. Anne J was the collector of subs for some time, until she found herself in difficulties over her inability to retain the funds intact between collecting them and handing them to the group worker; she found it difficult enough to collect the money in the first place. Another of the girls took it upon herself to be the one to collect the keys, open the door, and return them. Derek P and Jack V saw to the provision of a gramophone and records, which they not unnaturally used to suit their own temper and sense of rightness. Mrs. Andes worked through Pauline P to transmit messages to the others, but apparently the messages were not in fact passed on. For example:

I went to the P's. Mrs. P opened the back door; and I must say she looked very slovenly indeed. I said that I was sorry I could not go to the club that evening. She said, 'That's all right; Pauline will let the others know.' I asked, 'Do you think so, Mrs. P? If not, I'll go on to some of the others – the Joneses, Gladys K, and so on.' She said, 'Don't worry, Mary, you've got enough to do; she'll see to it.' 'Thank you ever so much. I now have to go to the caretaker to tell him.' Mrs. P said, 'No, Derek will go down on his bike – it'll be all right.'

The next evening I saw seven of the girls. They were very abusive about my not having turned up at the club the night before. They had waited outside in the rain. I asked whether they had not been told by Pauline P that it was not on. They said no – she was all right – *she* didn't have to come and wait in the rain.

When differences arose between participants they sometimes resorted to violence:

While they were dancing they were also eating the biscuits (which I had brought them as a present after my holiday) and stamping the crumbs into the floor. I said that someone would have to sweep up when we had left. Jane, who was standing next to me, said that she would like to do it. Janet, too, said she would like to. I said that would be fine. Janet, however, said she would not do it with Jane. When the evening was near its end Jane again asked me if she could sweep the floor; I said she might. Janet, Patsy, Tessa, and Anne, however, said they were dashed if she was going to sweep the floor. Janet tore the broom from Jane's hand and became very abusive. Jane also started to swear. Janet's face contorted in a quite terrifying manner and she said it was *their* club (not Jane's) and who was Jane anyway to sweep the floor for them? Jane insisted that she would sweep the floor. Janet said, 'I'll strangle you,' and her eyes grew very large as she started at Jane's throat. Jane was terrified and it was difficult to get Janet away from her. The others went off, still swearing they would 'get' Jane.

The next night Jane came again – showing by that great courage, I thought. After a while Janet, Patsy, Anne, Rosemary, and the rest came in. I left the room but was called back quickly by Anne, who said, 'There is terrible fighting going on in there.' I went in and saw that Janet was literally strangling Jane. Rosemary and Patsy were also fighting; Rosemary looked completely pale and beside herself; Patsy's blouse had been ripped off. Geoff tried hard to get Janet away from Jane, but Janet seemed to have superhuman strength; her eyes were completely distorted and she was shouting, 'I'm going to get her. I'll cut her tongue out and stamp on her eyes. I'm going to kick her so hard that she will be black and blue for years.' I managed to separate the other fighting pair; Patsy sat in the corner and just sobbed while Rosemary stood in another corner, quite white. Then I succeeded in parting Jane and Janet. Janet's face was scratched and bleeding, and Jane certainly had marks on her throat. Janet kept saying, 'She must go or me,' and she started at it again; she was like someone quite mad. In five minutes she was at Jane's throat again, shouting, 'You wait until my boy-friend comes home! Nobody else will stand up for me, but he likes me and he will.' During all the fighting Jane had been screaming, 'I have no parents; you have no right to touch me, because I have no parents.' Towards the end of the evening Gladys K came in, but she was hunted out, and I am afraid there was not much I could do at that moment.

Derek P and Ken H were swearing that they were going to round up a gang of friends to beat up Derek G and Dopey T.

I asked them whether they wouldn't like to come and talk it over with them, but they said they would not. Later in the street I had to pass Derek G and Dopey. I went over to them and asked whether they would not prefer to talk things over instead of fighting. They said, 'A nice little talk! Oh, no, not us!' and they talked about beating up the other two the next day – though I felt it was not serious.

A striking feature of the behaviour of some of the participants was the use they made of non-members to achieve their own ends against the wishes of other regular participants. In the early days of the club a definite decision was made that a list of members should be compiled and that 'members only' should be the rule on two of the three nights each week: Monday night would be 'visitors' night', when persons invited by members would be admitted. The decision to include any particular person as a member was taken in an informal kind of acclamation procedure by the original nucleus of the club:

Janet: 'I'm not coming if that girl (Jill) is coming.' *Rosemary*: 'Good riddance!' (Rosemary is Jill's sister.) They threatened each other with physical harm, swearing at each other. *Jill*: 'I'm as good as you are!' *Janet*: 'Are you?' *Jill*: 'I was born in Upfield.' *Janet*: 'Yes, but I don't know in which road!' *Jill*: 'Same road as you!' *Janet*: 'That doesn't mean a thing.' Meanwhile a general clamour had arisen for the undesirables to be thrown out. *Members*: 'Mary says you have to go!' *I*: 'No, you had better say whom you want to leave. It is for you to decide who the regulars are.'

Throughout successive weeks the problem of 'regulars' and 'visitors' continued unabated. Visitors provided the members with an opportunity of working our rivalries within the group itself. Dopey T and Derek G were on one side and Derek P and Ken H on the other. Dopey and Derek wanted to ignore the rules about visitors.

The group worker used the crises over visitors to point out to the members that, if they were to remain a group, they would have to deal with the problem of the visitors as a group and not decide as individuals or cliques to admit their friends when it suited their own convenience. The record of the next few meetings speaks for itself:

> A few non-members drifted in but nothing was said; nobody did anything about them and they were allowed to stay.

> I was greeted very warmly by the members, and there were only members there. 'No visitors,' they cried and locked the door. It all seemed to work well. Dopey and Derek soon came with some chaps from the Army and some other visitors. I stood at the door and said, 'I think it is no visitors tonight.' Beryl and Anne, however, said, 'Let them in; they are on leave.' I told them it was their affair and stood aside; the visitors came in but the Army chaps remained outside. There was a great cry from the other girls about visitors being let in. I really felt that they had decided on a no-visitors policy and were slowly going to keep it.

Once again, however, this apparent unity over visitors was shortlived. There were still more visits to be faced from 'Mugsy' and the long-haired boys. The Espressos still found the temptation of visitors too great to be able to make a united stand against them. Derek P, who had previously fought Dopey T over the original introduction of visitors, now joined with the long-haired boys rather than with the Espressos. The following extract describes an evening when both the long-haired boys and Mugsy's gang appeared:

> A gang of the long-haired boys appeared. The girls said, 'Quick, shut the door – they're horrible, dirty.' They locked the door. They kept on saying that if they had a Christmas party, they wanted only the group. Everything was really happy and it was a very pleasant atmosphere indeed. I remember the thought flashing through my mind that if I could only keep the group as a group, I felt all would not go too badly with them. But

Peter, who is really a bit of a fifth columnist, I should say, came in. Anne called to him, 'You don't open the door to let those other boys in to steal crockery.' But it wasn't Peter who opened the door this time. The group had warned him, through Anne, and also through the attitude of the others, that if he didn't do what was decent, they'd throw him out – they could cope with Peter.

But one of the girls went out leaving the door open, and some of the Long-Hairs came in. I remember one of the little girls, Jill, calling out, 'Those are the chaps you want to get rid of.' I stood quietly by the door, and slowly some of them drifted out. I was just feeling that the situation was really going to be managed all right when Pauline P and Gladys K came and literally grabbed me by the throat from the back, saying, 'Oh, what's cooking here?' and then they saw the boys and I think they were frightened of them, but at the same time they live in the same road and they do try to maintain friendly relations with them. They said, 'Do let them in; it's cold for them.' The ground was more or less cut from under my feet; so they came in. With them came Mugsy and his crowd. Janet J and Beryl B started to get rather rough, swinging from the windows; then somebody threw a chair. While we were all sitting round they suddenly decided they would pierce somebody's ear, and they had a needle. Then, fortunately, the sound of the gramophone gave out and they started to pack up quietly and go home; but not before Mugsy and a gang of seven had gone into the girls' lavatory in a provocative sort of manner and urinated on the floor (they shut the door, though).

Though this gives a picture of a set of young people who were very far from being a single 'gang' with a sanctioned mode of behaviour and a hierarchy of roles, or a series of such gangs, the above account would be distorted if it did not do justice to the fact that they at least preferred one another's company to that of other people – they were not very firmly attached to one another nor much interested in furthering one another's welfare, but they were more attached to one another than they were to anyone else. The quarrels were described by the group worker as being 'all within the family' – they fought each other, but did so in a brother-against-brother or sister-against-sister fashion. The outcome of the fight between Janet and Jane was that Janet called at Jane's home in the course of the week and effected a reconciliation. Geoff M was very derogatory about the club, but he fought for it, and apparently valued his connections with it. His first remarks were that he did not care about the club:

> He thought it was a pretty thick club we had here. It was full of people on probation, girls 'on the town', and sub-normal children (he laughed very pointedly), 'Paul here is one.'

He did, however, care enough about the club to write to the group worker from prison while awaiting allocation to Borstal in response to a letter from her:

> Thank you for the lovely surprise. I didn't expect to hear from you all so soon. I hope things are running well at the club. I was glad that you hadn't forgotten me nor my friends. Is Derek and Ken still larking around? Remember the records I used to bring down the club. Well, Mary, I hope the boys and girls are behaving and not giving you grey hairs. Don't worry about them, they are saints compared with some others I know. I hope you will write back and let me know all you can about the club.

The members had been encouraged by the group worker to write to Geoff, but never did so. They did, however, respond to his letter in a very friendly way:

> I passed Geoff M's letter around; it was surprising that though the letter had been a little bit critical, everyone said, 'Isn't this a lovely letter? Doesn't he write beautifully? Oh, we are his friends! We'll write to him again; we'll do something for him at Christmas.' They suggested boots, socks, or cigarettes should be sent to him, but Beryl B came out strongly in favour of a pair of boots, and they agreed with that.

When Geoff had been convicted, it will be recalled, he had caused a disturbance in the court, and it had taken five warders and three policemen to remove him from the dock. The sympathies of these young people were entirely with him.

The members used the opportunity that having a club room gave them to teach one another to dance:

> The atmosphere was very good; people were dancing and having a very good time; the dancers were teaching the non-dancers; there was a bit of horseplay (combs being hidden, girls being pulled on to boys' knees) but everybody knew it was fun.

Very often young people would be waiting for the club to open, standing about in friendly groups, waiting for Mrs. Andes to arrive and unlock the premises. After the meetings similar groups would be discovered by the group worker at their own street corners:

> I came to the club and Upfield Road was full of groups of young people. Madeleine S got the keys from me and she very proudly opened the door. The atmosphere was very jolly. Both Derek G and Dopey looked happier this evening and were chatting to members they had not chatted to before. After the meeting I went to the Angel corner, where Janet and Anne were standing with some boys.

One evening would be a 'bad' one as far as solidarity was concerned; the next would be one in which feeling between those present was one of friendliness and there would be a great deal of interaction between members. Thus, one evening would be like this:

> Attendance was very much down, and there was a general air of dispiritedness. Dopey said to me, 'It is a yellow evening.' Many others told me that the club was bad – that it had been nice before but that something had happened to the atmosphere, and the spirit had gone out of it.

While at the next evening the group worker would be able to write:

Two girls who had been courting just came in for a bop. It was most pleasant to see how much they enjoyed it – just rushing in to see their friends, and rushing out again to other friends.

THE QUESTION OF VALUES

The actual behaviour of these young people as described in the two preceding sections is similar in general outline, though not in specific content, to that of young people in other countries who are in similar positions in society and who come from similar homes. The most recent analysis of the elements common to gangs of delinquent boys in the United States is that of Professor A. K. Cohen (1956). It can be seen from his study that the Espressos in their behaviour are exhibiting traits which are far from peculiar to themselves, for five of the six characteristics which Cohen deals with apply without qualification to them – to girls and boys alike.

The first characteristic is the apparently non-utilitarian nature of their activities. Cohen deals in particular with the non-utilitarian nature of robberies carried out by gangs of boys, but extends his comments to all their activities. The girls' apple-stealing expeditions at the back of the Church Hall were of this kind.

The second characteristic is the gang's gratuitous hostility to contemporaries who are not members of the gang, as well as to adults. They are to be *flouted*, and there is an element of spite and malice, contempt and ridicule. This, also, is reminiscent of the Espressos at various times in the worker's narrative. The incident in the cinema, when some of the Espressos picked on a non-gang member whom they could torment, or the occasion on which two of the girls were walking down the street swearing at passers-by, may be mentioned.

'Making themselves obnoxious to the virtuous' is a third characteristic, which Cohen calls 'negativism'. 'The delinquent takes his

189

norms from the larger culture, but turns them upside down. The delinquent's conduct is right, by the standards of his sub-culture, precisely *because* it is wrong by the norms of the larger culture.'

Another characteristic of the 'delinquent gang', also shown by the Espressos, is that of 'short-run hedonism'. There is little interest in long-run goals, in planning activities and in budgeting time, or in activities involving knowledge and skills to be acquired through practice and study. The street corner for the Espressos is often at the *Golden Angel*; the candy store for them is the local fish-and-chip shop.

Fifth, the delinquent gang is 'versatile'; 'a generalized, diversified, protean "orneriness", not just this or that specialized delinquent pursuit, seems best to describe the vocation of the delinquent gang.'

I saw them plotting little schemes and went over and sat in the corner where they were sitting; the boys amongst them moved into another corner. Then they ripped the piano open and took out the notes. Derek P aimed very accurately, and started to throw the broken piano pieces at me. I saw on Anne J's face a look of amusement and pleasure that things were going wrong; but when she saw that I really was cross, her expression changed to one of concern. The other girls began to look concerned too; they sat in a corner and were quite cowed. Derek P went into the lavatory and urinated through the door, and people stood around laughing; others were peeping through the window—he was obviously exhibiting himself. Towards home-time some of the visitors whom I had never seen before turned out the lights and started to throw the furniture about violently. I got furious and *shouted*: 'Don't break the furniture here. It's very troublesome for us all if you do.' I think the girls were quite frightened by my having shouted in this way. There was a lot of mess to clear up, and Derek P, Ken H, Peter, another little boy, and two visitors stayed behind. Derek and Ken were very friendly with me at one moment, but at the next would get hold of some of the broken piano pieces and throw them about and also throw broken pieces of crockery about. Then they saw me to the bus stop, and on the way were telling jokes, quite clean jokes, like: 'What is black and white and read all over?'; and they then got slightly dirtier like: 'Two fleas were walking up the Duke's leg – where were they going?' Then Derek said, 'Will you accept our apologies for what happened tonight?' They got very constructive, deciding that the club should have members only, and that subs should be paid.

On another occasion:

Somebody (a visitor) was trying to pinch cups from the kitchen; then Dopey, Anne, and Beryl moved into the kitchen and tried to pinch cups also. I went in, not because of them, but because the lights had been switched off in the hall, but in their haste at my entry they threw a cup and broke the kitchen window. Beryl was hiding some cups and saucers, and so was Anne. I said, 'Well, you'd better put those back, hadn't you?' 'Oh, go on, my mother wants some!' Later, when I opened my bag I noticed that my purse was missing. Dopey said, 'The dirty rotters! You've had it! They'll pinch anything. They pinched the rent money off an old lady when she put it behind the mantelpiece. You won't see your purse again.' He was blaming the visitors.

In each of these five ways, then, the behaviour of the Espressos closely corresponds to that of Cohen's typical delinquent gang. But with regard to the sixth characteristic the Espressos deviate from the pattern of the typical gang. When Cohen writes of the principle of *group autonomy* he is referring to the gang as a separate, distinct, and often irresistible focus of attraction, loyalty, and solidarity. Though it is true that the members of the Espressos had strong feelings towards one another, their relationships varied in intensity and in character as the months passed, and there is little evidence to illustrate bonds of solidarity in the group. They are a loosely knit group by comparison with their American counterparts.

There can be no doubt, on the basis of the evidence gathered in the group work with these young people, that, whatever may be true of other young people, the Espressos and their acquaintances are a social problem – they are often a nuisance, and sometimes worse, to the people they come in contact with. Their behaviour is undoubtedly a *source* of stress and strain to others, but it appears also to be a symptom of stress and strain in the lives of the young people themselves. Is there anything in their circumstances, history, and native capacities or defects which will help us to understand why these adolescents behave in the way they do? They are apparently not unique, and we may therefore get some help from an appraisal of other students' views on similar sets of youngsters. On the basis of such an understanding of the sources of their behaviour, as well as on the basis of the fuller knowledge of the nature of the behaviour which the preceding sections have supplied, it may then be possible to tackle in a hopeful and fruitful way the problems posed both for society and for the children. These are the problems which will be considered in the next sections.

TRYING TO UNDERSTAND THEM

The first thing which helps to explain why the Espressos behave in the way they do is the absence of a clear, unified, and widely agreed set of beliefs as to how people ought to behave. This is, of course, very far from being a complete explanation, since it applies to everyone who lives in a modern, industrial, urban society; why these particular children succumbed to the difficulties of adaptation presented by a diversified culture while other children profited by them remains to be explored. The fact remains that where there are a large number of views as to the right and wrong ways of behaving, there is bound to be a problem of securing conformity which is not present to the same extent where there is only one view, or a few, of right and wrong. The American anthropologist, Margaret Mead, is one of those who puts the fact of multiplicity of moral standpoints in the centre of her discussions of modern social problems. She maintains that one of the most striking, and, from the point of view of law-abidingness, most important ways in which all isolated primitive civilizations and many modern ones differ from our own is in the number of choices permitted to the individual:

Our children grow up to find a world of choices dazzling their unaccustomed eyes. In religion they may be Catholics, Protestants, Christian Scientists, Spiritualists, Agnostics, Atheists, or even pay no attention at all to religion. This is an unthinkable situation in any primitive society not exposed to foreign influence . . . Similarly, our children are faced with half-a-dozen standards of morality: a double sex standard for men and women, a single standard for men and women, and groups which advocate that the single standard should be freedom, while others argue that the single standard should be absolute monogamy, trial marriage, companionate marriage, contract marriage – all these possible solutions of a social *impasse* are paraded before the growing children, while the actual conditions in their own communities and the moving pictures and magazines inform them of mass violations of every code, violations which march under no banner of social reform. Our young people are faced by a series of different groups which believe different things and advocate different practices, and to each of which some trusted friend or relative may belong . . . add to this the groups represented, defended, advocated by her friends, her teachers, and the books she reads by accident, and the list of possible allegiances, incompatible with one another, becomes appalling . . . And not only are our developing children faced by a series of groups advocating different and mutually exclusive standards, but a more perplexing problem presents itself to them. Because our civilization is woven of so many diverse strands, the ideas which any group accepts will be found to contain numerous contradictions (Mead, 1943, pp. 161–5).

It is not suggested that these kinds of choice are a matter of conscious and explicit intellectual difficulty; in most cases they

193

almost certainly are not. But it seems to be generally true that it is easier to secure conformity to any particular set of rules when there are not many alternative sets of rules being advocated. Furthermore, it has been argued by many writers, on the basis of their evidence and particular viewpoint, that the behaviour of an individual who has not a fairly clear and unchallenged view of the kind of life he ought to lead, which is supported by other people, is prone to deteriorate to the level of negativism, malice, pointlessness, and so on.

As Professor R. Wilson has suggested, a variety of ways of life and a multiplicity of choices are part and parcel of modern urban development, with all its advantages as well as its shortcomings; and since the problem cannot be eliminated within the limits of such a society, it is necessary for society to come to terms with it. Both the neighbour and the parent tend to abdicate their former role of imposing their own way of life on the child, and, Professor Wilson maintains, this is appropriate in a world of bewildering change, in which the neighbour and parent in any case no longer agree with one another, or parents among themselves, over which way of life ought to be imposed on the child. The education of the child to such a world must be the job of a flexible instrument – the school:

> Schools are places where we employ teachers to try to help the next generation to be effectively different from their predecessors ... (and) to negotiate the blind corners of life, unknown to previous generations (Wilson, 1952).

If this is taken as a statement of what is desirable and not as a description of the actual world, it is a point of view which coincides with that of Mead, who insists that she is not arguing for a return to primitive simplicity, but for 'education for choice' – education which enables children to face the world as it is.

Were the Espressos worse off than other children in this respect? It appears that in some ways they may have been. It will be seen from the Neighbourhood and Family Studies (Volume 2) that an area such as Upfield is not marked so much by the existence of a body of shared values as by the existence of a large number of different types of family and ways of life. The attitudes and practices of teachers in the locality suggest that 'education for choice' and a concern with 'the negotiation of blind corners' are not always in fact at the forefront of the schools' endeavour. In his recent examination of this problem, Ford argues strongly that one important source of the behaviour of the Espresso-type of boy and girl is this variety, and therefore indefiniteness and uncertainty, of rules of behaviour as far as they are concerned, and that this uncertainty is due in large measure to their unfavourable position in relation to the various social situations in which they have to operate:

> When the child leaves school he moves from one social grouping which, on one level at least, is out of adjustment with the community in which he lives, and passes to another social grouping in the workplace which is, if anything, even more drastically divorced from his home community. The transition itself and the necessary adjustments required of him are made more difficult by the lack of integration evident in both the educational process and the workplace situation (Ford, 1957, p. 168).

This is what Eisenstadt has called the problem of 'the generations' – the problem of securing the conformity of adolescents to the demands of respectable adult society when these adolescents have to contend with a marked break in their lives on leaving school. There is no easy transition from childhood, in the sense of the demands which are made on a person as a child, to adulthood, the taking up of the rights and obligations of a fully mature person. The observations of the group worker in the Project do not extend to material on this topic, and therefore there is little internal evidence on this point, but it is not unreasonable to suggest that a problem which other writers have argued is endemic in modern industrial urban society also affects the Espressos.

The teen-age gang is then seen to be one of the possible responses of young people to the uncertainty which besets them about the way they ought to behave; the members interact with others in the same position as themselves and give one another the satisfaction of 'knowing where they stand' – each knows what the other members of the gang think is appropriate behaviour in the gang. The gang is seen in this interpretation as a solution to a problem that society has set young people – the problem of an area with conflicting values, a social void, in their lives. Another possible solution is that of 'running amok' – of saying, 'A plague on all your rules! I shall make my own to suit myself.' Apparently American gangs tend to adopt both solutions; the Espressos, as has been shown, tend to the second more than to the first – their behaviour is less clearly that of individuals integrated into a tight gang pattern, and more that of individuals acting on their own with some support, but without strict gang control. Why the 'running amok' behaviour should take the precise forms it does take, and why the Espressos should be more of a gang than would be found in, perhaps, a professional neighbourhood, and less of a gang than would be found in the 'shook-up' neighbourhoods of the great cities of the United States, will be discussed below.

Whatever the complexity of and confusion presented by alternative ways of life in our society, there are certain values which are put forward with particular force and persistence. These are the values relating to material comfort, power, and prestige. What C. Wright Mills has said of his own country may be taken as true also of our own:

> Of all the possible values of human society, one and only one is the truly sovereign, truly universal, truly sound, truly and completely acceptable goal of man in America. That goal is money, and let there be no sour grapes about it from the losers (Mills, 1956, pp. 164–5).

It is not so much money on its own which is important, but money as it bears on prestige – on feelings of being respected by other people, and of being able to respect oneself. In a peasant society, a caste society, or any society in which there are different standards imposed on and expected of different segments, feelings of deprivation and of being 'underprivileged' do not arise with the keenness which characterizes them in societies like our own, where the *same* standards of worth and achievement are, by and large, imposed on everyone. Where do the Espressos stand in this situation?

They certainly see themselves as failures, and as coming from despised families and a despised district:

> Jane A asked me whether, when her brother came out of prison, he could come to the club. I said she would have to ask the others. They all said, 'Yes, he is our mate.' Someone said, 'But he is *rough*, Mary.' I said, 'That is all right' – and the boy who made the remark smiled happily at my response.

> Derek P said, 'You shouldn't have started a club in Upfield. You should have started it somewhere else, where it is nice. Upfield is a place for juvenile delinquents.'

> I met Gladys K and Beryl B. Beryl, in a very 'cultured' voice: 'Ugh, you going to the P's for tea?' I said I was. Gladys K said, 'You know what house?' I said, 'Ninety-one, I believe.' *Gladys*: 'You come down our street! A fine street it is! There's the man with the bald patch – he has been accused of murder, but they didn't have enough evidence. Two suicides we had lately. Two gone mad. Oh, a fine street! You just come down our street!' Her voice was bitter, and shrill, and melodramatic, like the Teds portrayed in a film. But at the moment, though rather exaggerated, the picture was nevertheless a true one, and it struck me just how melodramtic the plain truth was here. She pointed to the P's door, and said quietly and helpfully, 'There it is. Goodnight. See you Monday.' I waved to her as she went into the door of her own home, which is nearly opposite.

> I met Beryl B and Janet J. *Janet*: 'Where do you live?' *Self*: 'You know I live in Wellesley.' *Janet*: 'By yourself?' *Self*: 'I have someone staying there just now.' *Janet*: 'Oh, society ladies!' *Self*: 'I am no society lady. I work like everybody else.' *Beryl*: 'I suppose you wouldn't lower yourself to come to *our* house.' They were sitting on the kerb; I sat down by them and

197

said, 'I just about might!' They laughed, and the atmosphere became a little friendlier.

Later in the life of the club, when the group worker had become accustomed to the appearance of her charges, she was taken aback anew to find how noticeable was the contrast in general manner and appearance between them and other children from the estate. She wrote the following after a visit to a local youth club:

> I was struck by the great difference between the Espressos and this crowd who were sitting at table (it was the night of the club dinner). Though some of their jokes were good and hearty, their manners had very much an acceptable pattern about them. I was struck by the amount of ballroom dancing that was going on, and the great difference in appearance between these children and the Espressos.

It is true that some children 'rise above' this sort of background; it may even be that such a background is a stimulus to certain children, and it is in that sense a very real advantage in their advancement. This explanation of the behaviour of the Espressos is, therefore, by itself insufficient. But it would be very difficult indeed to maintain that this kind of background – what Cohen calls 'growing up in a class system' – is not a handicap to most of the children who experience it; that their own appearance and home address are not factors which lead them to be looked down upon by others; that they are not conscious of this, and that their violence, bravado, and spite are not understandable and indeed expectable responses to these facts. If we look further still, it may be that additional facts about the Espressos – perhaps their home backgrounds – may help us to understand why they in particular have been the ones to succumb to the negative aspects of their environment.

The Espressos were, in the main, failures at school.[1] Why this

---

[1] While all the evidence we have points in this direction, we cannot substantiate the conclusion by documentary evidence, since the Local Education Authority took the view that school records could not be made available for examination.

should have been so is itself a matter that would have to be understood in terms of the native endowment of each of them, their family life, their friends at school, and particular experiences with their teachers. As Mills points out, there is seldom any way of singling out a 'fundamental cause' of lack of success; it is nearly always a matter of several factors reinforcing one another, and this is as true of the successful, with their virtuous circle of cause and effect, as it is of the failures, with their vicious circle of cause and effect:

> Just as the limitations of lower class and status position produce a lack of interest and a lack of self-confidence, so do objective opportunities of class and status produce interest in advancement and self-confidence. . . . Energetic aspiration lives off a series of successes; and continual, petty failure cuts the nerve of the will to succeed (Mills, 1956, p. 111).

The fact remains that the Espressos were failures, and they had to pay the price of failure in the form of the withdrawal of public esteem and admiration:

> During the week Mrs. Wyatt, a social worker, phoned to inquire about Madeleine S. Madeleine was in trouble – stealing from her place of work. Mrs. Wyatt said that Madeleine's school report showed that she was very dull – she was D stream. I said I knew that. She asked what I thought of the child, and I said I had found her, in my personal contact with her, a pleasant girl – in fact, quite a delightful girl. There were great eruptions from Mrs. Wyatt, who could not understand how I could find a D-stream dull girl 'delightful' – obviously she must be very dumb, and that was the main thing.

The effect that this kind of failure is likely to have on the child's personality and subsequent behaviour is hinted at by Jahoda, when she writes:

> If an educational institution . . . is organized in such a manner that only the brightest students . . . are rewarded . . . all others

will be compelled to strive for the impossible with inevitable frustration and restrictions on personality (Jahoda, 1956, p. 575).

The Espressos are also clearly failures at work. Again it would be extremely difficult to separate out in the case of any particular child the extent to which his or her work failure is the cause of bad behaviour outside, and how far the general bad behaviour causes work failure. This point is not relevant just here. What is relevant and important is that work failure is almost certain to reinforce any existing predisposition to non-utilitarian, negative, and aggressive behaviour. The Espressos are failures in the sense that they are most often employed in the worst-regarded jobs (though not always the worst-paid jobs; it is necessary to stress once more that the level of pay is only one of the factors – the so-called 'status factors' – which lead people to think well of, or despise, a particular job; nevertheless, it is, of course, generally the most important factor). The girls almost without exception were not only not in clerical jobs but were in the lowest-status (i.e. most despised) factory jobs – in laundries and the sack factory. The following is an account of the drift of two of the Espressos from a fairly well-thought-of job to jobs such as their friends had:

> Heather and Pauline had both worked at Woolworths near the *Green Dragon*. Heather had got the sack because she was under age. Pauline had left 'out of loyalty', but I believe it was because she did not want to stay there on her own – she felt out of place. Heather got a job at the cleaners, but had not bothered to get a job for Pauline, who was still out of work. Desirée persuaded Pauline to try to get a job at her place (where Anne and Dopey also work); it is the sack factory, and the work is apparently very dirty, but you earn £3 18s. a week, which is more than you could get elsewhere. Pauline asked her mother's permission. Her mother said, 'Yes, it's all right – as long as you are with somebody.' Pauline said, 'Well, you know Desirée.' Desirée said to Pauline, 'Mind, they're very rough – but they are all right, and you have a good time.'

The boys were unskilled labourers in the building trade (often working on the same job as their friends), coal delivery drivers' mates, and porters of one kind or another – fish porters, and so on. They are failures, not only in that they are in poorly regarded employment but also in that they are often out of work altogether:

> Halfway to the club I met Derek P. He asked if I knew anything about a job. He sounded as if he had a cold (or he could possibly have been drinking). I asked him what had happened to his old job. He replied, 'Oh, I'll be getting the poke on Friday.'

A few days later the results of this threat were (in the opinion of the group worker) clearly discernible in Derek's behaviour at the club:

> Derek himself was in a very destructive mood indeed. I realized that it probably had something to do with his job and I asked him about it. 'No,' he replied, 'he's not poking me yet. He'll keep me for another week or two, perhaps.' I felt that this uncertainty had a great deal to do with his hatred this evening, because his job is very well paid (he gets about £9 a week) and it means a great deal to him. On the whole he is very affluent, and always told the others that he 'had money'. I remember his sister, Pauline, once saying when he had quarrelled with some boys that if they only made their peace with Derek, 'he would pay for them'.

Whether it was Derek's 'own fault' that he was losing the job is not at issue here; clearly the employer would have had some good reason for dismissing him – either because of his own failure in business, or because of the general economic situation, or because of some special lapse on Derek's part. Just as Derek's behaviour in the Espressos is explicable only in terms of a vast number of influences that impinge on his innate capabilities and defects, and a long history of development, so his behaviour at work would be understood only in terms of a large number of influences. There will be no disagreement over the reasonableness of the argument that the work failure of these boys, Derek included, has been one of the experiences that has been associated with their peculiar, and what may have been thought at first sight, motiveless and pointless reaction.

Professor Titmuss stresses this point of the problem of insecurity at work in a way which links it with the difficulties dealt with above arising out of the variety of appropriate ways of behaving in our type of society. He says:

> I have been particularly struck by the differences in the norms of behaviour expected of the worker in the factory and of the same worker in his home and in the community.

Whereas at home and in the community, stability and foresight are stressed, in the factory the worker is expected to reconcile himself to a week-to-week existence; the concept of stability is not an important attribute of the system either in theory or in practice. In general, the situation of many manual workers is basically a situation of uncertainty about tomorrow – a situation provoking 'immediacy of living' (Titmuss, 1958, p. 111).

THE WAY THEY ARE TREATED

The position of the Espresso-type boy and girl in the neighbourhood – the way that people in the neighbourhood react to them – is something which the group worker's research shows in rich detail. Two features of the reaction of local residents and workers in the locality are especially relevant in understanding the Espressos' behaviour.

First, attitudes range from praise and approval, through toleration and forbearance, to outright and uncompromising condemnation. Indefiniteness of expectations is itself, as has already been suggested, one of the circumstances which help to give rise to the problem behaviour of young people: they have to make their own decisions as to the way they ought to behave, and some of the weaker ones give up the struggle or experience personality difficulties which find expression in destruction of property, rowdyism, and so on. At one extreme in the neighbourhood are

202

the gangs of slightly older young people who look with approval
upon the delinquencies of their juniors; at the other are the sturdy
respectables, to be quoted below, who are firm in their conviction
that what these young people do is wrong and that they ought to
be punished so severely that they will be persuaded to cope with
their problems in a private way, instead of by being public
nuisances. The vicar in whose Church Hall the young people met,
and one of the local policemen, for instance, were tolerant and
understanding:

> I went to see Father Simpson at the vicarage, explaining how
> important it was that I should continue to meet the group, and
> that if we did not meet fairly often I would be losing the
> children. He said that the caretaker was threatening to resign
> (he sounded genuinely fond of him), and this would absolutely
> kill him, because he needed something to do – the Espressos had
> been quite a lot for him to withstand. He showed me the
> evening paper and asked whether any of the boys or girls who
> had appeared in court were members of the group. I said some
> of the boys were, but the girls were not. He was very sympa-
> thetic on the whole: 'Of course we're not turning you out.'

> I went to Father Simpson and told him about the destruction in
> the kitchen and the broken windows. He was very nice. We
> looked at the damage and I said we would make it good – that
> I'd 'phone the glazier' and so on. I must say that he was most
> helpful and understanding. I told him the members had done it,
> in a way because they liked the place so much. I thought that
> it would be difficult for him to understand, but he understood
> very well, and was most kind.

> I went to see Father Simpson. He was very distressed when he
> heard what had happened. On the other hand, he was his
> charming self – he was just having his supper, and said he did
> not mind being interrupted. He was really very kind indeed.
> He also treated Hazel, one of the Espressos who was with me,
> very courteously, making her wait not in the passage but in a

separate room, putting the fire on for her and so on. But at the same time he was horrified.

Called on Father Simpson, to explain that we may not be wanting the hall in future. He was interested to hear what I had to say about the girls. When I thanked him for all his help in the past he said, 'I quite understand the *problem* – it's the *method* I don't quite follow.' Throughout the conversation, which lasted for three-quarters of an hour, an expression of puzzlement and bewilderment never left his face, though at the same time he was very friendly.

Though the vicar was ridiculed by some members of the Espresso club on the first occasion on which he appeared, his tolerance and friendliness in spite of provocation soon ensured him a friendly reception. When, however, the Espressos were asked to find another place to meet, because the Parochial Council no longer felt able to allow them to use the hall, the reaction of the majority was to accept the facts lethargically, while the reaction of one or two was typically curt:

> I had produced a couple of Christmas cards (the children were obviously not at a stage where they would do a thing like that themselves) to send to the vicar and to the caretaker. Derek and Micky sat down and wrote them out most carefully, which is unusual for them, because as a rule they would just put their signature. But it was Anne who said after a bit, 'Is it them that want to put us out?' I said I was afraid it was – it was not really the vicar, but the people who talk round him. She said 'F . . . him!' (but at the same time I felt she accepted my word for it).

At least one of the estate policemen also was tolerant and understanding, not authoritarian, in his approach:

> Some of the children were using a bit of choice language outside. A policeman riding by on a bicycle came in to see me. He was a very pleasant chap – sort of chubby. He asked what sort of club I was running, and agreed I had quite a tough job, but

I think he realized that to try to instil fear into the children was useless; the only hope of doing anything with them was to treat them with kindness. He said, 'Mind you, you'd think that they'd show some respect for you in the language they use when they go out – but I know they think the world of you for all that.' Then he pointed out Tessa to me; he said she was quite dreadful – she had used the most awful language to him. He felt it would be much more appropriate if a policewoman dealt with her. 'It's only by having their confidence that you can really do something with them.'

But Upfield's reaction to the Espressos was in general one of hostility and disapproval. The first occasion on which the group worker's notes give an account of the reaction of a local resident to the Espressos was only a few days after they held their first meeting in the Meeting Rooms:

At this moment Mr. Franklin came in and told me to stop the people outside from swearing. I said they were not Espressos and I had nothing to do with them. He then went out and somehow shooed them off. He came back to me looking very agitated and pale. Pointing a shaking finger at me and in a breathless voice he asked me to open the kitchen door, which he had found locked. I had the feeling that he expected to see a really dreadful sight in the kitchen when the door was opened. He insisted: 'You must open the door. I am on the Bristol Social Project Committee, and I am entitled to know what is going on.' I said, 'Of course you are. I am trying to find the key – certainly you can look in the kitchen.' When I opened the door and he just saw people drinking tea, he went round touching the oven and looking at the windows. He then said it would have to be stopped; things had gone too far. The Goslings Club and this club would have to be shut. The girls told him how much they wanted the club. They said they were doing their best to keep it running in a fairly smooth way. They had in fact immediately cleared up the kitchen and were at their absolute best and were supporting me in any way they could. I did not

205

say very much to Mr. Franklin, letting the girls speak for themselves, and I think they did astonish him. Some of the boys came back and stood outside the door. He was just about to chase them when I intervened. He then started to talk to them. They told him they wanted this club, that they needed me, and if anyone organized a group without me they would not support it. They said that I knew what they needed. They began to swear again. Franklin started to lecture them on the wrongness of swearing. He also began to talk to them about God. At that they started to giggle among themselves. When I asked them to stop, however, they did so, and that again seemed to surprise him.

A week later one of the members of the research team, who at that time was living on the housing estate, had a neighbourly talk with a leading local resident. The informant was implacably opposed to the Espressos and to their treatment by group-work methods; he had the following things to say about their behaviour, about the behaviour of the group worker as he saw it, and about what he thought the solution to the problem ought to be:

I saw Beaver in his garden as I passed. He asked me whether I had heard what had been going on at the Meeting Rooms while I was on holiday, and I told him that I had just had a word or two with Bill Miller the day before. Beaver told me there was an uproar in the neighbourhood over Mrs. Andes's group: a committee was being held that night at which the matter would be thoroughly thrashed out.

Beaver sided with the objectors to Mrs. Andes's activities on three grounds: the behaviour of the members of the group, the behaviour of Mrs. Andes, and, to a lesser extent, the behaviour of the Director. The Espressos had damaged the Meeting Rooms – he gave me a list of the damage, which included pulling off door handles. They had been making so much noise that other meetings had suffered to the extent that their numbers were falling off; people came to enjoy themselves, and if their enjoyment was spoilt they would not come; the rock-and-rollers came to enjoy themselves as well, he said, but surely they could enjoy themselves without disturbing everybody else!

'One night I went over there, and in the small room there must have been *dozens* of them. It was an orgy! They were all crammed in there, rocking 'n' rolling to a gramophone. No one can say the Meeting Rooms were built for that! One night they were actually rocking 'n' rolling on the *roof* – did you hear about that? The boys go into the ladies' lavatory! You won't believe this – the *girls* go into the men's toilet. One night there was nearly a riot. There were two gangs in – they both had a gramophone and were fighting for the one room. I went over there one night and they were all hanging about outside, making a heck of a noise. I told them they had no right to be there. What a lot of cheek I got back! They turned round and said they darned well had, that they were waiting for Mary. I told them again that they had no right in the grounds until the club was due to start. Another mouthful of cheek! I told the culprit that I would give him a damned good hiding if he wasn't careful. I told them that if they didn't go straight away, I'd go for the police. That settled them! They went all right then!'

He went on to criticize the way the group worker treated the children:

'The trouble is,' he said, 'that the leader has no control over them at all. Do you know, one night Mr. Franklin went in to ask her if she would keep them a bit quieter, as his people couldn't hear themselves speak – she just said, "No, I won't!" He asked her if she would try to control them – she said she didn't intend to! She locked a couple of the members in the kitchen as a punishment. Mr. Franklin asked her to open the door. She just turned round and said she didn't have the key, and when he asked *who* had it, she said it was just lost! She was made to produce the key finally, and there was a *couple* in the kitchen *and water all over the floor*! Locking people up as a punishment! That is just using Teddy-boy tactics on Teddy boys. There is always a crowd of them there by half past seven; the club isn't supposed to start until eight. *She* never turns up until quarter past!'

His diagnosis and recommendations for treatment were that the trouble with these young people was that they have never had enough control:

'What these people need is *control*. If they are going to make a go of their lives they've *got* to accept discipline. They've got to play the game according to the rules. The matter with *them* is that they think they are the only people who count. They think the rules have to be made for their benefit alone, instead of everybody having a bit of give and take. You can see that down at the Meeting Rooms. If *they* are having a good time, it doesn't matter if they are stopping everybody else from having a good time. For them it's all take and no give. That's the saying, isn't it? – "The world is full of willing people – there's some who are willing to give, and there are others willing to let them." They ought to join the Scouts or Guides.'

He thought that however much there might be in the method Mrs. Andes was using, 'you've got to consider how much other people are put out by all this':

'The Meeting Rooms can be a place where people go for a quiet game of whist and where the Townswomen's Guild has its meetings, or it can be a place crammed with a lot of hooligans. It can't be both.'

Unfortunately his last point has a great deal of weight; indeed, it is irrefutable, given the quite legitimate motives of ordinary people in attending meetings in a building such as the Meeting Rooms – they do not go there to do social work, but to enjoy themselves. With limited resources, the question of a meeting place for unclubbables like the Espressos is itself a serious one.

The next night Mr. Franklin tried to stop the Espressos using the Meeting Rooms, and an ugly scene resulted:

Donald came running towards me [the group worker writes] and said, 'There's a man there who won't let us in.' Mr. Franklin was standing surrounded by about twenty-five members, who were arguing wildly with him. When he saw me, he did not greet me, but looked fierce – 'Mary, there will be no meeting here tonight.' We went into the Meeting Rooms alone to talk things over, after I had convinced him my suggestion was not a trick to get the youngsters inside the building. He shook his fist at me and said there would be no meeting that night. He said he had been there since seven o'clock trying to talk to the youngsters. They had told him they would murder him if he did not open the club. I said that as far as I knew there was a meeting of the club already arranged. He said that if I held a meeting he would see the chief officers of the Bristol Social Project Committee the next morning. Again shaking his fist at me he said, 'Mary, this has got to be stopped. There is nothing to talk over. I don't want to talk! I don't want to talk! I just want this stopped. There is not going to be any more.' I felt that although I could have insisted on my right to use the Rooms, under the circumstances it would not have been wise. I said that he might like to ring the Director about it, and he reluctantly agreed. As he went out Geoff and some of the girls shouted, 'We'll get you stuffed if you shut the club!' Geoff came and shook his fist at Franklin and said, 'You just try it on us! You just try it on!' Franklin turned to me, 'You see what is happening.'

The outcome of the phone call was that Mr. Franklin and Mr. Brown consented to allow the Espressos to use the Rooms, pending the final decision to prohibit their using them.

It is not difficult to see that the critics of the Espressos had a good case to argue. The Management Committee very quickly decided that the Espressos must leave the Meeting Rooms. The children, partly, the group worker believes, out of resentment at being excluded from the Meeting Rooms, did some damage to their new premises, which the caretaker listed:

> Five spoons missing from the kitchen, one card table slightly damaged, one blackboard and easel damaged – they belong to the Bristol Education Committee.

The group worker adds, however, that the caretaker was trying to be friendly and understanding: he 'obviously had been quite unaware of what a night it had been' – the night they had chalked 'We love Mary' on the walls. Within a week the caretaker's worst anxieties were, in his opinion, realized, and, though there were to be times when he was pleasant to individual Espressos when they called at the house for one reason or another, from this time on he clearly regarded the club as something which had been wrongly inflicted on him.

But in practice many difficulties were put in the way of the club, with, in the opinion of the group worker, detrimental effects on the Espressos. Before long, fear and hostility were the caretaker's only attitude. This attitude was shared by the deputy caretaker, Mrs. Sykes, who, on her first contact with the Espressos, had been charmed by them into giving them the key with the promise that they would not open the door with it until Mrs. Andes arrived, a promise which they at once ignored.

The Espressos in their everyday life are therefore faced, not with one response to their behaviour, but with a whole range of responses, from that which appears to condone or admire, at the one pole, to that which unequivocally rejects, at the other. The understanding showed by Father Simpson was rarely found in other community leaders. And this state of affairs not only tends to give rise to deviant behaviour, but also makes difficult the control of deviant behaviour when it appears. The same extremes of response (with moderate opinions getting less attention) can, of course, be seen outside the neighbourhood, in, for example, articles and letters in newspapers. On the one side, there are writers who condemn Teddy boys and Teddy girls, sometimes, it might be supposed, in the belief that all that is needed to make them into law-abiding citizens is harsh enough treatment, or even just a good talking to. On the other, with increasing frequency, are those who exhibit a slack and fashionable tendency to excuse them, either denying the existence of the troublesome because the majority are not troublesome, or maintaining that society has no right to inter- fere with such behaviour, even if it is troublesome, because it is the inalienable right of people to pursue their own course, so long as that course can be blessed by the shibboleth 'the culture of the Group'; or, from a relative standpoint, arguing that it is not possible to say that their behaviour is 'worse' than any other (an argument which is, unbelievably, current among some social workers); or, finally, refusing to *define* behaviour such as that described above as troublesome, on the grounds that the behaviour can be *explained* in terms of a bad family background, an unhappy childhood, and so on – an error in reasoning which, to use Pareto's phrase, oversteps the limits of comic absurdity.

The second feature of the reaction of local residents and social workers which is especially relevant in understanding why the Espressos behave in the way they do is that, the wide range of reaction notwithstanding, many of the most vociferous and paro- chially prominent people are condemnatory and repressive. As a matter of observation, the Espressos responded to condemnation and repression by behaving more destructively and aggressively than ever. Part of the reason for their behaving badly, it is strongly suggested, is their sense of inferiority and rejection in a society which values success in certain spheres in which they are conspicu- ous failures. It is, therefore, not very likely that their bad be- haviour will cease if their sense of worthlessness is exacerbated by public disapproval, and a perverse sense of their own importance is fed by public panic at the sight of their behaviour.

On the other hand, we would be foolish to expect the Espressos' behaviour to change quickly in response to acceptance and friend- ship. Indeed, acceptance is just as likely to be met with hostility, and friendship with distrust. It is this feature of their behaviour which is frequently so puzzling to the layman. Like the deprived children removed from their homes and boarded out with kindly foster-parents, who test out the love of their new parents, the Espressos also tested out the reality of the goodwill shown towards them by the vicar's offer of the Church Hall after they had been rejected by the Meeting Rooms.

It would be reasonable, perhaps, to place other people's needs and happiness far above those of the Espresso-type adolescent, and so decide to stamp out their delinquent activities at whatever cost to themselves. It would be reasonable to maintain (if the facts did not contradict the view) that the public got value for its money in the form of peace and quiet by locking away at great expense some at least of these young people. It would be reasonable to maintain that on the whole the best way to deal with the problem is to grin and bear them – as long as such a view was based on a realization that the young people themselves would not be helped at all by such a policy, and also on a realistic awareness of the fact that some people *were* having to bear them, so long, that is, as their segregation in certain housing estates, to some extent out of sight, was not taken as an excuse for denying their existence altogether.

It is not reasonable, however, to advocate a policy of sternness in terms of the Espressos' own good, on the grounds that this will lead to their reformation. An understanding of the origins of their behaviour completely negates such a solution – it is just not realistic and practicable, for all the talk of 'realism' and 'sound common sense' on the part of its exponents. It is certainly quite impossible not to feel that the reaction of people in the neighbourhood was more than justified by ordinary standards of forbearance. That does not alter the fact that such treatment aggravates the difficulties; it in no degree relieves them. All that it means is that in order to deal with Espresso-type children in a way which holds out some hope of success, time is needed, money is needed, patience quite out of the ordinary is needed, a deep care for the welfare of the children is needed, and a long professional training is needed. It is no good believing that 'the community', in the sense of ordinary people in the locality, can supply from among themselves this array of material resources, human qualities, and trained capacities.

There are two points being made in this examination of the re-action of people in the locality to the Espressos. The first is the central one here, that in the locality the Espressos meet with the confusion and contempt which they meet elsewhere, and which, it is argued, is one of the causes of their behaviour – their reaction to the caretaker was not that of conformity but of callousness. The second point is that it is tremendously difficult to do group work in an 'open' situation – the group worker is working along one set of lines, being permissive towards the deviant behaviour of her clients, and thus, consciously and purposefully, allowing them to act out more of their destructive and other aggressive tendencies than they would otherwise do; but others in the locality react in a markedly punitive manner to these public exhibitions of disturb-ance, and so aggravate the problem the group worker is trying to solve.

We have in this second issue a real tragedy. The group worker's centre of interest is her desire to make life fuller and happier for these disadvantaged youths, and she is convinced that the only possible way to do it is to reverse the processes which have led to their difficulties – too little love, too little respect, too little com-fort, too little power, and too little security in the enjoyment of even the little they have had. On the other hand, the people in the locality have never had real experience of children so asocial that they have yet to be brought to the stage where the ordinary in-centives and compulsions of society begin to affect their behaviour. They know in any case that *their* children respond beneficially to moderate and judicious control and chastisement. They find it difficult to realize that for some children, such as the Espressos, control and chastisement are petrol on the flames. The ideal so-lution would be the possession of the breadth of mind which would lead to the recognition of the fact that special treatment is necessary for special cases. But such breadth of mind is rare, and hardly to be expected.

The immediate effect of people in the locality on the attitudes of the Espressos can be observed, and the more general effect inferred, from the incident of the Boy Scouts' jumble, in which the conflict between Mrs. Andes and other equally worthy workers in the neighbourhood can also be discerned:

> There was a great deal of going in and out. Mugsy and his crowd discovered some jumble which the Scouts had piled outside their hut nearby. Mugsy and others started to dress up in various attires and came into the club. A lot of jumble was also just thrown onto the floor. The chief scoutmaster was quite understanding about it. But Derek P, who was in a very bad mood indeed, was asked by another of the scoutmasters to give him back the hat he was playing with. Derek would have given it back in a few moments anyway, but it was torn from his hand by this rather angry scoutmaster, with a look of intense hatred on his face: 'Give me that hat! We are trying to sell them for the Blind.'

But what is right treatment for a Scout-type of youth is not necessarily the right treatment for an Espresso. In the words of Edmund Burke, 'In all bodies those who will lead must also, in a considerable degree, follow. They must . . . conform their propositions to the taste, talent, and disposition, of those whom they wish to conduct.'

This account of the conflict between the neighbourhood and the Espressos is of little value if it does not provide us with experience for future work with the delinquent fringe of society. It is all too easy to see it as a battle between right and wrong, between the respectable and conformist majority and the non-conformist minority. On the other hand, it is clear that any worker engaged in trying to help a group such as the Espressos must incur the hostility – not the gratitude – of the neighbourhood. Hence our earlier suggestion that the worker needs support from her colleagues and committee if she is to deal with the community's reaction with understanding and insight. The Project's mistake was not that we failed to make explanations of our work to the community leaders during the period of the Espressos, but that we used the wrong structure through which to do it. We relied on the more formal types of neigbourhood association for discussion of the Espressos' behaviour, rather than on informal groups, as a means of 'working through' hostility and anxiety. As a result of this mistake our explanations were generally rejected and the local community's resistance was not seriously diminished.

PART IV

The Upfield Adventure Playground

CHAPTER 11

Achievement of the Playground

THE founders of the Project, however open-minded about the precise form that it should take, were clear in their intentions about three things: first, that the main focus should be on the 'stresses and strains' of a developing community; second, that the Project team should give help to the community through responding to some of the more potentially constructive needs; and, third, that the activities which were to be a vehicle for the fulfilment of these needs should continue, if possible, after the team had withdrawn.

As we emphasize elsewhere in this report, the achievement of these three aims demands compromise at various points. The story of the Upfield Playground makes this abundantly clear – the conflict between the felt needs of the community and the needs which a team of outsiders, the professionals as we have called them, consider to be most acute. There were, nevertheless, good reasons why an adventure playground should be chosen as one of the methods through which the Project attempted to fulfil the intention of the founders.

First and foremost, perhaps, because the community wanted it. Yet even this apparently unequivocal statement is open to argument if by the 'community' we mean the ordinary residents of Upfield. There was no deputation of residents, for example, asking the local authority to set up a playground. Indeed, even at the end of the first year of the Playground's existence some of the parents of the most regular users had little knowledge of its purpose. But there was, on the part of community leaders and of two chief officers of the local authority, a real concern for the development of an adventure playground. Second, since there was a feeling that Upfield, one of the first of the inter-war estates, had suffered from a lack of social amenities, the case for making up for this deficiency in various ways, such as the Meeting Rooms and an adventure playground, was a strong one. Third, as a result of the first year's study, the Project staff recognized that there was in the old estate at Upfield an appreciable number of families showing clear signs of 'strain and stress' in the upbringing of children. An adventure playground seemed to be one way of helping some of the children.

The fourth reason, which received the strongest emphasis in the Director's early memoranda, was to provide an opportunity for tenant participation through small local playgrounds for toddlers on six vacant sites adjoining some of the houses and also in an adventure playground in which the local authority and the Upfield Community Council were interested. From this point of view, however, the attempt to develop local playgrounds created and supervised by the tenants themselves was unsuccessful. Nor was the active participation of local parents in the Adventure Playground – with the exception of a tiny minority – in fact achieved, as we try to explain in this chapter. Experience taught us that, at least in the short run, in organizing a playground or a club so as to prove helpful to the minority of families and children whose stresses are greatest, it is difficult to obtain the interest and co-operation of the majority.

The Adventure Playground was primarily a contribution towards the happiness of Upfield children. During the first two years, the Playground leader, who had previously worked with 'unattached' young people in two pioneer experiments, was a member of the team. He kept a daily log-book of children and events on the Playground.

The recording of playground events presented no easy task. The work of supervising a busy playground, containing on some occasions as many as a hundred children, left little time for detailed and exact observations. But, in spite of many preoccupations, the leader was able to describe at least the main events. Not unexpectedly, the minority of unusual children who made the greatest demands on his help and understanding are mentioned most frequently in the log-book, while the majority escape notice. To some extent, therefore, the reader's attention may be diverted from the daily activities of the many to the distractions caused by the few. In writing this account we have tried wherever possible to let the leader's own narrative speak for itself and to add explanations only when necessary. In deciding what to include and what to omit, the main criterion has been the relevance of particular events for understanding the children at play.

WHY ADVENTURE PLAYGROUNDS?

Adventure playgrounds are still an unusual answer to children's leisure needs, existing mainly, as John Mays puts it in his delightful story of the Liverpool playground, 'on the lunatic fringe of orthodox recreation' (Mays, 1957). They are perforce untidy and often dirty places, which fit awkwardly into plans for making a city more beautiful through parks and open spaces. The variety of junk collected on them (hence their alternative title of 'junk playgrounds') gives them an air of neglect and disorder and an unfinished look. 'It will be nice when they finish it,' said an Upfield resident about a year after the Playground had opened.

Children, however, do not see the playground through adult eyes. For them its meaning comes from the dens they build, the games they play, the friends they meet, and above all else from the warmth and understanding of the leader. The Upfield Playground became known in the neighbourhood as 'Donald's', and it was of 'Donald' or 'Shorty', as some of the children nicknamed him, that they spoke first whenever the Playground was mentioned.

It is hard for children to create their world of imagination in

221

the crowded homes and streets of large industrial cities, and the desert island of the adventure story remains a distant dream. 'This is our island. It's a good island. Until the grown-ups come to fetch us we'll have fun.' So said Ralph, the leader of the group of boys left alone on the desert island in William Golding's *Lord of the Flies* (1954). Unavoidably perhaps, our towns have grown with the needs of adults rather than of children in the forefront of our plans. It is, after all, only too easy to forget the world of childhood as we move further away from it. The consequences of an industrial and urban civilization are felt most acutely by the child. The restricted and dangerous environment of the street, the limitations of crowded flats and homes, the monotony of the ready-made toys which fill the counters of toy-shops, constrain the energies and imagination of the child in his leisure hours. The adventure playground movement has grown up to meet such problems and needs as these.

Out of small beginnings in Copenhagen the adventure playground has become known in England very largely through the energies of Lady Allen of Hurtwood and the generosity of the National Playing Fields Association. In England adventure playgrounds have already been established in London, Liverpool, Grimsby, Crawley, and Bristol. Yet England, in common with many other highly industrialized countries of the West, has been slow to follow Sweden's bold and imaginative playground policy. In Stockholm, with a population of 800,000, the Parks Department has as many as eighty-five playgrounds located in housing areas throughout the city, with between two and five supervisors working at each and numbering about two hundred in all. These play supervisors are mainly young women with a social or educational training, whose primary function is to inspire the children to activities of their own.[1]

The aims of the movement, though hard to fulfil, may be simply stated. In essence the purpose of the adventure playground,

[1] Paper by Mr. H. Blom, Architect, Head of the Stockholm City Parks Department, to U.N. European Seminar on 'Playground Activities, Objectives, and Leadership in Sweden', May/June 1958.

unlike that of the orthodox playground with its swings and roundabouts and open space for ball games, is to provide children between the ages of about 5 and 15 with opportunities of expressing some of their imaginative and creative instincts in a safe environment – opportunities for building, for climbing, for cooking, for pretending, and for doing things which are impossible amid the hazards of the street and the confined space of back garden or courtyard. But most important of all – as we have come to recognize from the Upfield experience – adventure playgrounds depend for their success on the skill and understanding of the leader. Good leadership is the very heart of the movement.

It is all too easy to state ideals, and nowhere perhaps are they more deceptive than in the present case. The story which follows is an attempt to describe as fairly as possible what actually happened at Upfield, not what most of us would like to have happened, for theory and practice are often widely divorced. It is still far too early to lay down any rigid patterns of organization for the adventure playground movement, and experience will inevitably vary according to the place, the resources available of both money and skill, and the cultural background of the children.

THE EARLY HISTORY

The precise origins of the Playground at Upfield are hard to define. They are due in the first instance to the initiative and foresight of a small number of people, councillors and chief officers in the local authority, staff members of the Bristol Council of Social Service, and the community leaders of Upfield itself. The Playground was the result of a partnership between statutory and voluntary bodies and the local community.

In December 1953 the Community Council at Upfield had pressed the Education and Public Works Committees of the local authority for two playgrounds with supervision and, if possible, with equipment, one for each end of the estate, but at the time their pressure had no immediate tangible success. Five months later, however, there followed an important meeting at the

223

University Institute of Education addressed by Lady Allen and chaired by the Housing Manager. A playground exhibition and conference also took place at the same time.

Inspired and enlightened by this meeting, the Community Councils at Upfield and Boltwood each began a survey of vacant sites to be reserved as play spaces or developed as playgrounds on the two estates. The results of the very careful Boltwood survey had little or no practical effect. The claims of Upfield, however, met with greater success, and at a meeting of the Community Council in January 1955 attended by the Chief Education Officer, the Housing Manager, and the Organizer for Physical Education plans for an adventure playground were discussed. Overawed a little by the prestige of their visitors but convinced by their sincerity and enthusiasm, the Community Council accepted these plans by 27 votes to 2, and appointed a committee to act on its behalf. The initial tripartite basis of representation on this committee was agreed as follows:

Upfield Community Council	5 members
Bristol Education Committee	3 members
Bristol Social Project	3 members

Other members were added at a later stage.

THE SITE

Perhaps some day adventure playgrounds will be an essential element in town-planning policy. But until then it seems that they must be fitted into the vacant spaces which are still available. In its site for the Playground leased to the Trustees by the Bristol Housing Committee at a nominal rent of a shilling a year, Upfield was particularly fortunate. The $1\frac{1}{3}$ acres accepted by the committee are situated on the edge of the estate, separated from a middle-class area by a wood and a lake preserved for bathing by a private club. One end of the lake is invaded by Upfield children who defy the regulations and endanger their lives in the deep water by scrambling through the fence. The Playground itself is rough and hilly ground: through the far end runs a stream, a joy to children when swollen by heavy rain, but at most times no more than a trickle, and in dry weather completely empty. The bushes at the bottom of its steep banks and the long grass and undergrowth give encouragement to children in their games. The banks of the stream are steep enough for sliding on dandy-cars and on the chassis of discarded perambulators.

For a period after the leader arrived the site remained as it had always been – except that a number of holes were dug ('excavation' was specifically prohibited by the lease) and some dug-out and stone-walled dens were built. The children still knew it as 'The Banks'. Change appeared, however, as a hut was built and a fence erected, but at the end of four years the main natural features remain – the bushes, the long grass, and the hillocks. Only around the hut itself is there any change – a space has been levelled for ball games or the erection of a climbing frame.

PHASES OF THE PLAYGROUND'S HISTORY

It may be useful at this point to summarize the main phases of the Upfield Playground's history during the association of the Project with it, before going on to examine the events which took place and the methods adopted. We can describe this in two ways – first, the initial growth and the three phases of leadership and, second, the fluctuations in membership and activity imposed by the seasons of the year.

The pattern of the evening varied according to the season and the weather. There were, however, certain regularities throughout the year. At four o'clock the children would drop in to see the leader on their way from school. He would arrive about three o'clock to prepare the tools and the equipment. Some children merely came to say Hello, while others stayed to talk and play. Meeting with the leader after school was an invaluable point of contact for the children. This was, as it were, the peak period. Between four-thirty and five there was a steady drift homewards and the claims of tea and television attracted the majority away.

At six o'clock the return to the Playground began, until a call from parents drew some of the younger children home to bed. The Playground closed usually soon after eight in summer (in the winter between seven-thirty and eight) but for many children the games continued in the street until a much later hour. Saturday mornings were set aside for special activities, such as a visit to the swimming baths.

During the life of the Project there were three phases of leadership, though our primary concern here is with the first only. The life of the Playground started with the arrival of 'Donald', the first leader, on 16 May 1955. This first phase ended with his resignation two years later, in May 1957. Two years of such strenuous activity in all kinds of weather, he considered, were enough. The second leader, a retired school caretaker, worked at the Playground from June to November of 1957, when for reasons of health and other difficulties he resigned. The Playground then remained closed until May 1958 when it was re-opened on two nights a week through the good offices of the headmaster of a neighbouring junior school, also the treasurer of the Playground committee, and some parents from the school's Parent–Teacher Association, together with three members of the committee. During August and September 1958 the voluntary arrangement with the parents gave place to a new arrangement by which a rota of some fifteen teachers working in pairs and paid on a sessional basis enabled the Playground to be opened on four nights a week. As of the winter of 1958–59, the Playground was closed until the spring, with plans for re-opening on a sessional basis with school teachers.

Three main periods, therefore, are to be distinguished: (a) the full-time trained leader; (b) the part-time untrained leader; and (c) the collaboration of voluntary and part-time leaders. But the daily log-book of events concerns only the first two years during the appointment of the first leader. From this, eight distinct phases can be seen closely related to the two seasons of winter and summer. During the first two years of Donald's leadership we can discern the following phases:

226

Phase 1

This covered the first six weeks, during which worker and children got to know one another. The site was unfenced, still strewn with the relics of builders' rubble; there was no hut, and few tools at the start beyond three old pick-axes, two old shovels, a fork, a hammer, and an unserviceable wheelbarrow. Gradually entrenching tools were added, two small wheelbarrows, and some more tools. But the leader was the central attraction and great demands were made upon him. Of his introduction to the Playground, the leader writes:

The rain stopped again. I took off my coat, took hold of a pick and hacked away at a mound of earth near the pavement. I placed the sledge invitingly standing on its head on a small chunk of concrete. The Infants came out from school – stopped to watch me work – asked a few questions – and one of them tried his strength with the hammer – and succeeded in lifting it above his knees. Then the Juniors came along.

'What are you doing mister?' 'Digging for treasure,' I said, but they didn't believe me. 'Do you want to dig?' Did they! There was a rush for the barrow and it was empty. There must have been over thirty boys and girls around at that time (4.15). They wanted to know what I was doing. I said, 'We're going to make a playground – and anyone who wants to help can do so.' 'I'll help mister, I'll help mister, and me, and me.' So there we were. Some boys from Richmond School were there. Where would I get the men to help me – because I couldn't do it all on my own? I mentioned the bulldozer. 'Who's going to pay?' I said the committee would ask rich people for the money. Would there be tarmac instead of grass? No! A few had read in the local papers about a playground which would have motor-cars on it – was this the one? I said I didn't know about motor-cars. Was told about the steam roller. Meanwhile the sledge and hammer were pounding at the concrete – or flattening out tins. Bob, who lives opposite in Laurel Road, brought his own barrow and pick – both man-size – but had to take them in when his mother (or sister) came out to ask me whether I'd *sent* him to borrow them. The wheelbarrow, despite its tendency to tip over leaving the broken shaft in one's hand, went the rounds, picking up old iron and tins (to clean up the site), any burnable material (to make a bonfire on the first occasion that will be dry enough), or taking passengers for rides. The picks and shovels, after being used to level the first mound as a preparation to the erection of the fence, were used in attacking anywhere they fancied. All the time questions were being asked. Would we have swings? a slider? would we level it all? They warned me about 'the gang'. 'They've got Teddy boys too who would pinch anything. They'll get wire cutters to take the fence away to make pigeon cotes.' Where did I come from? Where do I live now? Do the police know that I'm digging here? Why don't I get a tent to stay there? 'I'll bet there'll be a watchman to chase us off!' One of them offered to build me a house. All but a dozen or so had gone by 5.15 – but many had said that they'd be there tomorrow morning. It rained again but none of those present left so we carried on talking and bashing concrete – until six o'clock when I thought it best to call a halt – because I want to give it to them in small doses. Half-a-dozen accompanied me with the wheelbarrow up the street to the school.

Phase 2

In July an international student work-camp arrived to build a hut for the Playground:

> This was a happy phase for the children. The weather was glorious, there was an interesting operation going on, and above all there were some friendly people who were interested in them. At the end of July the fence was started and after a little trouble was completed on 18 August.

The work-camp was successful in laying the foundations and in erecting the walls of the hut. The remainder of the work was completed by contract labour.

Phase 3

The disappearance of the work-camp and the completion of the fence around the Playground coincided with the children's holidays. During the holidays the numbers decreased.[1]

> Children tended to go farther afield on day outings or picnics, or in the really hot weather could not make the effort to get to the Playground, but were content to make use of their gardens or nearer plots of open ground.

But when the school term started again, the children returned in even greater numbers, on some occasions over eighty. This was a busy and active period, made easier by a welcome supply of junk.

Phase 4

The winter months quickly followed and with shorter days the large numbers dwindled:

> Time for digging and dam-building, etc., became less and less as the tools had to be brought in earlier and earlier. The weather became colder and wetter. Children called on the way home from school – unless it was too muddy – but no longer said they'd be back after tea except for the regulars – those children whom I could have predicted by September as being most in need of the Playground and the leader – and they came through thick and thin.
>
> Rain was our chief enemy. The cold we could keep at bay by playing a vigorous game or by means of a camp fire, but rain besides wetting us reduced the ground to a hopeless sea of mud which clearly showed the need for an island of surfaced ground. But, even on a dark winter's night, if the weather was fine, as many as thirty to forty children would come along to play chasing games and roast potatoes round a camp fire.

During this first winter the hut was kept as a second string – for those times when play outside was impossible. Inside there was

[1] By contrast with Upfield, the attendance of children at the Grimsby adventure playground tended to double in number during the holidays.

clay modelling and some primitive carpentry. The younger children fell off in number during the cold.

Phase 5

With the return of spring – and of longer days and warmer weather – the old faces reappeared, together with some entirely new faces. Numbers increased again, and by the end of March had risen to about sixty on a busy evening. The building of dens and dandy-tracks on the banks of the stream started once more. A new wire-fenced compound outside the hut provided some security for timber which had been given – but without 'the six bulldogs to guard it' that rumour had anticipated. Den-building was a slow and laborious process, for the dens once built were immediately the object of attack and destruction from rivals, above all from the Jones gang, of whom we write in some detail later on.

Whitsun holidays took the children farther afield into the woods, fishing for tadpoles and tiddlers. Summer saw the revival of den-building and the weekly visit to the swimming baths on Saturday morning. The girls' attempt to set up house in the dens was frustrated by the continual raids of 'cowboys' and 'Indians', but for the first time the dens withstood attack.

Phase 6

By the end of its second summer the Playground had developed a 'culture' of its own of which many features recurred from one year to the next. During September repair work began in earnest on the dens:

> We rebuilt those which had been partially destroyed and set about making them 'snug' for the winter. We put down a brick floor in one and built a brick fire-grate – using clay as a cement. It was a great success but even so has been pulled down half-a-dozen times. The usual dam-building at the stream – always washed away when the stream is in flood.

Gradually, through the second summer, the leader became ever more conscious of the distinction between the destructive and de-

230

manding few – that faithful minority of 'regulars' who had persisted throughout the winter cold and who during the succeeding summer had come to have a claim on his attention – and the majority of ordinary children who needed little more than the tools, the materials, and an encouraging word to set them at play. In his September 1956 report the leader wrote:

> Running through my work on the Playground is the theme of trying to help the more 'needy' children – who often prove to be the more aggressive and destructive. This means that obvious visual signs of constructive activity are not much in evidence. One can, perhaps, gauge the success of the Playground by the number of attempts at constructive activity and also by the length of time these constructions remain intact – but these signs would not be apparent to the casual visitor – neither would 'improved' behaviour of individuals be apparent. It would, I suppose, be possible to achieve fairly quick material evidence of the 'improving nature' of the Playground by excluding the aggressive and destructive child or by exercising a rigid control (if these things are possible in this particular situation) but this in my opinion would be avoiding the real issue. The Playground obviously cannot be a therapeutic centre for difficult and aggressive children (though there might well be such places set up) so we must compromise and try to cope with all types together in whatever mood they may be.

Phase 7

During the second winter, however, the leader began to change his role on the Playground. He recognized that the permissive policy which he had adopted did not meet with the committee's general approval, and he was anxious to leave the Playground, at the end of his second year, in a form in which constructive activities could continue. The hut he still reserved, as in the previous winter, for specific activities.

In spite of the leader's and the committee's policy that the hut should be used as an additional feature of the Playground and not

231

as the centre of group activities along the lines of a more formal youth group, this proved difficult to maintain, because of the design of the building. The equipment of the hut was sparse and the furniture limited. Nevertheless, there was an increase in the activities carried on in the hut, such as painting and crayoning, rough woodwork, and impromptu concerts. Just before Christmas there was a special show at which a mother of a family of 'regulars' came along to make up her children, five of whom took part. Screens were made of wood and covered with old lorry tarpaulins and coloured by the children with powder poster paints.

These inside activities did not take place in an ordered 'quiet' all the time. The outdoor games of 'touch' and 'cowboys' intruded when the chased ran in pursued by the chasers and, once inside, found it more fun to stay inside and play. The leader changed the chasing games into singing games and this at least kept them in one spot. The dens with fires and candles burning provided the kind of meeting place where the children liked to sit and talk, sing, or listen to stories.

As in the previous winter, the age of the boys was higher than in summer time – several working boys of about sixteen were regular users, and these the leader attempted to direct to neighbouring youth clubs.

Phase 8

As the days grew longer, again the smaller children returned and a sunny half-term holiday in March brought a renewal of den- and dam-building. Many of the older boys, however, who had been coming regularly during the winter months, went off farther afield on their cycles, rather scornful of playing near the younger children.

But perhaps most significant as a sign of progress was the security of the new dens from attack. One, for example, the leader reported as having remained partially built for two days without destruction: 'A year ago it would have been knocked down if it had not been quickly completed.' Small changes such as these are hard to recognize from casual observations.

For the smaller children the hut offered light and protection for extending their play beyond the hours of daylight, but in general the better weather brought a revival of activity in the open, with the stream once again – while the water lasted – as the centre of attraction. Some of the children, too, made a successful start on a bed of flowers around the base of the hut. The older girls still wanted to enter the hut so long as the attraction of the older boys lasted. They liked a place in which to chat and talk and the hut fulfilled to some extent the function of the shopping centre.

In May Donald resigned to take teacher's training. His departure was celebrated in the hut on 26 April by a farewell tea-party and concert organized spontaneously by one of the 'regular' mothers on a stage erected by her husband. Three busy weeks of rehearsals preceded the great event. Donald was succeeded shortly afterwards by a second leader.

CHAPTER 12

Children, Neighbourhood, and Committee

THE most complex and controversial issues arose, not from the discussion of property, playground, hut, and equipment, but from the human aspects of the Playground. It is here, perhaps, that the social scientist should be able to make his main contribution. Although he has no special expertise on the design of playgrounds, he is trained to look closely at the way in which an institution actually fulfils the purposes which it sets out to achieve. The social scientist looks beyond the manifest and expressed aims to the latent purposes which lie beneath.

It often happens that a service set up for one purpose in fact appears to have other more pressing functions to fulfil. Professor Simey, for example, quotes (Simey, 1952) the interesting case of the Maternity and Child Welfare Service which was originally set up to raise the level of physical care of young children. In the course of time this purpose is achieved and a declining rate of infant mortality is evidence of its success. But it is also possible to see the Service as a method of dealing with the emotional strains and stresses often found in families with young children which are a frequent cause of unhappiness and perhaps even of ill health. The clinic might be utilized as an educational service of benefit to the family as a whole, and thus become an even more important source of well-being to the community than it is today.

This example of the Maternity and Child Welfare Service is not in fact as irrelevant to the issues involved in the Playground as it may at first sight seem. For the observations on the Upfield Playground which follow do in fact raise the same kind of question. How best can an adventure playground meet the particular needs of its users? Do the stated and manifest aims of 'providing opportunities for creative and imaginative play and for the development of a spirit of adventure' in fact achieve this end? Are there not equally important latent purposes in addition to those which are generally stated and for which the Upfield Playground was instituted? What light does Upfield experience, of committee, of leader, and of children, throw on these questions?

In the short account of the seasonal cycle of events we have already hinted at some of the problems involved in answering these questions – at the apparent conflict of needs between the nonconforming few and the conforming many, and at the difference in emphasis placed on these needs by the Playground committee and by the leader supported by the Project team.

The first question to consider is: do Upfield children need a Playground in view of the open spaces which already exist? Although Upfield had certainly been starved of social amenities, it was in fact well supplied with open spaces for play, as we have seen. The leader, who had previously been working on the Clydesdale Road Adventure Playground in North Kensington, wrote at the end of his first year:

When I first saw Upfield and was shown the location of the Playground, I had my doubts about the need for an adventure playground in the area. Upfield seemed to me, especially after the congested areas of London, to be amply supplied with open spaces, so that the need for space as such did not apply. But we all have our ideas about what an adventure playground is, or what it should be, and one of the chief needs I felt that it should meet was the need that children have for a play space in which, to put it simply, 'anything goes'. I should qualify that by saying 'anything within reason goes'. What I mean is a place in which they will not feel constricted or restricted by notices which say 'keep off the grass' and where they will not be subjected to adults constantly yelling 'don't do this or that'. My year at Upfield has shown me the need here for this type of ground.

I believe that it needs more than a caretaker. It needs workers with special understanding of children and aptitude for work with them, and enough of them to be really helpful to the children.

Why do I think these workers are needed? Because from the hurly-burly of the Playground are thrown up problems which are a challenge, and cases that cry for help. I believe that it is in trying to solve these problems that it becomes more than just a playground.

Not every child needs an adventure playground and not every child needs a youth club. Every child might derive some pleasure, even benefit, from attending an adventure playground or a youth club, but there are some unfortunates who *need* these places, and these are the children who need extra help and care, though not to the exclusion of others. This is one of the problems that workers face. Aggressive children must not be kept away; yet these aggressive children must not be allowed to drive others away. Not all aggressive children are problems, nor are all problem children aggressive. There are those shrinking, defenceless children – isolates – who come looking for friendship, who are far from being aggressive. But one must be prepared for aggressive action on a playground, and try to meet it with patience, and try to seek the causes. Robust activity is the rule rather than the exception.

The Playground for most children is a place where they come to 'let off steam'. They find themselves in an atmosphere created by themselves, and moving in a society structured by themselves, and they behave accordingly. They form their own groups, selecting and rejecting. They decide their own policy. They are social and co-operative, or antisocial and hostile, with much interplay and what may seem to be confusing changes of attitude.

Many children come looking for the affection and sympa-

236

thetic understanding of an adult. Most of these would rather play with the worker than use any of the tools or materials provided for them, and any adult visitor who stays for a while is eagerly seized upon. That is why an understanding and sympathetic adult is invaluable in the Playground situation, if we are in any way to meet the real challenge.

Our evidence suggests that in spite of the attractions of neighbouring playing fields, the woods, the 'Little Field', and the forbidden lake, Upfield children both use and need the Playground. But this is an easy suggestion. More difficult, however, are the questions: Should there be an agreed order of priority as to needs? Can the Playground really contain the nonconforming few and the conformist many, the very destructive and attention-seeking minority with the happy and stable majority?

This dilemma of needs gradually emerged as the central theme of the Playground's history, yet it was never resolved. The excitement and novelty of the Playground in the first three months masked the diversity of standards among the children, but by the end of the summer the conflict was already apparent. During the winter it was the minority of destructive and withdrawn 'regulars' who stuck to the Playground through wet and cold. They did so because of their feelings for the leader. He fulfilled for them their need for a friendly and accepting father. But when spring came and the majority returned, the dilemma as to priority of needs again became acute.

The leader's aim – as he suggests in his first annual report to the committee – was to try to meet the needs of *both*. The committee, however, felt that he was giving priority to the 'difficult', encouraged in this policy by the Project team which had a special concern for the 'stresses and strains' of Upfield. Some committee members were critical of his failure to develop the constructive and creative activities of the Playground. They saw the Playground as providing an extension of the opportunities for development of initiative and imagination provided by the schools, and tended to judge the Playground behaviour by the standards of the schools. Considered in this way, the leader's achievement fell short of their expectations.

It was in October 1956, six months before the termination of the Project's grant and the leader's resignation, when future plans were under discussion, that the conflict of opinion over this problem emerged most clearly. To quote from the minutes of the committee meeting of that month:

> There was some difference of opinion as to the function of the Playground.
>
>   Some members felt that provision should be made for all types of children, that there should be more constructive work and more discipline, that the predominance of more difficult types had driven away other children.
>
>   On the other hand it was urged that one of the functions of an Adventure Playground was to help difficult children, that types dealt with on this Playground included a wide age-range with no limits to membership. The dens did show some positive constructive work, and there was some appreciation from people of the district of what was being done.

These short paragraphs in fact conceal a frank and lively discussion in which the diversity of committee opinion was clearly revealed. Although the item on the agenda was 'Conditions for Leader and salary after May 1957', the discussion which in fact took place was predominantly concerned with past and present, and the atmosphere was heavy with dissatisfaction at the leader's methods, his inability to use tools, and the lack of constructive achievement.

Looking back on these events nearly two years later we may fairly raise the question: Was the committee right in the policy presented to the leader? Was not a scale of priorities essential? Was it ever really possible for one man with limited equipment to provide for the needs of *all* types of children? The dilemma remained unresolved although the minutes had concluded: 'It was generally agreed that more help and equipment are needed.'

Perhaps the main lesson to be learned from the first two years

238

of the Upfield Playground is the need to set limits to the aims of the Playground in the light of the resources available and of the culture of the neighbourhood. Of the resources available, both human and material, we have already written. For the remainder of this chapter we are chiefly concerned with the children, their families, and the neighbourhood.

THE CHILDREN

Although it is unwise to generalize from particular experiences, certain simple facts emerge from the records of attendance about the use of the Playground which seem uncontroversial and important. To keep a strictly accurate register of the users of the Playground was an impossible task for a single worker, but the records do provide at least a rough guide.

The Catchment Area

The catchment area of the Playground was highly localized. At Upfield over three-quarters of the children lived within a quarter of a mile of the Playground; about one-third lived between 220 and 330 yards from the Playground. The population of the catchment area was approximately 3,000. A very small number of children came from farther afield. But these children had special needs which were in part met by the friendliness of the leader, and none of them could be called 'regular' attenders.

Sex, Frequency of Attendance, and Age

The Upfield Playground made a greater appeal to boys than to girls. Of 202 children whose names were recorded by a teacher visiting the Playground during the three-month period September–November 1955, some 70 per cent were boys and 30 per cent girls. Among the children who attended most frequently the proportions were about the same, but among the less frequent attenders the proportion of girls was higher though still less than half the total number of children. We can do no more than speculate as to what might have been the proportions had there been a female

239

rather than a male leader, or at least a substantial group of female helpers. One helper who came regularly for a period observed that, even allowing for domestic work at home, the girls were never present in large numbers. They disliked the den-building but enjoyed practising home-making in the completed dens, if the boys allowed them. Many spent a good deal of time around the leader, taking part in the jumping and other games.

It was to the eight-year-olds that the Playground made its biggest appeal. There were, of course, seasonal fluctuations. During the dark and cold winter evenings the peak age of the children increased to about fourteen. But the older boys never considered the Playground as their own. They thought of it as a 'kids' playground' and tried to perform as supermen while the others watched and admired. Of the very young children who came, the majority were in the charge of elder brothers or sisters.

Groups

The majority of children played together in groups of four and five. On one occasion there was a group of eleven. The girls played mainly in pairs. Most of the groups were of boys or girls only. They changed frequently in their membership with the exception of the Jones gang (described below) who remained constant in their loyalty to one another and who swept through the Playground like an avalanche leaving destruction and tears behind them.

The Sixteen 'Regulars'

One of the outstanding aspects of the leader's diary is the persistence of names of a small group of 'regulars', through summer and winter, fair weather and foul, holiday and term-time. What was it, the leader and the Project team continually asked themselves, that brought this small but ever faithful group of children to the Playground in spite of all the obstacles of season and weather? What did the Playground mean to them? Certainly there was no compulsion of any kind to attend from school or parents, committee or leader.

The short answer to this question is in the character and the understanding of the leader himself. He turned no one away, made no reports to the police, and offered no discouragement to children who made a nuisance of themselves, beyond warning and disapproval. The assumption which the Project made – though it is unfair to claim that the Playground committee necessarily agreed – was that the culture of the Playground would reflect the culture of the immediate neighbourhood at Upfield. Our analysis of the catchment area of the Playground shows how localized are the leisure activities of children. Inevitably, therefore, an adventure playground reflects the culture of the immediate locality.

In general the Upfield Adventure Playground proved to be no exception, but there is one important qualification. The culture – as we argue continually in this report – was not a homogeneous one. Rough as well as respectable families lived in the locality surrounding the Playground, sometimes but by no means always segregated according to streets. *Both* kinds of families had a legitimate claim on the services of the Playground. But did both make equal use of it? Ideals and practice are frequently in conflict and our evidence suggests that however much the ideal of the committee was that the Playground should not become overweighted with children from one type of family, in practice it tended to attract those children coming from the rougher homes where the standards of care and aspirations of parents were weak. Of the reasons for this we say more elsewhere.

To provide some evidence on the social and family backgrounds of the 'regulars' – it was clearly impossible to collect evidence on *all* the users – a small study was carried out in the summer of 1956 of sixteen of the most regular attenders. The three questions which we asked were: (i) What is their family and social background? (ii) What are the attitudes of their parents to the Playground? (iii) What are the effects of attendance at the Playground on them?

To provide some answers to these questions the worker drew on as many sources of evidence as he could. He talked with all these children on the Playground, he visited all their homes, meeting mothers in most cases but both parents as well as brothers and sisters on certain occasions, and he talked with teachers and social workers who knew the children and their families.

Once again we must point out that these children chose of their own accord to attend the Playground. They were not directed there. It is of interest, therefore, to see that three-quarters of the families in this group were known to at least one social worker and half of the families to more than one. More specifically, eleven were known to the School Welfare Officer, one to the Family Service Unit, and six to the caseworker of the Bristol Council of Social Service. One boy was on probation for his second offence (his two best friends in the group were subsequently committed to an Approved School in November 1958 with two others for a series of burglaries).

A statistical analysis of the families in so small a sample is clearly of little value. Our remarks are therefore predominantly descriptive in character. Over three-quarters of the children in the sample came from large families. All of these families lived in streets adjacent or very close to the Playground. Fourteen of the sample were boys and only two were girls. Very regular attendance at the Playground certainly appears to be a male prerogative, though we can only guess as to how far this was due to the personality and sex of the leader.

Of the children's intelligence it is hard to be certain in the absence of test results. But judging by the comments of teachers and social workers these regular users were – with the exception of two ESN boys – of average intelligence for the junior and secondary modern schools which they attended.

Eight of the children had brothers or sisters who also visited the Playground, though some were less regular in their attendance. Their fathers were mainly dockers and labourers. Only one was in skilled employment. Four came from broken homes, in one case temporarily during a prison sentence. The worker attempted a general assessment of the relationships between the children and their parents on the basis of what he heard and saw from his visits and observations. His comment was that 'although relationships with the mother appear generally to be good among over half the children, those with the father were poor or father was absent from the family'. This reflection certainly adds weight to our general assumption that it was a substitute father that the children sought most of all—albeit unconsciously – from the Playground.

An accurate assessment of family relationships on the available evidence is hard to make. The general indication from head-teachers and social workers is of a group of families characterized by financial difficulties though also by a variety of social standards and with limited aspirations for their children's future education and work.

The dominant impression gained of the attitude of these parents to the Playground is the passivity of their response. Only two mothers were critical; the remainder thought it a useful place which kept their children off the streets and away from the dangers of the woods and lake. They knew where to find them and had confidence in 'Donald's' care. Many spoke affectionately about him:

> 'Oh well, you know where they are, don't you? I think it's good like that but they come back so filthy, all covered in grease and oil; that's the only thing I got against it.'
> 'It keeps them out of trouble now Donald is there.'
> 'Well there's one thing about that place – you do know that they're not wandering about and you know where you can find them.'

Replies such as these were typical of all the parents. None of them had thought about the Playground beyond the question of safety. They had few positive suggestions to make about its function or how to improve it. Though none of this is in itself surprising in the light of their background and intelligence, it is important in contrast to the general aims and objects of the adventure playground movement.

One mother, Mrs. H, a large woman with a weather-beaten complexion, was critical of the Playground. She did not *allow* her children to go there though she could not prevent the two elder boys, who were frequent attenders. She explained to the worker how strict her husband, a building labourer, was with the children. One of the boys was given a cycle which he was told he could ride only in the garden. But he kept taking it out into the street, so they sold the cycle. Her husband, on the other hand, looked forward to the boys' going to work as soon as possible: 'We need the money, they must leave at fifteen.' Only grudgingly did they allow the second boy to enter the technical class of the Secondary Modern School, as it usually meant another year, and an apprenticeship was ruled out because they paid so little.

Proximity to the Playground was no doubt the main cause of Mrs. M's hostility. It was the children on it whom she complained of:

> 'They get in on Sundays and make a lot of noise. I have complained several times to the police. It is untidy and dirty. Donald isn't strict enough with them. They need somebody who can control them. I'm surprised they picked on a man like that. Mind you I like Donald – he's very nice and he must love kids. But he ought to be stricter with them. I had expected to see cricket pitches and tennis courts for them to play on.'

Mrs. M also admitted that it kept them off the streets. At a much later stage in the Playground's history after Donald had been succeeded by a new leader (the retired school caretaker) Mrs. M was able to see the contrast in methods of control.

The worker's visit to the F's, a family living no more than three hundred yards from the Playground, throws light on an important problem of the housing estate – that of communication. The Playground as a new and unfamiliar institution did not easily become a topic of local discussion. The 'grape-vine' is very selective in the topics which it transmits. Mr. F, for example, in spite of the fact that his boy was a regular user, was virtually unaware of the Playground's existence and certainly ignorant of what it was intended to do:

> A small middle-aged man still wearing his working overalls invited me in even before I told him why I was there. The

eldest girl was present and Mrs. F soon came in. Father had told Fred to come in. This gathering of the clan was soon explained as I was invited to sit down, when Mr. F said, 'Well, what's the trouble?' I assured him there was no trouble and explained why I had called. But he knew nothing about the Playground and his well-concealed belligerence was not yet dissipated so he answered by telling me how dangerous the woods are: 'If I could only get to a meeting of some sort I'd soon tell 'em.' I was unable to get any opinion of the Playground – I doubt whether he knew it exists.

Asked about help on the Playground, Mr. F, a carter, said that he was quite willing to do anything he could to help – if there were jobs to be done rather than with actual Playground work. So I asked him if he would care to meet Donald. This more specific approach rather put him off at first but as I was leaving he decided to come down to the Playground with me.

He became much friendlier once we were out of the house. I asked him how the children got on at school: 'Oh, all right except that one of them quite often does not want to go.' He said it rather quickly and it seemed better not to pursue it.

When we got to the Playground he made no comment about it but had a slightly stunned expression – as though he could not believe his eyes. Donald came over and Mr. F promptly told the children to go away as they wanted to talk business. He seemed to like Donald and he left looking much more amenable than when I first saw him.

Several points of interest emerge from this encounter with Mr. F – his willingness to undertake simple but clearly defined tasks, the absence of communication on certain subjects of local significance, and the assumption that the stranger has come with a complaint about the children's behaviour. This interview throws light on the kind of educative work that is required before parents' understanding of the Playground's objects can be secured.

Yet none of the families of the 'regulars' could be said to be typical, and it is the diversity of opinions, particularly on how children should be brought up, that is so characteristic a feature of this group. Mrs. O, for example, whose garden and home are 'rough', is the mother of a very large family. She always sends them to the Playground to have them out of the way. Round the corner is Mrs. L, who apologized to the worker because the house was 'upside down' when in fact it was spotless. She strongly criticized the Playground and had complained several times to the police. While Mrs. O believed in children 'sticking up for themselves', Mrs. L thought that they should be subject to strict discipline. A mother with nine or more was undismayed by the size of her family. The mother of three (of whom two are twins) was certain that 'That's enough; I don't want any more'. One housewife was willing to talk to the worker only when 'dressed up' complete with make-up. Another did not mind being interviewed in her bare feet. A third permitted an interview while washing her hair.

The culture of the neighbourhood allows children freedom to roam about the streets until late at night. Yet one father insisted that his twenty-two-year-old son be home regularly by 11 p.m. Another (Mr. H) was even stricter with his fourteen-, twelve-, and six-year-old boys. The families of the 'regulars' contain numerous examples of such diversity of behaviour.

Understandably enough, the third question as to the effects of the Playground on the 'regulars' proved difficult to answer. It is seldom easy in human behaviour to ascribe particular changes to particular causes, and the Playground was no exception. None of the parents seen by the worker actually *expressed* the opinion that it had effected any positive change in their children, and some stated that it had not. All of their opinions, however, were diffidently made and it was clearly a subject to which they had given little or no thought. Neither the teachers nor the social workers who were interviewed thought that the Playground had influenced behaviour. The teachers contrasted the Playground's influence with that of the school, which they considered to be positive in its effects.

The leader himself was modest in his statement as to how far his own relationships on the Playground had a positive effect on the 'regulars'. But over one particular boy – Peter, a withdrawn and demanding child – he was emphatic in his view that there were real signs of greater independence and security. For the Director, at least, who spoke with Peter quite regularly for two years, there can be no doubt about the change in his behaviour.

Peter was certainly the most isolated of the sixteen 'regulars' and in many respects typical of the other isolated children who used the Playground though at less regular intervals. For two years he was seldom absent. 'He took more out of me,' the leader said, 'than any other individual on the Playground.' Throughout the intense cold of the winter months he was always there, never far away from the leader.

His home had little to offer in the way of material comfort or of the closer ties of affection. His mother was nervous and anxious. He was known by the other children as 'Slimy', his running nose and mouth and unattractive appearance made him the inevitable 'whipping-boy', a target for teasing and ridicule. And clowning, whether in school or on the Playground, was his way of seeking attention. The first record of him in the diary was: 'His asthma seemed bad to-night.' On this occasion he had been sent home early from school because one of the teachers couldn't stand him any longer.

He was fortunate in the friendship of his regular school teacher and of the Playground leader, and he developed from a boy continually seeking recognition into a person who could join successfully in the group activities of other children and even turn down an invitation. This growth in security was reflected also in his manner and appearance.

The leader at one point tried to 'push him off' too early, after comments from the committee that he was spending too much time with the minority. The effect was a period of hatred from Peter, who in due course returned. But at a later stage he was able to move on to a local youth club where he became a regular member. Thus the Playground was able to fulfil the very important function of a half-way house through which children

247

moved in their own time to other organizations which would make greater demands on their ability to conform.

Peter's story shows perhaps more clearly than that of any other single child on the Playground the patience and understanding that are required in such a setting.

The Gangs

More difficult, perhaps, than the isolated and demanding children who made great claims on the time and attention of the leader was the problem of the destructive and marauding gangs who swept down on the Playground leaving a trail of destruction behind them.

The Jones gang was outstanding for the trouble which its members (a core of six, but sometimes numbering eleven) created. Three of them are included in the sixteen 'regulars' whom we have discussed. Their reputation in the neighbourhood certainly preceded the creation of the Playground:

> Three of the older boys took a hand at digging the pond. Their attitude was one of scorn that I should be daft enough to think that we could do anything here. 'Look at him,' said one, pointing to Barry Jones.[1] 'Give him a hammer and he and his gang will knock a council house down in no time.' 'They'll pinch all your tools.' 'This pond'll be full of stones and rubbish before the morning.' All this in the hearing of Barry Jones. 'I'll have to attend a meeting tomorrow afternoon,' I said to Barry, 'so I'll give you two picks and two shovels to take home with you to-night and you bring them along tomorrow and carry on with the job until I arrive.' This in the hearing of the others. 'You'd better take his name and address,' they said, 'or that's the last you'll see of 'em.' At about 7.15 they began to tire of the constructive effort and were beginning to fill up the pond with stones – so we packed up the tools and moved up to the top of the site – Barry took his tools off home and returned to join in our game of Cat and Dog. Left site at 8 p.m. As usual that's the

[1] Barry was the leader of the gang.

signal for the four or five who stay behind to climb onto the roof of the hut and shout after me until I'm out of sight. Barry returned punctually at 4.10 with his tools the following day.

The leader was determined not to take them at the neighbourhood's estimation of their reputation and his trust was thus immediately rewarded. But the second recorded episode gave an indication of future troubles:

Two boys were crossing the site with a sheet of zinc each and were spotted by the Jones gang, who immediately went after the spoil and took it without much resistance. But young Jones (Mervyn) threw a stone which hit the head of one of the others and he spouted blood. He was standing in the middle of the road when he was hit (he is not a regular attender on the site). Mrs. M came out and took him in to render first aid and cleaned him up – after which he went home. Young Jones was scared – in tears and worried lest his father would tan him. His older brother came for him and took him home – but he came back later and announced with a grin that he didn't get a beating.

Events of this kind in the early months of the Playground were common and this was but one of many episodes in which the gang left behind them on the Playground children in tears and dens in ruins. Their own den, however, always remained intact, even when they were all absent.

The main body of the gang was recruited from two families, living near one another in a street adjoining the Playground, both with the name of Jones but in fact unrelated. On the fringe of the gang were four boys ranging in age from 13 to 10 years. They too lived within hailing distance, next door or across the street.

They conformed to the classic pattern of the gang as described in particular by American observers – a leader, his lieutenants, and the followers, a group in revolt against the established code of society – similar in many ways to the Espressos but more cohesive in their loyalty to one another. Perhaps most significant of all, and most ominous for the future, was their young age – 13 to 6 years.

The oldest, Jack, stood aloof from the gang's activities, to be used only, like the hydrogen bomb, as a deterrent to all who threatened them: 'Our Jack will beat you up.' Thus they were clearly within the Playground age.

Leaving aside Jack, whom the gang reserved for special occasions and who belonged to the first Jones family, the nucleus of the gang consisted of three boys – Archie, Barry, and Robin – from the first Jones family, and three – Ken, David, and Mervyn – from the second. The four members on the fringe – Harry S, Paul T, Charlie B, and Tommy D – outside the Jones families were attracted to the gang as a whole though there were also certain individual friendships. Charlie and Tommy were warned by their parents against associating with the gang, though with only temporary success.

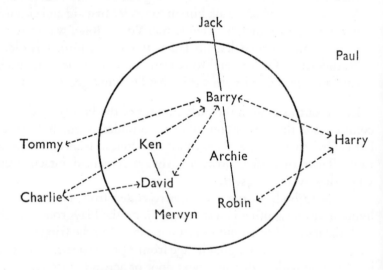

Circle contains hard core of gang

——————— indicates brothers

←----------→ indicates particular friendships

The diagram points clearly to the significance of Barry Jones as leader. It was upon Barry that the gang depended for leadership and initiative. He was small, sturdily built, and 'as hard as nails'. Cheerful, aggressive, and fairly open, he was always prepared to take physical risks and quickly mastered new activities. He would fight and beat opponents far bigger than himself.

Barry's family consisted of two older brothers, and a sister and one younger brother, both users of the Playground. His parents, then in their forties, both worked for the same company, his mother working from 7 a.m. to 3.30 p.m. Both Barry and an elder brother had previously been on probation. Their home did not give the impression of an unhappy one, nor were there signs of material neglect. Neither parent, however, had the time or inclination to devote attention to the children. Their father appeared as a passive individual from whom it was difficult to evoke any positive response. He remained a remote figure in the children's lives, appearing only on occasions as an ultimate sanction in the event of certain kinds of behaviour. Their mother had felt the constant need to work full-time since the war. She seemed harassed by her financial affairs.

The activities of the gang were sometimes initiated by Tommy D, in the early days a 'fringe' member but nevertheless an important figure. Tommy was a highly emotional child, always acting as the victorious conqueror. It was evident from the constant warnings given to the leader about him that he, too, had a considerable reputation among the children of the neighbourhood.

The log-book is full of entries of the gang's exploits both inside and outside the Playground. They would commandeer all the tools, hide them in the bushes, and then disappear, leaving the leader and the other children to search for them. The serious work – on the rare occasions that they joined it – they soon turned into a game at the expense of the others, shovelling dirt, splashing water, or throwing mud all over them. On one occasion they appeared on the Playground with white sticky-paper bands around their legs calling themselves the 'White-Band gang'. On another they were rifling a locked hand-cart left by the Gas Board near the Playground when a policeman rode up on his bicycle. All fled except Barry, who stood his ground. He knew from past experience that 'all I'd get would be a talking to'. Their independence as a group was illustrated by the way in which they built a den on the Meadow – an open space almost adjoining the Playground – using materials they had purloined from the Playground, and used that site as their own adventure playground for a number of days. Of their exploits off the Playground, they spoke of 'nobbing' expeditions to the orchard, of visits to the golf course to seek balls to sell back to the golfers, of shop-lifting in the city, of setting fire to bonfire piles in neighbours' gardens, and of climbing the roof of a local chapel hall and their subsequent ejection for creating a disturbance.

The leader wrote:

> I have seen them hanging on to the backs of lorries, throwing stones at street lamps (near the Playground). I saw them teasing some girls who had a guy outside a public house. I have seen Barry dodging his bus fares when we have travelled together on a bus – and I saw him put all his spare coppers into a collection box to save an old horse from the butcher.

Much of this suggests perhaps that the leader was no more than a passive observer of their behaviour. Nothing could be further from the truth. By friendship and understanding he gradually removed their innate suspicion of adults in authority in spite of the fact that he had continually to fulfil the role of defender of the weak and had on one occasion smacked Charlie B's bottom, an event which precipitated a visit from an angry mother.

During the winter months of 1955–56 the members of the gang gradually became less of a problem though the prestige of gang membership still gave rise to fear or respect. The leader came to know them as individuals, and the smaller numbers and higher age-group in the winter evenings reduced the potential nuisance value of the gang, though there was still the odd occasion when they would chase another group from the Playground (they themselves never fled but always fought on the retreat, thus providing the leader with a chance to intervene). There was more time in which to know them, particularly two of the fringe members –

Paul T and Harry S – who during the summer had stood rather aloof from the leader.

Then at the beginning of May the Jones family (II) moved to the 'better side of the estate'. The fighting potential of the gang was reduced and the core became the Jones family (I) with the addition of Fred G. Big brother Jack was now invoked rather more frequently but as a cry for help rather than as an added weapon. Although the boys from the two families met at school, their interest in one another seemed to diminish, and during leisure hours the partnership was broken. After their move the Jones family (II) paid occasional visits to the Playground, but never joined in the activities of the gang. Moreover, two of the fringe members, Paul T and Harry S, spent more time away from the gang.

During the second winter the leader reported continued progress, a lessening of the gang's destructiveness and a greater willingness to take part in joint activities and small building projects: 'In this way they tended to fit more easily into the general background of the Playground, whereas formerly they stood well out in the foreground.'

This story of a gang prompts several questions. Is environment the very important factor that it seems to be, and is removal from environment at least part of a cure for antisocial behaviour? Could more use be made of a conscious policy of movements in similar situations? In the present instance removal was the result of a decision on the part of one of the two families: its results were noticeable throughout the whole gang.

Equally important questions arise about the function of the leader and the problem of the destructive minority. That the Jones gang in the early months kept numerous children away is abundantly clear, but their own antisocial behaviour, through their relationship with the leader, lessened in the course of time.

Even so, the story is not entirely one of success. In human affairs the end of one chapter is but a prelude to the next, and to do justice to the events of these two years they should be seen in the light of the boys' subsequent history. As of January 1959 the two brothers, Barry and Archie, from the Jones family (I), and Harry S, also one of the 'regulars', had recently been committed by the Juvenile Court to an Approved School for breaking and entering. This was the culmination of a series of similar delinquencies. One of the Jones brothers admitted that his share of the proceeds was somewhere between £50 and £60. There seems little doubt that during the first two years of the Playground's life the gang confined its energies to behaviour less serious in its consequences.

SOME ASPECTS OF THE NEIGHBOURHOOD CULTURE

The extracts from the leader's dairy which follow give some indication of the culture of the neighbourhood. They are open to criticism to the extent to which they fail to reflect the diversity of standards that characterizes the estate, but they do, nevertheless, provide some evidence of the standards of behaviour characteristic of the rougher section of the Playground's children.

Playground Material in the Eyes of some of the Neighbours

The Playground was seen as a source of supply of wood, particularly at times when a new load had been received from an outside donor:

> Mr. B's lorry brought wood and corrugated zinc sheets. Mr. Y came over to try to buy hut sections for a pigeon's cote. I explained that it was for children to erect and that though it was so frail that it would not be with us long I was afraid he couldn't have it. He understood but said, 'Don't blame me, mind, if it's missing – just because I've asked for it. You know what they are around here.'

> Mr. W came along to make a dandy for his two girls. Earlier in the week he'd asked for a plank – said he'd buy it if he were in a position to do so – but because he was an epileptic and couldn't work he had no money. Told him then that he could bring his wheels down and make dandy on site.

Mrs. P came over at about 3 p.m. to ask for wood to make hutch for guinea pigs. And later when children were out from school she came in to tell me that some boys were cutting wire round compound. I went and found Dick with wire cutters happily cutting away. We used his pliers to fasten it together again.

Tony brought along a pram and said, 'Dad's asking if he can have some wood because the baby's ill.'

The Trade in Scrap Metal

Many of the children were aware of the money to be made from scrap metal. Any material which was rich in scrap metal had a short life on the Playground.

Car chassis had been left on the Playground during my absence yesterday at the Playing Fields conference in London. It looked very bashed about. Ralph and his two younger brothers came up through site from stream (he said his mother's legs are bad again so he can't go to school). He told me that as well as chassis there had been a 'station wagon' body. He and one or two others had made a den of it – 'It had doors and handles and everything.' It was now in the stream – smashed. No valuable scrap metal left. Metal had also been removed from chassis – lamps, etc.

Jack told me how he'd taken scrap – he'd written a note saying, 'Please take this scrap from my son because I'm out of work', and signed it R.H.W. 'Got to be careful that you don't write it like a boy – but like an adult – scribble it.'

Peter told me his mother took his scrap to yard last Saturday – because he'd heard that scrap merchant couldn't take scrap from children under 14.

Norman and brother Mike had been caught by a man trying to remove valuable metal from a derelict car near Arley bus stop. 'There's nothing of value on it,' said Norman. 'No', said someone else, 'Norman had taken most of it before.' He had, he said, removed the brass headlamps. But – and he told us this with relish – he discovered that the man who caught them is the scrap-metal merchant himself, so he can't take the headlamps to be sold after all. Apparently the man had slapped the boys about a bit and had knocked the lens out of Mike's glasses. Norman said he'd twisted his arm.

The Rough Treatment of Property

To write an exhaustive description of the damage to Playground property would indeed be tedious. We quote a few examples from the leader's records, after some large drain pipes had been delivered at the Playground:

> The pipes arrived in two separate loads, the first while the children were in school. These I placed end to end to form a tunnel and when the children came from school I watched to see what they would do. The Infants walked on them and sat astride them and asked me what they were for. The Juniors did the same thing and threw stones at them to see if they would break. The Seniors discovered that they could roll them by standing on them and that they could roll others inside them. They helped to unload the second lot and put them in position.
>
> While I remained near, children of all ages played happily with the pipes, but when the time came for me to leave the area to collect tools etc., within five minutes of my departure another concrete pipe was rolled down the bank to the stream and only my rushing back prevented more damage.
>
> The following day (Saturday morning) we again lined up the pipes, joined them together and closed the collars up with clay and drove in iron stakes each side of the pipes to hold them in place – and the children really enjoyed crawling through the tunnel. But on Monday all the 'clay' pipes had been – despite the stakes – rolled down to the stream and smashed. This was done, so I am informed, on Sunday evening. The concrete pipes are still intact.

The leader's return to the Playground on Mondays frequently met with reports of weekend damage. Thus:

> Warm sunny afternoon. Children came in with me. Lock had been smashed off; protection we had put round flower bed missing, front window holed, and dens bashed in. Mrs. M told me she'd seen boys breaking lock and had gone to stop them. Barry brought in lock and told me names of breakers whom he'd seen at work.

Both the hut and the fence were the object of vandalism and the committee minutes reflect the considerable proportion of time spent on discussing repairs.

Attitudes to the Leader

Of the children's and their parents' attitudes towards the leader the log-book is almost entirely silent, although some evidence is available through the study of the sixteen 'regulars'. The best indication, perhaps, of neighbourliness was the daily tray of tea and a bun which Mrs. M prepared for the leader. There were numerous other similar acts of kindness. For example:

> About 6.45 Harry S[1] brought over a pasty which his mother had just made and sent over for me. Is it perhaps a return gift – acknowledgement of the fact that I give Chris (then aged $3\frac{1}{2}$) a bun when I get my tea. Chris, when I first knew him, was an ill-clad, neglected-looking child who was always out in the streets. Impossible to approach, instantly on the defensive, and very aggressive. After a long period I established a friendship. He now waits for me to come – even on Sundays – he has become quite friendly and allows other adults to approach him. Lately he has been much better clad and receives more attention at home. Have been told by other children that he used to receive beatings at home. Has an older brother who is mentally defective.

There was recognition, too, from the Jones gang when the news of the leader's forthcoming resignation spread around:

[1] One of the sixteen 'regulars'

By 7.45 all had gone except Barry. He told me he was making
something for me in craft lessons. Said that he and Archie were
going to collect for me before I left – because I'd been good to
them.

The farewell concert and tea-party with a large iced cake with
two candles and 'Donald' written in silver balls, organized with
such care by one of the mothers, ended in this way:

Towards the end of the programme I was sent to appear on
stage and was presented by one of the troupers with a pen and
pencil and wallet and the address which she read. Tremendous
and prolonged cheers. I thanked them and Mr. and Mrs. D said
it was their wedding anniversary – and they took front stage to
tremendous and prolonged cheering. Sang (according to Programme) 'Auld Lang Syne' and 'The Queen'. Exit 7.50 p.m.
Troupers remained behind to share the load cake.

THE COMMITTEE

The Playground committee initially consisted of representatives
from the Local Education Authority, the Upfield Community
Council, and the Project. In the course of the first three years certain changes occurred in the membership of the committee and
by the conclusion of the Project in September 1958 local interests
were rather better represented. The decision to include at least one
representative from the parent-teacher association of a neighbouring primary school was a happy choice.

A word about representation may be useful, particularly in the
case of an experimental or pioneering venture. Where objectives
are not generally understood a committee has to face both apathy
and opposition. The very strangeness of the adventure playground
makes this inevitable, and in the face of difficulties even a moderate
achievement carries its own reward.

What stands out from the work of the Upfield Playground
committee is the enthusiasm and hard work of many of the local
authority members, both official and elected. It is clear that the

Playground could never have developed without their generous help, or the tenacity with which they pleaded its cause. But it is doubtful whether the committee was constituted in such a way as to be able to call on other sources of help. A steady supply of material equipment, one of the outstanding needs, was seriously lacking. The committee badly needed the representatives of business interests who could have helped them in this matter.

The addition of a parents' sub-committee, entrusted with the responsibility of simple tasks, such as the organization of jumble sales, the collection of money, and the repair of equipment, but not with the actual supervision of children, might have strengthened the sense of local responsibility in the neighbourhood. The committee was indeed fortunate in the representatives of the parent-teacher association of the local primary school whose help was invaluable. Nevertheless the fact remains that parent-teacher associations are generally attended by the élite of parents specially interested in their children's education and welfare. On the Upfield Playground it was the rough children from the larger families who predominated. The committee never really succeeded – as the interviews with the parents of the 'regulars' indicate – in enlisting the support of the rough parents. The dilemma remains a very real one. Those parents most competent to help children found that their own children used the Playground least, and some of them were disinclined to devote time and money to the children of their rougher neighbours.

Earlier in this section we posed the difficult and controversial question of priority of needs. It was natural that the Project's interest was in the Playground as a 'practical means of tackling stresses and strains' and we have tried to make some analysis of the committee meetings in the light of this particular objective. An objective analysis of the minutes reinforces the impression of the team members that the committee devoted a lot more time to administrative matters (finance, equipment, hut, lighting and paving, fencing, etc.) than to a consideration of policy in the light of the real but conflicting needs of different children. The Upfield committee is by no means unique in the proportion of time it devoted to finance and administration; it is common experience of distinguished committees that fundamental policy issues get pushed out by the pressure of immediate practical detail. And the financial troubles and problems of property of the Playground were both difficult and continuous. The fact remains that, in so far as the Playground was established as an approach to 'stresses and strains', the committee found itself giving very little time to consideration of the work in this respect. It did not really wrestle with clarification of the Playground's purpose and an assessment of its achievements. It worked hard as an enabling agent to give the appointed leaders tools for the job, but it was not able to work steadily towards clarifying its own corporate conception of exactly what the job was and why there was uncertainty.

This was, at least in part, due to a failure on the part of the Project team to present persuasively enough the need for clarifying the issues of principle. For underlying all the committee's discussions there lies a fundamental divergence of assumptions – the claims of *activities* as contrasted with *personal relationships*. In the middle-class Copenhagen suburb of Helrup, where the first adventure playground was created, no such conflict arises. The family background of middle-class children is such that most of them are able to take part in the creative activities that a playground aims to encourage. Thus the object of creative activities is part of the culture of their homes. In Upfield, on the other hand, and in other neighbourhoods with a similar background, there is a diversity of cultures. The predominant assumption of the committee was that the Playground existed to carry on where the schools left off for all local children. Their criticism of the leader derived from his failure, in their view, to promote these activities.

To extend the work of the school in leisure hours and to develop the spirit of creativity and adventure are indeed legitimate purposes, the success of which depends on the ability of the children to achieve them. As our narrative suggests, there was a substantial group of Upfield children whose need for a playground was very different. The appeal that the Playground had for them was the difference that it presented from the school. As one boy said: 'It's the place where I can come and do my mischief.' What we believe he needed, if he was to grow responsibly, was the experience of being destructive and yet not losing the confidence of a stable adult – the experience which most children get in a reasonably disciplined affectionate home, and which these children lacked. Some might get it at school, but this is a chancy business in classes of over forty, where the nuisance is easier to suppress than to treat.

In February 1957, for example, when the leader began to change his policy and to place greater emphasis on the development of activities, one of the boys remarked: 'Come off it, Donald, you're turning this place into a bloomin' school.' The analogy of a school is a misleading one. Imagine, for example, a school with only the head-teacher and no other staff available, with only a playground and one classroom provided, and with all the school regulations removed.

The Playground was in fact complementary to the school. It was an 'escape valve' where many of the children came to let off steam after school. Though many of the most difficult children on the Playground were also difficult in school, there were others who were well-behaved, apparently model children in school, yet up to every kind of mischief while on the Playground.

As an extension of school and the encouragement of activities developed in school, the condition and life of the Playground were not always easy to justify – particularly in view of its untidy appearance. Yet it was on these grounds that the committee had to face the criticism of public opinion. The signs of better personal relationships, on the other hand, just because they were less visible and less obvious, were harder to demonstrate. Of these the children themselves and the leader were perhaps the only witnesses.

CHAPTER 13

Suggestions for the Future

FROM so short an experience in one particular area it would be presumptuous to make recommendations. There are, however, some suggestions for the future, simple to state though hard to achieve, which deserve emphasis.

The organization of an adventure playground is neither simple nor cheap. It may be useful to relate some of the main features of the experience at Upfield as a guide to future policy.

FINANCE

Perhaps it is the fate of many pioneer experiments that they are run on a shoe-string and must prove their worth before adequate finance is made available. An adventure playground inevitably suffers from a shortage of money, and the Upfield Playground is certainly no exception. During the first two years the financial position was better than in the following years. The withdrawal of the Project's annual grant of £300 towards the leader's salary of £450 per annum and £50 towards running expenses coincided with the full-time leader's resignation in May 1957. At this point the Education Committee of the local authority increased its previous annual grant of £150 to £350, and this made it possible to appoint a part-time leader at £300 per annum.

But at the end of 1957 the Primary Sub-Committee of the Education Committee felt obliged to withdraw its grant, and the

262

financial situation was indeed serious. The National Playing Fields Association, which had already given £300, promised a further £175 provided that a similar sum was forthcoming from the local authority. The Housing Committee promised £75 to be given in the form of maintenance to the fence and the hut. The full Education Committee responded by inviting the Primary Sub-Committee to think again about its recommendation, but again the Primary Sub-Committee turned the application down. It took the whole of the first half of 1958 for the Education Committee to find a way of contributing £100 to stand alongside the £75 which had been at once forthcoming from the Housing Committee. Meanwhile the local press had on its own initiative taken up the cause of the Playground and the threat of closure for want of £100. Finally, in June 1958 the Chairman of the Playground committee was able to report that the Education Committee had finally agreed to the grant but on the understanding that it would not be repeated. The struggle was at last over, at least for a while, and the Playground had been reprieved.

To meet the needs of the children during the summer at a time of financial uncertainty the Playground was opened by the headmaster of the local junior school and by two parents in his parent-teacher association for two evenings a week. But this could not be regarded as a permanent measure, and a circular letter was sent to Bristol teachers inviting applications for part-time work on a sessional basis of 18s. per session. Fifteen applications were received and the new arrangement operated during August and September, when the Playground closed for the winter months. The estimated cost of opening the Playground on a part-time paid sessional basis, assuming a week of four sessions between 6 p.m. and 9 p.m., was £273 12s. for a year of thirty-eight weeks. The assumption was that it would remain closed during December, January, and February.

In December the good news was announced that the Education Committee would renew the grant of £100 for a further year. The committee made plans for re-opening during the spring of 1959.

Of the two main sums involved in the initial capital expenditure the six-foot chain-link fence with concrete posts was £565 and the hut £671 (towards the cost of which a firm of contractors gave £500 and the Housing Committee £99). The type of supervision, it is clear, must depend on the size of the committee's budget, and the initial policy of a full-time leader could not unfortunately be maintained after the withdrawal of the Project's grant. The annual maintenance cost of the Playground (excluding salaries) for such items as water, electricity, fire insurance, heating, equipment, and repairs amounted to about £100. The rates were raised in 1957 from £18 10s. to £26 5s.

But to any formal balance sheet must be added numerous gifts in kind from the local authority, from business firms, and from private people, of sand and bricks, tree trunks and drain pipes, ropes and climbing apparatus, while from local residents in the immediate neighbourhood came paper-backed books, bed frames, bicycle frames, and an organ.

FENCE

Whether to fence in the Playground or to leave the site in its original open state was a difficult problem for the committee and one of the earliest on which a decision had to be taken. There were some doubts as to the absolute necessity of a fence all round, particularly in view of the high cost that was estimated. Protection of children from traffic on the busy road was clearly essential, as was the safeguarding of property from marauders. On the other hand, there would be the inevitable loss of informality and of casual visitors. Subsequent experience showed that parents generally seemed apprehensive about entering the gates of the Playground. Many of them stopped short at the entrance. But the deciding factor was insurance against accidents. No company would accept liability unless the Playground was fenced and locked when there was no responsible adult on the site. The leader wrote in his annual report:

My view is that it is an unwelcome necessity. There was a nice atmosphere about the site before it was fenced. People came quite casually into it. There were a number of paths crossing it which were used. Occasionally a mother with a pram would stay for a while and watch. There were no such questions as I've had since from children who stop at the gate and say, 'Hey, Mister! Can anybody come in?' I suppose that ideally there should be no fence – but when we reach that happy state we will have no need for adventure playgrounds.

Our fence does not keep out children, who can get under in many places and over almost anywhere. It has not prevented them from taking pieces of timber, etc., but it has, I think, a limiting effect.

In subsequent years when there was no full-time leader it was suggested that the Playground should be left open even though unsupervised. This policy was never in fact adopted though on occasions there were large numbers of children playing inside the closed gates. The insurance policy was considered to present an obstacle to any such plan.

HUT

Some form of building on an adventure playground is essential. There are certain minimum demands of any building, such as lavatories, a tap for drinking-water, a room in which to lock up tools, equipment, and first-aid material. But given the money and the facilities for winter opening we can go beyond these minimum demands. A room for the leader where he can talk with children and prepare for the evening's play is particularly useful, but above all there is need for covered space where children can model or paint or read in wet and cold weather.

The Upfield Playground committee received from an architect a design for a building containing a covered play space of just this nature: a flat-roofed concrete and brick building containing storage space and a play room open on two sides. But primarily

265

for reasons of economy, and thanks to the help of the Housing Manager, a pre-fabricated asbestos hut resting on concrete blocks, some sixty feet in length, was erected by the student work-camp. The method of heating was through an old boiler and radiators, which resulted in cracked pipes in the frost when the complicated ritual of draining the system was not rigorously observed.

In retrospect it appears that as a committee we were never clear about the precise function of the hut, confusing two views of the way in which it could be used. One view is to see it as a club in which the normal type of club activities takes place with a list of members and rules as to membership. But in this case, the building should be designed for the purpose and not located on the Playground. The alternative view is to see the hut as an extension of the Playground into which children retreat from the wet and cold. But the Upfield pre-fabricated hut, with no space open to the Playground, provided the worst of both worlds. In the leader's words at the end of the first year's work:

> The fabric itself is too fragile for its site – it is on a playground and not in a street. It was hopeless to try to cope unaided with the numbers of children who wished to come into a hut which was being used as a storehouse for timber and which had no more than hammers, nails, and clay to offer in the way of activities. Furthermore, the children expected to be able to carry on, with the same energy inside the hut, the games which they had been playing outside. It was impossible to supervise inside and outside.
>
> For what it is worth I should like to offer the suggestion that a more suitable type of shelter for a playground would be a large, solidly constructed, concrete pavilion structure – open at one side. Into this building the children could retreat from bad weather and still retain their outdoor mood.

A hut of this kind would, in fact, have required more helpers on the Playground than were available, and is likely to be successful only under conditions where there is independent supervision of children both inside and outside.

Whatever building is constructed will have to be built within a small budget. But a building of the wrong design is a mixed blessing. A pre-fabricated hut, for example, has many handicaps. Any building constitutes a challenge to children to climb, and glass windows are all too easy to break. The structure must be solid and secure; ideally it should give the appearance of being a quite natural feature of the playground – itself part of the adventure implied elsewhere on the site.[1] A well-designed building

---

[1] Because the designing of a playground building appeared to provide such an important challenge, one of the professors at the Royal West of England Academy School of Architecture gave as a training exercise to first-year students during 1957 and 1958 the design of an adventure playground shelter on two sites in central areas of Bristol in process of reconstruction. The Director of the Project was invited to collaborate in this exercise. The brief to the students included the following instructions:

'The project consists of providing a playground shelter on the site together with fencing, screen planting, and such landscaping as may be required. The City Authorities have promised a grant for the construction of the project on condition that the work is carried out by voluntary labour. The Committee has therefore decided to accept an offer of help from a student work-camp. The volunteers will be unskilled but they will be supervised by a retired Clerk of Works who will be employed specially by the Committee.

As a designer you are limited to using very simple techniques of construction in order that the building and layout may be completed by the camp of some twenty people within the set time of six weeks. The cost of the project must be kept to a minimum compatible with all the functional requirements being adequately met. The techniques employed in constructing the shelter will necessarily be limited: concrete, brick, or stone can be used for flooring, paving, or walling fairly easily, but for roof construction the only practical material is timber, and you will be strictly limited to it in your design. Also for partition and walling, timber has the advantage of speed of erection, but here other factors weigh against its use.'

At the end of the second exercise Mr. Stephen Macfarlane, a Lecturer at the School, wrote: 'The design of an adventure playground including a shelter building is a valuable exercise for training architects. The building type is unique and the designer needs to free himself from preconceptions and conventions. The design should grow in answer to the children's needs rather than be an adult interpretation of those needs.

We found when seeking advice from people with experience that "the best playgrounds just seem to have happened" (e.g. bombed sites).

The designs judged most successful have been those that tended to be non-representational in form. Abstract form may be handled to stimulate imagination in a variety of ways and to be useful for many different kinds of game and make-believe. An object identified from the adult world – a railway train or a castle complete in detail, for example – would be an influence towards aims different from those of the adventure playground.

The designer's personality should be hidden in the building, he should be able to encourage activity through forms he builds and not allow this kind of building to be a means of self-expression.

We must admit, however, that the value of our work, so far only projects on paper, cannot be properly judged.

As a new direction the R.W.A. School of Architecture at Bristol has carried out several "live projects" in which students carry through the whole process of designing and building. An adventure playground would be an excellent "live project" and we are anxious to build one.'

267

can greatly facilitate the leader's task. Short-handed, he may wish to keep an eye on activities both inside and outside the building. Part of it, therefore, can best take the form of a shelter rather than a hall, open to the playground but with cover from rain; some kind of fireplace or open hearth with chimney for primitive kinds of cooking and the fascination of a camp fire would be important for the winter months.

Building policy must inevitably depend on decisions as to winter opening. If the playground is to be open during the whole of the winter, good lighting and heating will also be needed. Perhaps the lighting should include the flood-lighting of some part of the playground at least. Many of these suggestions may involve expenses beyond a normal budget. They are certainly exciting possibilities for the future.

EQUIPMENT AND MATERIALS

Unlike the orthodox children's playground where the swings and seesaws, slides and merry-go-rounds are fixed equipment requiring only the minimum of maintenance, adventure playgrounds require a continual supply of material: logs, tree trunks, bricks, bits of wood of all kinds, nails, tools for making things and for digging, wheels, corrugated iron for roofing, drain pipes for climbing inside and metal frames or steel scaffolding for climbing outside, sand and water, ropes and ladders. There is no end to the ingenuity of the children under the inspiration of the leader and to the range of material which is needed. Some of the material is obviously junk and of little use for building purposes – the product, for example, of demolished houses – but much of it has a value in certain quarters. In areas where children and their parents have good contacts with the scrap-metal merchant, there is money to be gained from stripping the derelict motor-car of its metal parts. Wood, for example, is useful for firewood or for making rabbit hutches or pigeon lofts. A wide range of contacts with people of goodwill, able to provide material of this kind, is essential.

The Upfield Playground, in spite of the generosity of numerous individuals, was never able to maintain an adequate supply of materials, and there can be little doubt that the quality of the play suffered in consequence. It was the constant demand of everyone who worked there, whether full-time or part-time, paid or unpaid.

Looking back on this problem in retrospect, we see two issues, other than shortage of money, which stand out. The first was the difficulty of transport. Although several firms expressed their willingness to give discarded timber and other material for play, few were able to supply transport. The services of a lorry would have contributed materially to a better supply. The second was the composition of the committee, which was weak in its contacts with the world of industry. We would go so far as to suggest that at least one-quarter of the Playground committee should have been representatives from the field of industry and commerce.

TIMES AND SEASONS FOR OPENING

Here also the variety of local needs and resources must make generalizations impossible. The period following the end of school until about 8 p.m. is an obvious characteristic of term-time during the summer months. Some special activity, such as a visit to the swimming baths, is a possibility for Saturday mornings. On Sundays the leader will need a rest from a strenuous week's work. During the school holidays, however, the time-table may be altered and the hour of opening fixed earlier in the afternoon.

Winter opening raises different considerations. Much depends on the social background of the area and the terms of employment of the leader. In an area where children use the street as their playground in dark winter evenings as well as in summer, arrangements for winter opening may fulfil a real need, but covered or indoor facilities can accommodate only a limited number. With facilities for a smaller population and activities of a different kind the winter programme would be similar in many ways to that of a youth club. The younger children will inevitably be less numerous.

Some restriction on numbers will be essential if available material is to be used with some degree of order in the building.

But should an adventure playground become a club? This is a policy question on which opinions vary. The Upfield policy was to retain the playground idea as far as possible throughout the year. In any case, winter opening makes essential some expenditure on indoor equipment, modelling clay and paper, pencils and paint, clothes for dressing up, packing cases, tables, chairs, a gramophone, PT apparatus, and so on.

If the playground is open only for the summer, provision must be made for winter employment of the leader. To combine leadership of a playground in summer with teaching or youth work is a sensible measure, though for reasons of lack of staff local authorities may be unwilling to make arrangements of this kind. A strong case can be made for the employment of teachers with an interest and aptitude for work with children in the informal surroundings of a playground. Unless we can achieve the acceptance of some policy of this kind, we must become resigned to the fact that few men and women with the right qualities of skill and understanding will be prepared to undertake so arduous a task.

LEADERSHIP

Good leadership is the very essence of the movement. At first sight it appears as if the handy ex-sailor with a fund of stories, or the retired school caretaker with some experience of children, is the kind of leader whom we can usefully recruit. Without denying that there may be some situations where this is possible and that there are men possessing the necessary feeling for the needs of children at play, we must nevertheless be more realistic and set our sights higher.[1]

[1] To run an adventure playground with part-time leadership is exceptionally difficult. We must add, however, that during the summer of 1959 the Upfield Adventure Playground had a most successful season under the general supervision of a teacher from an Upfield secondary modern school assisted by a small group of teachers and by two fathers living nearby. It was a strenuous job but the teacher in charge had the advantage of knowing personally not only many of the children using the Playground, but their parents also. The Local Education Authority paid these workers on a sessional basis.

In the foreseeable future adventure playgrounds in England (by contrast with Scandinavia) are most likely to be established in those urban areas where the needs of children are greatest. This will probably mean either or both of two things: first, that the area is densely populated and poorly equipped with open spaces or parks; and, second, that the social standards of the families in the area are such that the children are left very largely to their own devices. It is from a minority of the homes in these conditions that a large proportion of delinquent children is drawn.[1] The adventure playground which tries to meet the deprivations of these children is thus one way of helping children to grow up as responsible citizens, and should properly be an integral part of the whole educational system, though trying to do something different from what the school itself does.

For this reason the possession of skills as handyman, though extremely valuable, is not enough. More is required of the leader. He becomes, in effect, for many children, a part-time parent, and whatever he helps them to create or build or express has virtue by this relationship with them. As adults we may deny the relevance of this aspect of his work, but the children see him otherwise. As a part-time parent the kind of person that the leader is, whether man or woman, needs careful attention. Personality alone, however, is not enough. To understand and meet children's needs, and particularly the needs of deprived children from underprivileged neighbourhoods, requires training and experience. *To entrust an adventure playground to the untrained is to run the risk of failure.*

But without the assistance of voluntary helpers the leader takes on a heavy task. Where are these helpers to be found? One source of supply is the parents of the children living in the neighbourhood. With their help the playground becomes a neighbourhood institution. Their interest and support are invaluable. But we must not expect too much. Probably more disagreement is created in a neighbourhood by differences over children at play than through any other single cause. It is the exceptional parent who can understand, as if by instinct, what the adventure playground sets out to

[1] See, for example, the illuminating study of Croydon by Morris (1958, Chapter 7).

271

achieve. The leader, therefore, has a responsibility for educating parents in the ideas and methods of the movement and for building up good relations between the playground and the neighbourhood. Nevertheless he can at least expect from some of them the performance of simple tasks, the guardianship of property, for example, as Mays (1957, p. 21) describes, the repair of tools, or the collection of equipment. Yet even here, as the extracts from the log-book showed, many local parents do not recognize rights of, or their responsibility for, other people's property. Working with parents will constitute yet another demand on the worker's skill.

But ought we not in our search for helpers to cast the net rather wider than this? To help with a playground might well be one of those opportunities for service to the community among the older boys who are working for the Duke of Edinburgh's Award. Here, indeed, is a challenge to qualities of leadership and to the exercise of physical ability and craftsmanship. Students at universities and training colleges, too, can gain much in understanding about children at play if arrangements for introducing them to the playground are wisely made with their tutors, and in turn they can give useful help. The organization of this kind of help, however, is yet another claim on the full-time leader.

There can be no hard-and-fast rules about the use of helpers; so much will depend on circumstances. The lessons of the Upfield Playground, however, seen in the light of the principles of social group work described in Chapter 4, certainly point to the need for greater contact between adult helpers and the gangs and individual children using the playground. Ideally, what would be desirable would be to promote a link between helpers and particular groups. Thus the 'White-Band' gang' (as the Jones gang called themselves one day when they appeared wearing white paper bands on their legs) would be the responsibility of Mrs. X, and the Spring Grove mob the responsibility of Miss Y. Through such a process of decentralization, intense competition for the attention of the leader would be lessened. The leader, on the other hand, would have general responsibility for the encouragement and supervision of the helpers.

COMMITTEE

Perhaps the most important aim in forming a playground committee should be the range of interests of the members. A playground is essentially a local neighbourhood institution – few things are more localized than the activities of young children at play, and the catchment area predominantly covers the streets in the surrounding neighbourhood – but it requires a far wider range of interests than is possible from a neighbourhood committee.

First, there are the representatives of the various departments of the local authority who are likely to be concerned and able to give help, the education, housing, and parks departments, both the elected members and the official staff. In the second place, local leaders also, such as clergy, doctors, head-teachers, and social workers, as well as the members of local associations, may have much to offer. Third, there is the need for those business men in the city through whose good offices a continual supply of equipment and play material may come and whose advice could be so useful. Fourth, we should be wise to include also some people who by training, experience, and inclination are primarily concerned with children and their families. The temptation to become immersed in the business of administration to the exclusion of nearly all else is strong and by the nature of the work almost inevitable. We need also people who are more detached from the local scene than parents are likely to be.

But there is an important place too for a parents' committee. If the playground is to become a neighbourhood institution with a meaning for the local residents and a place for which they themselves have a sense of caring and responsibility, a local committee of parents entrusted with some of the simpler tasks of organization has a very real contribution to make. There would be, presumably, some form of cross-representation between the two committees. Certainly, representation from among parents on the main committee is desirable. To work with a parents' committee will make yet another demand on the time, and above all on the skill, of the leader. Unlike the teacher in school who works within the framework of an established institution, the playground leader when facing the parents must expect to find among them a bewildering and often conflicting variety of expectations of what purpose adventure playgrounds are designed to fulfil. The playground in fact carries with it opportunities for community organization in addition to the more obvious purpose of providing a place for children to play creatively together.

At the present stage of development it may be far too ambitious and unrealistic to advocate the extension of playground aims into so wide and difficult a field. In the present stage of public opinion, of finance, and of ideas on the provision of playgrounds, we may have to be content with more modest objectives. But it need surely not be the final answer. The Project was asked to consider the strains and stresses of developing communities, but the functions of neighbourhood in modern society are severely limited. Work, leisure, shopping, and a large part of our social activities, are no longer localized as they once were. But the children's playgroup remains, and this – at least to judge from the catchment area of the Upfield Adventure Playground – is entirely a *local* activity.

Through developments of this kind there is an opportunity of learning to live together and of sharing in a common task. Through the sharing of their feelings about children at play, adults have a real meeting point, but one in which emotion is often more decisive than reason. On the question of standards on the playground, few residents are likely to remain neutral. There will be the advocates of stricter control, on the one hand, and of greater freedom, on the other. The leader's standards may differ from those of both the committee and the neighbourhood. Provided, however, that there are opportunities for discussion in which differences may be acknowledged and feelings shared, the experience can be a creative one and the foundation for new achievement.

But we must emphasize in conclusion a point which we tried to bring out in the discussion of the Upfield committee, that it is the business of the professionals concerned with adventure playgrounds to see that committees discuss children, their needs, and how they can be met. This, of course, means that some reorganization of the committee programme is required so that there can be more time devoted to the discussion of children and less to problems of administration. If committees can, with professional help, achieve this difficult aim, they will go beyond the function of enablers to the professionals, and will contribute to the general extension of greater insight into child development in the neighbourhood.

PART V

Conclusions
and
Recommendations for Social Policy

CHAPTER 14

The Nature of Stress and Strain

UNDERLYING the work of the Project have been two convictions: the first is the belief that a planned and democratic society must take responsibility for its 'sore spots' and for the situations in which stress and strain are particularly acute; the second is the necessity of social research as an essential basis for policy-making and for devising methods to put the decisions of social policy into action.[1]

The Project was founded on the belief that society cannot displace its responsibility for dealing with stresses and strains onto an army of social workers or a team of back-room boys, and the object of the work described in this report has been to learn more clearly the most effective methods of discharging this responsibility. In the conclusions which follow we try to bear in mind two things: the importance of lay responsibility in a democratic society; and the very considerable degree of professional and expert knowledge required in dealing with stressful and troublesome situations.

Much of the group work discussed in Parts II and III implies a commentary on the problem of relating these two ideas, above all

---

[1] In our report to the Carnegie Trust we presented our recommendations for social policy as a coherent whole, in the light of our experience of action research as well as of the built-in research on the neighbourhoods and the ordinary families. For the purpose of publication, however, we are compelled to divorce the conclusions of the action research from those of the studies of the sociologist and the psychiatric social worker. When presenting these latter studies in a second volume we hope also to discuss their implications for housing and town-planning policy, for the community association movement, and for health and welfare services dealing with the family and the child.

in the work with the Espressos, who constituted so threatening and troublesome a group to Upfield residents. Again and again we have tried to emphasize the fact that the understanding of the layman is essential if the professional worker is to be successful in reducing the level of stress in the group, both among the members themselves and also in relation to external society.

The second point is the role of social research, of which action research is one particular form. It is perhaps a relatively new idea that social policy, social welfare, or social service – the precise label is unimportant – require a foundation of psychological and sociological knowledge for their formation, application, and evaluation. Policy-making is no longer purely a matter of making the poor richer. In the words of Professor Titmuss (1957), 'since the nineteenth century we have lost our psychological innocence and, with it, our economic naïveté'. The content of man's needs has been enlarged and redefined. The significance of doing things *with* people instead of for them has become clearer. At the same time, the value of social policy which rests on an analysis of such cold and uninspiring data as occupation, age, class, or size of family, has been continually illustrated.

What, then, is the role of research in the field of social welfare? Titmuss (ibid.) has suggested three roles, which in his view are among the most important: an educational role, a policy-making role, and a protesting and critical role.

Much of the main body of our report certainly falls into the third category. The Project has assumed a critical role, because we believe that there must be informed studies of how a 'developing community' – we have generally preferred the more neutral words 'neighbourhood' or 'locality' – in practice understands and deals with its stresses and strains.

Neighbourhood and family provided the focus for our work. We were charged with the task of 'taking part in the life of a developing community in an attempt to establish practical means of tackling those "stresses and strains" which arise in such a community in the form of delinquency and other disturbances'. Of the three neighbourhoods of Bristol chosen, after an initial survey, for the Project – the two housing estates of Upfield and Boltwood and the old central neighbourhood of Mount View – our main work has been in Upfield, which contained within its boundaries a more than average share of stresses and strains (see Appendix VI). In these conclusions we try to examine the primary lessons of the Project and their meaning for social policy. For reasons of space we confine ourselves chiefly to action research, leaving the studies of the neighbourhoods and the ordinary families to a second volume.

One of our objectives has been to understand the problems of the neighbourhood against the background of the whole city, and to see the characteristics of Upfield, Boltwood, and Mount View in the light of the total industrial and social structure of Bristol.

Concern about stress and strain defined in the initial terms of reference as 'delinquency and other disturbances' was the reason why the Project Committee called on the services of the professional team. This definition was deliberately vague and it was the team's function to clarify it.

In the first instance we took the definition to mean symptoms such as adult crime, juvenile delinquency, persistent truancy, problem families, and problems of child welfare. This interpretation of stress and strain, though greatly oversimplified, made it possible to make some assessment of the distribution of these symptoms in Bristol and so to help in deciding on the precise neighbourhoods in which the team might operate.

A short ecological survey was, therefore, designed to answer the question: Are the families which give rise to symptoms of stress and strain scattered throughout the city, or do they cluster together in particular neighbourhoods and streets?

The results of this short preliminary survey showed that *there was a clustering of these symptoms in three areas, two of them housing estates on the periphery of the city, and the third an old central area* (see Appendix VI). Though an important conclusion from the point of view of social policy, as we discuss later, this was no new discovery. Several studies, both in the United States and in Great Britain, have pointed to the concentration of these symptoms of

Conclusions and Recommendations for Social Policy

stress and strain – or indices of social and family disorganization as they are sometimes called – in particular areas and particular streets. It is a matter of common observation that in the crowded slums of our large cities stress and strain of the kind which we mention are particularly high.[1]

What does emerge from these studies and is confirmed by the Bristol study is the difference between American and many British cities in the distribution of symptoms. The typical American pattern is a clustering of symptoms in the areas adjacent to the central business district – areas disintegrating in character, with lax social standards and a mobile population. In England, on the other hand, several observers have noted that the process of clustering is not confined to the centre of the city, but is found also in housing estates on the periphery. The simplest explanation of this lies in the development of public housing in England, where building has taken place to a large extent on the outer ring of the city. As a result of slum-clearance programmes, there have been substantial movements in population from the centre to the circumference. Thus social problems which had in the past been concentrated in old central areas, in which the property was owned mainly by private landlords, were transferred to housing estates built and managed by the city corporation.

The symptoms of stress and strain selected for the ecological survey were primarily those which give rise to public concern and hostility, classifiable broadly as antisocial. Certainly these symptoms had brought the individuals and the families to public notice, and it was through the helpful co-operation of local government officers that the early survey was made. Information was also available on the distribution of 'problem families' and of mental defectives in Bristol. Similar clustering in the case of these two indices was also observed.

But the method of ecology – or the 'epidemiology of morals' as one committee member called it – is no more than a pointer to

[1] Wootton (1959, p. 70): 'In general, therefore, it may be said that ecological studies have succeeded in establishing that things are very much what one would expect them to be: birds of a feather flock, or at any rate are found, together. But it is the interpretation of these findings which is the critical issue; and this remains a matter for speculation.'

further thinking. Ecology is concerned with place, and the locus of stress and strain is only one framework within which to view the problem. To focus discussion, moreover, only on symptoms which are a nuisance to society is to single out only one particular aspect of a much more complex issue. It is also to concentrate attention on a particular social class[1] characterized by low incomes, unskilled jobs, and low status in the community – a fact of which the Project team was very properly reminded by some of its critics.

Viewed in a broader context, however, the symptoms of stress and strain constitute a more complex problem. The symptoms are of many different kinds. Some are respectable, such as duodenal ulcer. Others, such as juvenile delinquency, are stigmatized by all except very unusual groups. Some have a high nuisance value and are the subject of public action, whereas others are contained within the family and attract less attention either from the family or from the various services of the welfare state.

Many symptoms are excluded, however, from policy considerations because they are regarded as falling neither in the medical nor in the criminal field. Trouble with housing, trouble with neighbours, a bad employment record, and defective personal relationships – all appear in this category. These were among the symptoms of stress and strain used as criteria in our Family Study.

These quasi-medical, quasi-criminal stresses and strains tend to get the worst of both worlds. On the one hand, they fall outside medical justification for expenditure. On the other hand, since manifest harm does not extend much beyond the individual's family, they are not considered as appropriate objectives of criminal policy or of the penal and reformative services.

The roots which sustain both kinds of symptoms, however, lie beyond the individual – in his family, in society, in the way he is treated by others, and in the deprivations and rewards he has suffered and enjoyed.

[1] Symptoms of stress and strain are differentially distributed both in character and number according to social class. Social class differences, however, were not the special subject of the Project's investigation and our knowledge is therefore based on the conclusions of other workers. See, in particular, Hollingshead and Redlich (1958).

Conclusions and Recommendations for Social Policy

The shape of the urban community today is one of fragmentation and mobility. This is the social background to stress and strain and it is in this context that social policy must be formulated. Place of residence is now increasingly on the fringe of the city. The movement, which in Bristol began with the growth of the 'tramcar suburbs' like St. George at the beginning of the century, has been greatly accelerated during the past twenty-five years.[1] Industry, similarly, has scattered to the periphery of the city. The likelihood, therefore, of finding people with similar interests in the neighbourhood is considerably diminished.

Equally important consequences for the character of neighbourhoods have been brought about by the social revolution. The relief of poverty, the improvement in transport, and the extension of vastly elaborated means of communication have multiplied out of all recognition the possible loyalties of the ordinary workman. This implies not only the physical separation of people with similar experiences but also the superimposition of opinions from the outside on existing attitudes.

Then, too, there are the consequences arising from the fact that the labour force has become more diversified and there has been a growth particularly in white-collar jobs. There is also the revolution in the employment of women. All the other influences mentioned, apart from the considerations of occupation, affect the woman equally with the man, and these permeate her attitudes and behaviour through her relationship with her husband, the most important adult person in her life.

The weakening of neighbourhood ties and the corresponding strengthening of the impact of the national culture on the individual compel us to emphasize once again the importance of the family, not only in the different ways in which families give rise to stress and strain, but also in the manner in which they deal with the symptoms.

For many working-class families the housing estate presents many unfamiliar experiences which are alien to established modes

[1] The central areas, which in 1931 contained 40 per cent of Bristol's population, contained only 20 per cent in 1951.

of living – separation from 'Mum', from the support of the kinship group and the close ties of neighbour relationships built up
through the need for mutual aid under social conditions different
from the present. Anxiety over status, for example, and uncertainty as to the appropriate ways of behaving as neighbours are the
natural concomitants of movement to new surroundings. Where
the traditional criteria of status arising from length of residence
and old acquaintance are removed, new criteria, which often give
the appearance of speciousness to the middle-class observer – the
possession of the TV set or the three-piece suite – take their place.

It is deceptively easy to mourn the disappearance of past tradi-
tions and to exaggerate the consequences of movement. All new
estates in the course of time grow old, and although Boltwood
and one-half of Upfield were not finally built until the early
fifties, building in the older part of Upfield was commenced in
1931. The important point is that adjustment to new ways of
living in itself makes demands on the family's capacity to deal with
stress. The Family Study shows that *families are confronted with a
variety of standards and that the roles of father and mother, husband and
wife, are not clearly and unequivocally defined by the neighbourhood.* It
is in this context that the family faces the problem of stress and
strain.

In her analysis of the 'ordinary families' the psychiatric social
worker related certain clearly recognized symptoms of stress and
strain to four types of family functioning. *The distinctive feature of
these four types of family functioning is the nature of the fit between the
roles of spouses.* It is this factor (i.e. the 'marital fit') which seems
to constitute the decisive influence on the family's capacity to contain the symptoms of stress within the family as contrasted with
their overt expression against society.

Some families – to which we gave the label 'integrative' – seem
to provide a secure framework in which new ways of living
might be worked out. They are able to contain stress within the
boundary of the family and to deal with it from their own resources. Others, however, the 'disintegrative' families, in which
there is a wide discrepancy between the internal values of the

family and the values of the outside world, are unable to cope with stress and strain. They rely on help from outside, from the wider kinship group, from the general practitioner, and from workers in the health and welfare services.

The largest number of symptoms of stress and strain were observed in the 'disintegrative' families, and the majority of these families lived at Upfield. An independent rating of these families by the sociologist showed them to be in the lowest status group.

It will be clear, we hope, from what we have said that the problem of stress and strain is much more complex than was assumed in the original definition of the Project. The forms which it can take are more varied and the roots deeper and more extensive than we recognized at the planning stage.

The clustering of symptoms of strain and stress which carry with them a public stigma and give rise to public anxiety still exists in a large city such as Bristol, in spite of the vigorous and enlightened housing policy pursued by the city in both the pre-war and the post-war years. The persistence of such clustering seems to be an inevitable consequence of the mobility of modern life. A slow process of social selection or, more accurately perhaps in certain circumstances, of social rejection takes place in which the 'respectable' citizens move away from the 'rough'.[1] A small study carried out in 1953 into the reasons for movement away from Upfield and Boltwood (the percentage of tenants moving either off the estate altogether or to another street was 10 per cent at Upfield and 5.6 per cent at Boltwood) indicated that the most important reason for movement was hostility and trouble between the neighbours. There was also a statistically significant difference between the social class of those who moved away and the social class of those who remained behind.

The belief that certain strains and stresses – in particular, juvenile delinquency – are no more than the inevitable consequences of slum conditions and that the slum 'breeds' delinquency, with its corollary that better housing will *ipso facto* lead to its dis-

---

[1] Compare also the observations of Kuper in a study of a housing estate in a Midland city, in Kuper *et al.* (1953).

appearance, is unfortunately too simple. We still have to face the difficult social problem of what one may call the 'residual' area, that is, the area of minimum choice with low standards to which families characterized by stress and strain of a predominantly anti-social pattern tend to gravitate, or from which their more respectable neighbours move away. This is a difficult problem which every public housing programme has to face, and we discuss it further in the second volume.

The evidence, however, suggests that it is a serious mistake to see the problem in clear-cut terms of black and white. The findings of the Project, for example, do *not* support the stereotyped ideas which many people in Bristol appeared to have of Upfield. The public reputation of an area, it is clear, may be seriously affected by even a small proportion of 'black sheep'. *But the stereotyped idea of a 'problem sub-culture' (Morris, 1958, p. 177) in which the whole area subscribes to a set of values different from those held in the wider society certainly does not apply to Upfield, nor, we consider, to estates of a similar social structure elsewhere.* It may still be true of certain old central slum areas, though our study of the Mount View area indicates that it is by no means a universal characteristic of central areas and is less and less likely to be true as the neighbourhood becomes more related to the national culture and to the standards of the wider society. In its extreme form the idea is most likely to persist on a street basis, but even here our sociologist has drawn attention to the diversity of standards within streets generally stigmatized by the outside world as uniformly 'black'. What is characteristic of the so-called 'black' streets, in which so many of the stresses were concentrated, is not that antisocial behaviour is approved of, but that it is not condemned so openly and so often as in other areas.

CHAPTER 15

Group Work

ONE of the main arguments of this report has been the value of group work[1] as a means of helping people to deal with the stresses and strains of a developing community. The growing areas of the large modern city do not provide the same traditional methods for helping the development of social relationships that were available in the more isolated and self-contained communities of the past. The urban neighbourhood is characterized by a wide diversity of attitudes and a fragmentation of outlook. It is no longer an appropriate catchment area for many social groups. Group work, therefore, except for certain special groups such as mothers with young children, and for the children themselves, should be developed on a wider basis than that of the neighbourhood. It is on the small group of some eight to ten members meeting under trained leadership that we place the major emphasis.

At this very early stage in the development of group work in

[1] We have used the general phrase 'working with groups' or 'group work' rather than the more precise titles of 'social group work' (used in American schools of social work) or 'group therapy'. It is clear from even the Project's limited experience that the way in which the worker may use the group can vary widely. In a sense, all group experience is potentially therapeutic. In our view the essence of the distinction between group work and group therapy lies not in the setting of the group or the professional training of the worker, but in the emphasis which the former method places on improvement in the role performance of the members and the latter on the specific object of helping the members to deal with recognized sickness. We do *not* suggest that the setting of the group or the training of the worker are unimportant but that these are not the most fundamental elements in distinguishing between the two. In group work as contrasted with group therapy the object is not to deal with something specifically labelled as 'sickness' but to help the members towards *better* performance of their social roles and improvement in the relationships which the performance of these roles requires.

this country, however, we believe that it would be unwise to be dogmatic about the precise method to be employed. One of the most interesting points which arise from the Project experience is the diversity of approaches of the various workers and their advisers. The American principles of social group work certainly are carefully elaborated, well-documented, and based on an extensive body of practice. We ourselves are greatly indebted to Professor Wallace for his friendly help and teaching. However, an eclectic method is likely to prove the most useful approach in Great Britain at the present time.

For our advocacy of eclecticism in the development of group work in Britain there are two main reasons. The first lies in the difference between British and American culture; the second in the question of authority and control. The first is a sociological, the second a psychological, problem.

Readers of Whyte's *Organization Man* (1956, Chapters 25 and 26) will no doubt contrast the culture of the Chicago suburb of Park Forest with the social life of the housing estate in recent British studies. Whyte's emphasis on popularity among neighbours, on giving and receiving invitations to the best parties, on knowing the right people, and on belonging to the right groups, contrasts rather strangely with the British ideal of 'keeping oneself to oneself', of retreating from neighbourhood relationships, and of maintaining barriers to close and friendly communication among neighbours. Among adolescents on the delinquent fringe of society, the well-organized gang of *West Side Story*, typical of the underprivileged areas of the larger American cities, may be compared with the much looser group of Espressos. Group work must be related to the cultural background of the society in question. The readiness to join groups varies, not only from one country to another, but from class to class and from area to area. Housing estate studies have emphasized the difference in the characteristics of group membership on the estates as compared with some of the old slum areas of large cities.

The Project's experience in working with groups raises also the second question of authority and control. It is in the use of authority that the special skill of the professional group worker is to be found. So much is clear. But what kind of authority and what degree of control are to be exercised? The answer to this must depend not only on the setting of the work but also on the personality, training, and experience of the worker. There can be no single pattern. But a few general observations may be appropriate.

As regards the setting, group work will seldom take place in isolation. It may be inside an institution, such as a hospital, school, or prison, or in an ordinary residential area, in church hall, community centre, or youth club. A generally accepted pattern of control will be present in all these situations, and the group worker will be expected to work within the traditional framework.

Here the experience of the Project and other recent experiments are relevant. Readers of the group work described in Parts II and III will have noticed the contrast between the Espressos, the Mothers Group, and the Goslings Club. While working with the Espressos the group worker was the object of continual criticism and hostility, whereas with the Goslings she was regarded as a useful figure in the neighbourhood. Her own estimate of her work, however, was the very reverse of that of the neighbourhood – she regarded her work with the Espressos as the most important of the three groups.

It follows from this that the setting and the character of the group are particularly relevant to the question of authority and control. From her experience with the adolescents at Upfield, the group worker came to see that the methods used with the Toffs and Bums presupposed a measure of organization and control which made greater demands on the Bums than they were able to understand. The apparent freedom which she allowed the Espressos was the result of regular discussion with her psychiatric consultant. This freedom was misunderstood by the neighbourhood as licence. In actual fact there lay behind it a very clearly defined policy – the attainment of control of behaviour as an individual choice rather than as a response to the pressure of external authority.

Group work with the nonconforming minority requires very different methods of control from work with the majority who are able to conform to the demands of society because their early childhood experiences have given them no reason to be in conflict with it. With the majority of conformers the authority of the group worker differs little from the normal pattern of leadership. The group worker is an enabler or facilitator who helps the group members to achieve objectives and purposes towards which they can work.

But the capacity of groups to achieve objectives and purposes, and their ideas of what are appropriate objectives, vary considerably. The group worker's skill consists, among other things, in recognizing what their capacity is and in understanding the cultural background of their ideas. Some objectives are approved by the wider society, others are disapproved. A group which requires help to achieve its aim of a football team or a music circle is very different from the delinquent group for whom even a rock-and-roll session at which no one is hurt nor property damaged is a positive achievement.

The skilled group worker relates the degree of control which he uses to the capacity and level of understanding of the group. We may distinguish, moreover, between the authority of the worker analogous to that of the father-figure in a family, predominantly active in character, and to that of the mother-figure, more passive in her approach. The authority of the group worker in relation to the Espressos was largely that of the mother-figure.

THE GROUP, ITS WORK TASK, AND THE INDIVIDUAL

In Part II we suggested that the emphasis in group work could be placed on one of three aspects – the individual, the work task, or the group itself. It is dangerous to be categorical about where the primary emphasis should lie. In the first groups with which the two members of the Project team worked there were differences in method. Neither of the two workers was concerned primarily with the work task. In the case of the Mothers Group, for example, the group worker did not maintain the work task of the National Institute of Houseworkers, which was instruction in home management and housecraft. But whereas the group worker was concerned with the needs of the individual members of the group, the psychiatric social worker placed the emphasis mainly on the group itself. Admittedly the composition of her two groups was different in character; they were professional workers, teachers, and social workers.

The psychiatric social worker's object was to help the two groups of teachers and social workers to learn more about the here-and-now situation of the group of which they were members. But to reach this rather sophisticated stage is a long and slow process. The pace cannot be forced, and the group can learn only through its own efforts and mistakes. No amount of 'telling' on the part of the worker will produce the desired result.

Thus the final phases of both these groups were an attempt to move towards this stage of here-and-now learning. What did this mean in actual fact? In their initial stages both groups concentrated their attention mainly on what we have called the work task. For the Teachers Group this was the job of collecting information through a questionnaire. For the Social Workers Group it was the role of the ordinary advisory committee – advising the social worker of the Bristol Council of Social Service at Upfield as to the help required by cases who applied to her for assistance of various kinds.

In the course of the two groups, achievement of the work tasks became less and less important. The emphasis shifted twice – first to the ordinary process of learning through the method of the seminar, and second to the sharing of feelings associated with the various roles which the members performed in the course of their occupation. At that stage the groups began to adopt the method which is the very essence of this process, of looking frankly at the feelings associated with these roles and especially with their relationships with one other.

The experience of the Social Workers Group may be cited as an example. The social workers, as members of both voluntary and statutory bodies in Bristol, were conscious of certain underlying tensions between the two services and the effect of these on their own relationships with one another. The group was able, with the skilled help of the worker and in the mutual confidence which had gradually been built up through shared experience, to discuss freely the meaning of these tensions. After the episode of the 'minutes' (see page 128), for example, the group was able to look more closely at the implications of the differences in background among the members. The effect of such shared experience led in turn to greater confidence in the group in dealing with further problems. Unfortunately, it was at this point that the Project terminated and the worker had to withdraw from the group.

SOME PROBLEMS AND METHODS OF TRAINING

The opportunities for group work are far wider than the limited experiments carried out in the Project. The members of our groups were either living or working professionally at Upfield. Beyond group work with this kind of population, there are many other more specialized needs to be met, particularly in institutions of various kinds. The recent report of the Younghusband Committee (1959), one of the most important documents on the development and training of social workers, recommended the development of group work (and community organization) as part of social work training in such fields as centres for the physically handicapped, clubs for the mentally disordered, hostels for unmarried mothers, in the responsibilities of home-help organizers, and in the encouragement of many forms of voluntary help.

In considering the problem of training, there are certain essential matters to be kept in mind. The first is the relationship between theory and practice. The history of training for social work in this country points to the need for a close relationship between the two, in which the teaching of principles and the practical experience under a competent supervisor are planned and organized in a co-ordinated policy. A proliferation of small-scale experiments is not an adequate substitute for the development of a national policy in which universities, national voluntary bodies, and government departments ought to come together to work out a plan of training.

Perhaps the most satisfactory method will be under the auspices of a National Council of Social Work Training, as the Young-husband Committee has proposed. The question arises, however, whether such a body would provide training for the wide variety of fields in which the group work method is appropriate. Our own experience certainly points to the value of the group work method in youth work, and we are anxious to see provision made for the training of youth leaders in working with groups.[1] One important step in ensuring adequate representation of all the bodies concerned with youth leadership in the training process would be the setting up by the Ministry of Education of a Central Youth Leadership Training Council analogous to the Central Training Council in Child Care at the Home Office.

A second important consideration relates to what has been called the 'generic' nature of the social work method. By this is meant the common body of knowledge underlying the three specializations of casework, group work, and community organization. The basis of the social work process is the relationship between the worker and the individual, group, or community and the worker's skill in using that relationship constructively for the benefit of individual, group, or community, as the case may be.

'The fact that these distinctions exist in context and method, side by side with a fundamentally common purpose and the common assumptions and approaches of all social work, is a strong argument in favour of having both a common basic course of training and a subsequent more specialized course' (Kuenstler, 1956, p. 101). Training for group work will be most effective when it is grounded in this body of common assumptions about human needs and behaviour, and it is specious to see it as a technique that can be quickly learned. As in all professional social work

---

[1] As a result of the recommendations of the Albemarle Committee, a useful beginning has now been made in the provision of this training.

training, the opportunity which practical work under supervision provides for the student to gain some understanding of his motives and emotions is a *sine qua non* of the learning process.

We do not believe that the teaching resources available will enable more than a minority of workers to have this professional training, at least in the early years. Moreover, the co-operation of the voluntary social services in particular will be necessary in providing a number of appointments with appropriate salaries and conditions in which the trained group workers can make use of their training. This will require considerable reorganization of the existing structure of many of the services. It is not a method which can be imposed on a situation in which policy is directed to quite different aims and purposes.

We wish to emphasize the necessity for professional training and to recommend that the provision of adequate facilities should be regarded as an urgent matter deserving of the attention of departments of social work and education in the universities, of the appropriate national voluntary bodies and government departments, and, we hope, of the large trusts and foundations.

Shorter methods of training will also be required. It is at this point that the method adopted by the psychiatric social worker in the final phases of the Teachers and Social Workers Groups deserves careful study. For a number of years the Tavistock Institute of Human Relations has pioneered in the development of what it has come to entitle 'the study group method of training'. The principles are in many ways similar to those on which the psychiatric social worker based her work.[1] The value of this type of training depends largely on the skill and training of the consultant to the group. He is in fact a kind of group worker. *We should like to recommend that further work of this kind should be developed along*

[1] In Dr. Sutherland's words: 'The participant in a Study Group does not require prescriptions for "handling" others or for removing stress from group life. Stress is inseparable from group life and, indeed, has many positive functions in stirring people into necessary activity . . . At the same time there are benefits in a better appreciation of the nature and forces in groups. If those who have had the Study Group experience can learn to be more tolerant and understanding of the emotional aspects of the groups with which they work – and their own "personal equations" as members of those groups – they will be more likely to mobilize the positive forces which lie within them.'

the same lines. In our view the experience of the Tavistock Institute is of great potential value in the field of group work and of community organization.

COLLABORATION BETWEEN GROUP WORKER
AND FAMILY CASEWORKER

In the description of the Espressos we drew attention to the fact that we should have welcomed an opportunity for collaboration between group worker and family caseworker. Our experience with the Espressos in particular pointed to the need for a caseworker working in close collaboration with the group worker. The amount of contact which the group worker was able to have with the families of these underprivileged adolescents was severely limited. She was able to visit them only on those occasions when there was an obvious reason for the call, and the visit was generally on their terms – the worker came as an invited guest. The group worker learned from experience that even casual visits to inquire about the health of a member of the group who was sick often gave rise to strong feelings of jealousy and rivalry on the part of the others in the group. On occasions, such visits to an individual's home even led to the temporary exclusion of that member from the group.

Yet not every group will respond with such intense feelings of jealousy to individual visits. The Mothers Group, for example, showed less intense feelings of rivalry, though even there the worker wrote of the competition between mothers for her attention. Adolescents, in certain respects, are a special case and are at a stage in development when they resent the contact between group worker or youth leader and their parents. Such visits are often felt to be a threat to their desire for independence.

But there are other reasons for our advocacy of collaboration between group worker and family caseworker. Our study of the histories of Upfield families from all the case records which were made available to us confirms the conclusion *that, in spite of all the lip-service to the role of the family as one of the essential units in our society, in actual fact no social agency, whether voluntary or statutory, appeared ever to have worked with these families as a group.* Most of the workers had had contacts with particular members – father or mother, son or daughter – at particular times. But when the crisis had passed the contact was discontinued. No one had worked with the members of the Espresso families as family groups. All the work had been with individual members.

Perhaps no one could have done otherwise. Indeed, with such families on the very fringe of ordinary social relationships in society, collaboration with social agencies on none but their own terms is a notorious characteristic. It would be strange if it were not so. What we advocate is certainly family casework of an extremely difficult character, and it is wise to have modest expectations of what can be achieved. *Close contact between group worker and caseworker is of great potential value in strengthening the relationships of individuals in their family setting, at the same time as the experience of group membership with the worker's guidance helps the individual, adult or child, in dealing with his own problems.*[1]

THE ADOLESCENT GANG

Of the disturbing activities of the adolescent gang, the Teddy boy, the *Halbstarken*, or the 'Shook Up Generation', to use Harrison Salisbury's phrase, there is abundant evidence in the press of nearly every country in Europe and America – and increasingly in the industrialized areas of Asia. 'The gang is youth's last-ditch answer to adult pressures and conflicts far beyond juvenile powers of diagnosis or resolution.' In spite of the Romeo-and-Juliet legend of *West Side Story*, there is little romance to be found in its activity – it is more often the story of frustrated lives and restless and misdirected energy.

'Gangs', wrote Thrasher (1937) in a well-known study, 'represent the spontaneous efforts of boys to create a society where none

---

[1] The group workers and caseworkers on the staff of the Shoreditch Project (sponsored by the Nuffield Foundation) have worked concurrently with families, and also with some of their children, in therapeutic groups (see Halmos (Ed.), 1962).

adequate to their needs exists.' The gang is a struggle for recognition, an opportunity for gaining status in a society where status is continually denied. The worker's diary of the Espressos contains frequent references to the feelings of these boys and girls towards a world which seemed to reject and hate them. Outside the door of an Upfield public house the notice appeared: 'Teddy boys are requested not to use the saloon bar. They are only admitted to the public bar.' A polite notice, but one more reminder of society's attitude towards a group to which a stigma has become attached.

Side by side with this denial of status and opportunity for achievement has gone a rise in material standards and of wage rates, not only among the adolescents but in society generally. On all sides these young people are bombarded by the blandishments of television advertising, the glossy catalogues of the hire-purchase firms, and the attractive display of the shop windows. For the underprivileged boys and girls, however, at the bottom of the ladder, the consequences are disturbing. 'A permanent improvement in his social status is unlikely, and high wages will provide not security for tomorrow but pleasures for today. The carrot is there all right, and he may even get a nibble, but it may be snatched away at any moment' (Morris, 1959, p. 982).

Of the Espressos' behaviour towards society we have written earlier at some length. At this point we wish to emphasize the place of group work as one method of helping these adolescents. It is certainly not a panacea for social problems of great complexity and far-reaching consequences. Nothing could be more foolish than to see it as such. Nevertheless, our proposals are relatively new in this country. Certainly there is little in the way of specifically British experience to guide us, though there is a fair amount of American literature.[1]

This proposal rests on the assumption, which we believe the episode of the Espressos has clearly proved, that the orthodox youth club and the uniformed club fail conspicuously to cater for the underprivileged and for the emotionally deprived. This failure

[1] See References, Parts II and III, and especially the publications of the New York City Youth Board.

arises for many reasons but not least from the high standards which these clubs demand from their members. The Upfield Youth Club had a greater appeal for the Toffs than for the Bums. Only one of the Espressos was attracted by it.

The recommendation we make concerns these underprivileged adolescents on the delinquent fringe of society. They have been variously labelled as the 'unattached', the 'unclubbable', or the 'hard-to-reach'. Though outside the organized youth service, most of them are sociable people: the lonely or isolated children are few in number. *Our proposal is that there should, as a matter of considerable urgency, be serious and sustained experiments in appropriate methods of gaining contact with hard-to-reach youth.* In particular we recommend the appointment of 'street workers', that is of men (or women) trained in group work method, mature in personality, and well versed in the customs of Teddy-boy society who will be prepared to seek out these adolescents in their gangs, some large but the majority small in size, at the street corner, the dance hall, the fish-and-chip shop, or the cinema.

We do not underestimate the magnitude of this task, which calls for character and ability of a very high order. Initially, at least, offers of friendship and help will be met with hostility and suspicion, not only on the part of the adolescents but also from the neighbourhood. It will be wisest to institute small teams of workers under experienced leadership and with the support of an enlightened and understanding committee. These workers will need both the support of their colleagues and the backing of their committee.

The emphasis is on people rather than on buildings, and the first stage of any enterprise of this kind should be one of research, learning about the ages, habits, cultural background, and the haunts of these boys and girls. An estimate of the probable number of gangs at work in an area is also an essential preliminary task. We recall that in working with the Espressos the group worker faced her greatest difficulty from rival gangs. We should have liked to have a worker at the disposal of each of the gangs in the neighbourhood.

Buildings follow afterwards. In well-planned areas we hope that sites will have been left vacant for the erection of huts and halls. It is at this point that these vacant sites can be so useful, and the gang's own creative instincts employed in the preparation of the building. The well-known fact that we respect what we create for ourselves is abundantly true. Let the gang do as much of the building and the decorating as it can. Carefully designed and well-built huts provided from outside are less respected than property which is the result of hard work on the part of the user. Successive gangs, moreover, do not necessarily treat kindly the buildings created by their predecessors. How to formulate a flexible policy in which, as one committee member put it, 'oases of unstructured-ness' can be preserved is one of the most difficult problems facing the town-planner.

We doubt whether group work of this kind is a proper responsibility of the local authority at the present stage. But our proposal offers a great opportunity for a voluntary body to pioneer in a bold and imaginative manner. But first and foremost must come the search for suitable men and women, the planning of their training, and the possibility of a reasonable scale of payment for their labours. *We commend an experiment of this kind to the attention of a charitable trust or foundation.*

CHAPTER 16

Community Organization

ITS NATURE AND PURPOSE

ALTHOUGH the Project was never specifically called an experiment in community organization, there was nevertheless sufficient similarity between the basic ideas of action research in a local community and the process of community organization to justify discussion of the main issues. Yet we must be cautious in drawing conclusions from a single experiment. Circumstances differ, between town and country, between agricultural and industrialized societies, between one culture and another, and between areas of predominantly different social classes. Ross defines community organization as follows:

> . . . a process by which a community identifies its needs and objectives, orders (or ranks) these needs and objectives, develops the confidence and will to work at these needs or objectives, finds the resources (internal and/or external) to deal with these needs and objectives, takes action in respect of them, and in so doing extends and develops co-operative and collaborative attitudes and practices in the community (Ross, 1955, p. 39).

Basically the task of the social worker, whether with individual or family, group or local community, is the same – to help the clients to deal more effectively with their needs and problems. The 'essential feature of this process', in Ross's words, 'is the involvement of the community itself in determining the nature, method, and pace of change or innovation or reform'. The achievement of goals is of lesser importance than the process by which these goals are obtained, and the assessment of success or failure should not be made purely in terms of the goals which are achieved but rather by the growth in the community's ability for further work.

This process is related to our knowledge of social change. People will change their behaviour only if compelled to do so or if they have good reasons (good, that is, to themselves) for doing so. Since the use of force and compulsion is clearly excluded, the problem becomes one of conditions and ways in which this motivation for change is achieved. Many factors are relevant, such as the personality of community leaders, the nature and effectiveness of associations for securing community action, and the social structure of the local community itself. Nor can past success or failure in community activity be neglected. Ross emphasizes two distinctions, both of which are of particular importance in the case of the Bristol Project – the factors of time and of objectives – and contrasts work on which a strict time-limit has been placed with work to which no specified limitations of time apply.

The process of community organization is certainly a job for the trained worker, though at the present moment in this country – unlike North America – there is no professional training available. The role of community organizer is not an easy one to describe in precise terms, combining as it does so many different functions. The community organizer may assume in the course of his work such diverse roles as enabler, expert, guide, and social therapist. To some, indeed, he may appear to be the paragon of all virtues and they may ask whence such virtuous characters are to be recruited. To others the possibility of conflict or confusion between these roles may seem too great for such a diversity of functions to be assumed by a single worker.

As an example of the possibility of role conflict, the roles of enabler and social therapist may be quoted. In the role of enabler, the community organizer performs many daily tasks of a quite

302

simple kind, e.g. collecting building materials for a hall and digging the foundations, delivering chairs to a hall for a show, helping to distribute a local news-sheet from house to house, and so on.
As social therapist, on the other hand, he faces the much more
difficult decision of knowing the appropriate moment when to
refrain from giving straightforward and obvious assistance of this
kind and to place the responsibility for action on the members of
the community themselves.

To some extent in the Project these roles were divided, each
member performing a different function. Certainly there was a
division of responsibility between the members of the team and
their relationship with different sections of the estates. The sociologist worked with the Boltwood Community Association; the
enabler, with the Upfield Community Association; the Director,
with the two Community Councils; and so on. Whereas the two
Community Associations were organized by what we may call
indigenous or informal leaders, representation on the Community Councils was weighted largely in terms of professional or
formal leaders. Where community organization is the responsibility of a single worker, the possibility of conflict is correspond-
ingly greater.

The community organizer is in no way concerned to usurp the
legitimate political function, or to do things which properly are
the responsibility of local government. The very reverse is the
case: to help the elected members and the officials and to direct
people to use them when in need of help, and to encourage local
associations to make adequate use of the resources available. In this
capacity the community organizer works as a kind of local
'citizens' advice bureau'. But this function, though useful and important, remains a minor one. His main role is that of helping the
community to identify its needs and to take action in respect of
them.

The crucial question here is in the word 'needs'. Whose interpretation of needs is the yardstick – the worker's or the community's? The two interpretations will not necessarily be the
same. The situations, however, in which there is agreement and

disagreement will vary according to the circumstances. It is right that both parties should have their own values: the idea of neutrality over values on the part of the community organizer is as unreal as it is on the part of the caseworker or group worker. What is important is that the worker should not impose his scale of values on the community, but rather help the community to see its needs more clearly. Just as the psychiatrist does not *tell* the patient what he ought to want, but confines his role to that of giving his patient greater insight into his conscious but also – most important – his unconscious motives, so the community organizer carries out something of the same process, though at a simpler and more conscious level.

THE PROJECT'S EXPERIENCE OF COMMUNITY ORGANIZATION

In the first instance at least, Upfield's problems, or its 'stresses and strains' as these problems were called, were defined from outside, not inside. Though 'delinquency and other disturbances' were the problem which the Project had attributed to Upfield, the leaders of Upfield did not want help with what outsiders considered to be their 'problem' but rather help with other things. Either the 'problem' should be removed or, they felt, they should be allowed to forget about it.

Upfield identified its 'needs' as for such things as Meeting Rooms, the Adventure Playground, the newspaper, and the Goslings Club. None of these was wanted for its potential contribution towards help with stresses and strains, but in helping Upfield to get them the members of the Project team acted as community organizers: we were concerned as much with the *process* or method of achieving these objectives as with the achievement itself, believing that in this way the community would be better fitted to continue further after the withdrawal of the team.

We have emphasized the limitations placed on community organization by time and place. For the purpose of dealing with some of the more complex stresses and strains, those about which Upfield was most sensitive – delinquency, for example – the time-limit of five years set upon the Project was too short. We only began to reach this point towards the end of the period.

Throughout this discussion we have spoken of 'the community'. But who precisely is the community? In this section we use the term to signify the body of formal leaders known as the Community Council, and it must be said that the Project was indeed fortunate in finding such a body in existence at Upfield. Through the two Community Councils at Upfield and Boltwood the Project was able to communicate some of the observations which emerged from the team's work and also to make suggestions for social action. We give two examples:

(a) At Upfield the Director threw out casually to the Community Council the idea of holding an annual exhibition of local paintings. The idea was discussed with enthusiasm and the festival has now taken place for two summers. The Director was able to act as intermediary with the Head of the Royal West of England Academy, who agreed to come to judge the paintings. Apart from this, the Director took an active part in the organization of the exhibition, which was planned and arranged by members of the Upfield Community Council and by residents and workers on the estate.

(b) At Boltwood, towards the end of the Project, the sociologist talked with members of the Joint (Community) Council about their own method of work. He tried to show how they unconsciously switched their interest from the more important but less manageable problems to those which were easier to handle. The vigour with which the Joint Council had handled the problem of Boltwood Square was an important exception.[1] The consequence of the talk was an encouraging demonstration of the value of 'expert' diagnosis, and its effect was renewed interest and initiative by the Council in looking at its method of working and in pressing for better facilities for the large adolescent population on the estate.

[1] The Joint Council at Boltwood will be examined in Volume 2. The reference here is to the local controversy over the planning of a central open space on the Boltwood estate.

Conclusions and Recommendations for Social Policy

These examples illustrate two of the three senses of social change described earlier in this report. The first example (a) is an illustration of change in the first sense. The Director acted as an enabler, and in this instance in the simplest possible way, by suggesting a new activity for the Community Council and later by acting as intermediary with the appropriate local government department.

The second example (b) illustrates change in the second sense. The sociologist, by reporting to the Boltwood Council on his observations of their meetings and way of tackling their business, helped the group to look more closely at itself and to clarify its ideas on its objectives. At first there was resistance to his interpretation of what had taken place, but the vigour with which the Council subsequently applied itself to the current needs of adolescents at Boltwood indicated that the time taken up in self-examination had been well spent. This role of interpretation and examination of objectives is one which the sociologist is well equipped to perform.

SOCIAL PROBLEMS OF NEWLY DEVELOPED AREAS AND THE ROLE OF THE COMMUNITY ORGANIZER

There can be little doubt that community organization is a difficult process requiring training in social diagnosis as well as the ability to work with people. There is a real need for men and women entrusted with responsibility for community organization in areas which have been newly developed. The traditional policy of community centre wardens does not, in fact, meet the need. *The main weight of our proposal is on the flexibility of the worker's approach to the community, and we believe that it is unwise to tie the worker down to a specific building such as a community centre.*

How then might the role of such a worker be defined? He would have, as it were, a roving commission with responsibility for a particular area. His first task would be to learn about the social structure of the area, the occupation and social class of its inhabitants, their age structure, the size and composition of the

306

families, the proportion of old to young, and so on. Such information is an essential preliminary in the process of 'identifying needs', which we have defined as the first step in community organization. Side by side with this will go an analysis of community resources, not only in terms of buildings, but also in terms of the characteristics and activities of groups and associations and their officers.

So much by way of what we may call the formal analysis. The next stage in diagnosis is more difficult and consists of an identification of the needs of the community in less precise and measureable terms, a personal knowledge not only of the formal leaders (the leaders by status, as we have also called them in this report) but also of informal leaders, and of the social problems of the area. The Project experience has taught us to be as alert to those concealed stresses about which little is said as to the obvious stresses on which everyone is vocal and frequently hostile; for example, to the adults and children who suffer in silence as well as to the vandals and the delinquents.

For this task the earlier discussion of action research is relevant. The community organizer should distinguish clearly between the three kinds of change. His role will be different in each case. For the third kind of change – a change in the community's emotional attitudes to stress, particularly to stress in the form of delinquency and destructive behaviour – it is important for him to make use of the group work method, and to give special attention to the structure of the groups in which hostile feelings are worked out. The community organizer, in helping to facilitate change of this third kind, has the difficult role of interpretation – he is an interpreter between the respectable leading citizens and the delinquents and, as such, he must resolve the difficult problem of avoiding over-identification with either group.

His role of interpreter, however, can be seen in a context wider than that of the local community. He has the task also of facilitating communication and acting as interpreter between officers at the city centre and in the locality. He is, in Brooke Taylor's (1959, p. 148) phrase, a 'lubricator of the body politic'. This task calls for tact as well as insight. Here also the difficulty of avoiding over-identification with one party or the other arises.

FRAMEWORK OF COMMUNITY ORGANIZATION

By whom should the community organizer be employed – by the local authority or by a voluntary association? What size of area should he cover? Should certain kinds of neighbourhood be given priority, such as neighbourhoods with a particularly high incidence of stress and strain?

In the New Towns the Social Development Officer, whose function is in many respects similar to that of the community organizer, is a member of the New Town Corporation. His task of social development is closely linked with that of public relations, and the Public Relations Officer of Hemel Hempstead has written most interestingly about this work (Taylor, ibid.) In the newly developed areas of large cities, particularly the housing estates, some measure of decentralization will be necessary. The combination of community organization, moreover, with public relations is less appropriate here. In cities with a Council of Social Service this combination of functions could most usefully be performed by a voluntary body – as was formerly the case in Bristol – for which a grant from the local authority would be necessary.

Some of the simpler functions of community organization are already performed in certain estates by the area officers of the Housing Department, called Resident Agents, each of whom is responsible for Corporation housing in a sector of the city. The Resident Agent, for example, in the sector of Bristol in which Boltwood is situated has been chairman of the Boltwood Joint (Community) Council. At Upfield the Resident Agent was treasurer of the Upfield Youth Club and took a keen interest in the old people's homes.

Nevertheless, the role of community organizer, as we have defined it, demands a more specialized training and includes a wider range of functions than a busy housing official can reasonably be expected to perform. Community organization, to be effective,

308

requires an administrative framework which enables the worker to maintain close relationships both with the appropriate departments of the local authority and with voluntary associations of various kinds. This we regard as essential, and any pattern of administration must make this close relationship possible. We commend the pattern of the Bristol Youth Committee, consisting of elected members of the Council, of representatives of the voluntary organizations, and of individuals interested in work with young people. The secretary of this committee is an officer of the Local Education Authority responsible for the development and organization of youth work in the city. *We recommend that an analogous administrative framework for the work of the community organizer deserves careful attention.*

In the city, the community organizer's function is certainly *not* to 'build community', in the sense in which that phrase is frequently used. It is rather to recognize the interdependence of neighbourhoods and the specialization of interests. Certain activities, such as mothers' and young children's groups, very properly belong to the local community. But others, such as special interest groups or sports clubs, draw their members from a much wider area. It is important, therefore, to delineate the areas for which the community organizer is responsible in such a way that people are helped to cross the boundaries of their immediate locality and thus to extend the range and scope of their social relationships. In terms of population, however, there is a limit to the amount of work which the organizer can do, and a maximum of 30,000 or 40,000 seems to be essential.

In the foreseeable future, however, and with present resources, population limits are unrealistic. The more important question relates to priorities as to areas. So far in our argument we have assumed that it is the newly developed communities which have priority, and this in effect has implied housing estates and New Towns. But why should publicly owned housing receive priority? Are not privately developed areas also of importance? And what constitutes new development? Is it, for example, the first ten years in the life of an area? There is certainly abundant evidence from the literature on estates to show that the pattern of local activity alters in the course of time. The tenants' association, born as the result of a movement of protest against inadequate amenities, changes in character as these amenities become available.

One answer lies in the character of the housing estate population. Housing estates in the past tend to have drawn their residents from the poorer income groups, though we should not assume that this is a static position.[1] As social work with individuals originated from a concern for the underprivileged, so also it was the underprivileged neighbourhoods which became the main focus of the social movements such as the Settlement, which may be described as the forerunners of the more modern concept of community organization.

It is, however, in our view, a serious mistake to regard the community organizer as appropriate only for newly developed estates or for areas which contain a high concentration of stresses and strains. We will recall that Upfield felt self-conscious over the Project's attention. The work of the community organizer will be more effective if it is not tied down exclusively to poorer and underprivileged areas. *Priorities indeed there must be, but it would be wise to see community organization as an important adjunct to the ordinary process of healthy social living rather than as a predominantly remedial community service.*

TRAINING

Outstanding in the conclusions and recommendations arising from the Project's experience in community organization is the need for training. Enough has been said to indicate that the role of the

[1] See, for example, the figures contained in the Report of the Bristol Housing Authority, 1 April 1956–31 March 1958:

Income Group	31 *March* 1956	31 *March* 1958
£9 or under	16,730	12,506
£9–£10	4,725	3,641
£10–£11	4,125	4,249
£11–£12	3,118	4,201
£12–£13	1,958	3,395
over £13	3,039	9,174

community organizer is neither simple nor easily learned and makes considerable demands on the skill of its practitioners. *We should like to recommend the development of courses of training sponsored by universities in collaboration with national bodies with responsibility in this field.* A curriculum in which theoretical teaching is closely integrated with practical experience is essential, and the experience gained from training courses for community centre wardens and neighbourhood workers provides a useful beginning to the training of community organizers.

It is particularly encouraging, therefore, to find that the Younghusband Report (1959) made several references to the need for training in this branch of social work. The Committee comments on the fact that of the three kinds of social work – casework (social work with individuals), group work, and community organization – so far only casework has begun to reach a satisfactory stage of development in this country. They recommend the teaching of community organization and of group work at the proposed National Staff College. Training in community organization, they suggest, would be valuable to officers with administrative responsibilities in enabling them to identify unmet or inadequately met social needs, and to help to mobilize local community resources to meet these needs (ibid., para. 629).

CHAPTER 17

The Project's Experience of Action Research

THE small group of Bristol's leading citizens who made plans for the Project described herein embarked on a social experiment of which existing knowledge was slight and the course ill-charted. There were many sceptics both in public life and within the universities who doubted the wisdom of linking together research and action. It was, therefore, a bold decision on the part of the Carnegie Trustees to respond so generously to the proposals.

LESSONS LEARNED

Clarity of Purpose as to the Level of Operation of the Project

In retrospect it is clear that there was, in the early stages at least, a variety of opinions as to the precise level at which the Project was expected to operate. Some members of the committees and also of the team favoured a predominantly social interpretation. The initial sketch for a social experiment had aimed at 'a higher quality of community life and a greater readiness to undertake such activities as fall within the capacity of local leadership and local initiative'. The marks of success, it was hoped, would include an initial readiness on the part of Corporation committees and administrators to

312

encourage local initiative, an improvement in the 'feel' or atmosphere and an increase in the local pride of the community in question, and an increasing readiness on the part of administrators, local social workers, and residents to make their needs and problems articulate.

Others, among them the Director, sought the main emphasis in the terms of reference 'to establish practical means of tackling those stresses and strains which arise in such a community in the form of delinquency and other disturbances'. The second emphasis was on relationships and was predominantly psychiatric in its implications.

The history of the Project may be seen as an experiment in transition from the first to the second objective. We concentrated at first on those functions which were simple and relatively straightforward in their object, such as the building of the Meeting Rooms, help in the creation of an Adventure Playground, the publication of an estate newspaper at Upfield, and then moved on to the more complicated – and controversial – work with groups, such as the Espressos, where the object was less easy to understand. Emphasis shifted from change in the sense of better social facilities and a greater understanding of public affairs (what we have called change in the first and second senses, see Chapter 2) towards a deeper knowledge of stresses and strains and of the quality of social relationships. To have plunged right at the outset into problems of relationships would have confused and disappointed the expectations of Bristolians connected with the Project. They were looking for tangible and overt, rather than intangible and concealed, results. The demand was for concrete plans for social action, and the Director was continually told in the early months that his statement of objectives was insufficiently related to a practical and clearly defined programme of social action.

The transition from one level to another is inevitably slow and many doubts and conflicts of opinion are bound to arise. We say this deliberately, to emphasize the inevitable diversity of expectations and the apparent slowness of the pace of action research.

The Relationship between Local Communities and the Political and Administrative Centre of the City

It is a common assumption of local community projects that the primary focus of attention is the local community itself, and the strengthening of 'local initiative' and 'local leadership' was one of the main objectives in Mack's sketch for a social experiment. Our experience during the Project compels us to examine very critically the validity of this assumption. The whole argument of the Neighbourhood Study (Volume 2) has been to question the idea of the local community and to see neighbourhood relationships within the wider framework of the city. Local policy is closely bound up with central policy, and decisions taken at the centre have important consequences for the locality. Health, education, whether formal or informal, housing, town planning, and parks, are dependent on policy formulated at the centre of the city, influenced by decisions taken *in camera* by a party caucus, and administered by officers of the local authority. Thus the scope of action research in the purely neighbourhood context, especially of the housing estate, is strictly limited. *To effect change at the level of the neighbourhood it is necessary to begin work at the centre of the city.*

One of the major lessons of the Project was the Director's failure to take adequate account of this principle during the initial planning and diagnostic phase (Stage I). His early contacts were mainly with the senior administrators of the city's services and with the formal leaders of Upfield and Boltwood. But he failed to establish any working relationship with city councillors beyond the six members appointed at one time or another to the Project committee. The consequences of this mistake are best illustrated by the events in Stage II leading up to the appointment of the psychiatric social worker. The plan for close collaboration between this worker and the Maternity and Child Welfare Clinic serving the Upfield area encountered strong resistance from the City Council, expressed formally through a committee decision. It is difficult to say whether the feeling behind this decision was a general one, shared by the City Council as a whole, or was a feeling primarily of the party in power.

The manifest reason for this resistance was the belief that confidential matters should not be shared with workers not responsible to the local authority. But there were also certain latent feelings and opinions that deserve mention.

First and foremost, perhaps, was the view that certain housing estates had received an unfair share of attention and publicity, particularly in the press, and should be left undisturbed by the interference of a team of social scientists. There was a desire to protect the Upfield families from the kind of inquiry which the psychiatric social worker would be trained to make.

There were other attitudes which lay behind many of the arguments used: a suspicion of the social scientist as someone intent on searching for skeletons in a cupboard without producing any very obvious or tangible benefits in return, and a feeling that as a voluntary body the team was not directly responsible to the citizens of Bristol through their elected representatives. By some the team was seen as prying into other people's affairs.

These attitudes were strongly held, and a series of meetings between the Director and some of the Executive Committee with leading councillors, though useful in bringing about greater understanding, did not in fact dispel many of the fears about the Project's aims. The outcome of these discussions was a change of plan by the medical sub-committee of the Project Executive and the decision to use the psychiatric social worker in a purely research role working in parallel with the sociologist on the Families Research.

We quote this experience as an illustration of a general principle which the Project has clarified. *Action research in the neighbourhood, if it is to be of maximum value, must be related to the pattern of civic policy-making and administration in a thoroughly acceptable way.*

The Strength and Weakness of Delinquency as the Initial Problem

In Chapter 2 we emphasized the fact that action research is essentially problem-centred. It starts from the 'problem' about which the community is anxious and needs help. In some ways juvenile delinquency fulfils this criterion admirably. The local committees on juvenile delinquency, set up by many local authorities in England and Wales as a result of the invitation from the Home Secretary and the Minister of Education, produced a number of very useful results. But as a starting-point for an action research project the value of delinquency is open to argument.

Let us state as baldly as possible some of the conflicting attitudes about criminal and delinquent behaviour which we experienced at Upfield. First, is the mixture of indifference and inferiority on the part of the delinquents themselves. Some can see no point in the fuss and bother that occurs: 'We have to live somewhere, leave us alone in peace.' Others are acutely aware of a sense of rejection, and the Espressos were frequently puzzled by the group worker's continued work with them: 'Why come to Upfield to work with us?' They were determined to live up to their bad reputation. Second, is the hostility of residents who suffer at their hands: 'Why does the local authority send these families to Upfield? Why can't they be sent elsewhere? Why must we get more than our fair share of the trouble?' They deal with this difficulty either by pleading for the removal of the delinquents, or else by applying for a transfer for themselves to another area: 'The quicker I can get myself out of this place, the better.' Third, is the attitude of denial: 'This estate isn't as bad as it is painted.' 'It doesn't deserve this reputation.' 'The majority have to suffer for a minority.' 'We are trying to build up a good reputation and only want to be left alone and not reminded of our delinquent minority.'

This, briefly, was the background of social attitudes to juvenile delinquency. The Project's approach – 'We must learn about the roots of delinquency and take positive action towards the delinquent: rejection and hostility only make the problem more difficult' – was an unpopular attitude. The group work with the Espressos is an example of how perplexing and threatening the worker's acceptance of their behaviour appeared to the neighbourhood.

But more important was the stigma which some leaders of Upfield felt at having the attention of the Project directed at their estate. In spite of our emphasis on the 'strengthening of growing points' and the shift in focus from delinquency *per se* to strains and stresses in family and neighbourhood, the anxiety about stigma remained and was certainly increased by the ever-present risk of press publicity. Inquiry into behaviour at Upfield was always likely to be news; the 'strengthening of growing points' was not.

The Relationship between Publicity and Research as a Barrier to Coincidence of Intentions and Achievement

The Director came to recognize towards the end of the Project, when the distinction between the three kinds of social change was being clarified, that to have the greatest possibility of effecting change *in the third sense* it would have been better had there been no publicity of any kind of the existence of a Project or of a grant from the Carnegie Trust; no public commitment to the publication of a report; no social or psychiatric research programme (such as the Families Research) built into the Project; a director with more clinical experience.

The plea for informality in the structure of groups associated with an action-research project and for an absence of public scrutiny is grounded in quite clear principles. The object is to secure conditions in which spontaneous – not imposed – change can occur and in which resistances to change can be worked through. The fear of publicity, the apprehension aroused by a future publication, and the entrenchment of defensive positions on the part of groups whose security seems to be threatened are none of them conditions that facilitate success. By highlighting some of the situations in which the Bristol Project found itself, and the lessons learned through past mistakes, the lines of future policy may perhaps emerge more clearly.

RECOMMENDATIONS FOR ACTION RESEARCH IN THE FUTURE

The Level of Working

The confusion most likely to arise is about the level of working in an action-research project. Participants will hold very different expectations as to the nature of the change which is intended. In our view, the term 'action research' should be applied only to change in the third sense. But it is necessary for the professional team right at the outset to make this clear to the clients employing its services.

The process of clarification will be long and slow, but it is an essential first step in any operation. The visible and tangible signs of change will be, for the clients, the test of achievement; the professional team, however, will assess achievement by such criteria as greater self-awareness and sensitivity to the social and emotional forces at work in social relationships.

For this reason the scale of the Project should be small, based on intensive work with small groups rather than extensive work in a large area. The intensity of the work varies inversely with the scale of the project.

The Initial Introduction of the Professional Team

At this level of working there will need to be a clear definition of the roles of the professional team and the laymen. The motive for action research should be: 'We should like to employ you to help us in dealing with our social problems' not 'Come and deal with our social problems for us'. Dr. Turquet (1949) rightly emphasized the weakness of the 'knights in shining armour' role of action-research committees. Committees themselves must be involved in the process of change. The task of introduction is itself a long one. Society is pleased to have a doctor for its sick, its nonconformists, and its delinquents, but it is less willing to accept the idea that the doctor's help is also useful at the preventive stage.

Action research, if it deserves the name, is a process which severely tests the commitment of its participants. Nothing less than the spontaneous wish of people to take part in a project is adequate. There must be freedom to withdraw at all stages. Moreover, the nature of action research is such that no entirely adequate explanation of what is involved can be given at the outset. It is a process in which the participants learn by experience. Much of the experience is

318

painful, and there is certainly no short-cut to the attainment of the
objective. The closest analogy is to the process of psychotherapy,
of which the therapist cannot give the patient an adequate explanation at the outset.

Hence the emphasis on the significance of problem-solving in
action research. Without a problem giving rise to stresses and
strains there is unlikely to be a patient asking for help. But the
professional team are not magicians able to remove the problem:
what they can do is to help the client to understand it and in this
way to come to terms with it.

Who is the Client?

The initial demand for an action-research project is likely to come
from individuals who already have some understanding of the
value of the process. As a way in, this is indeed feasible, but it is
no more than a method of entry. The basis of the project is not a
series of unrelated individuals but the group. The assumption of
change is based on knowledge which we possess of change in
group attitudes and its effect on the individual members of the
group.

In action research the client is the patient. By saying this we
certainly reverse the natural order of things. The ordinary temptation is to call in the experts to deal with someone else, rather than
with ourselves, and to cast the experts in the role of missionaries in
the foreign land. But the foreign land, especially if it is a so-called
'delinquency area', doesn't want the missionaries, even if they come
bearing gifts to win over the natives to their side. It distrusts their
motives and resents their interference, believing that they would
employ their time better in converting the people who sent them.

The first task, therefore, is how to induce the client to seek the
help of the professional. *Unless this help is willingly sought (in the
jargon of the trade – unless the client is motivated to seek help), the professional meets with resistance and hostility and the process of change
becomes more difficult.* As Tom Sawyer was astute enough to recognize when faced with the laborious task of whitewashing his

aunt's fence, the job had to be presented to the other boys passing by in the street so as to look attractive.[1]

Where to Begin?

A major weakness of delinquency as the focus of action research, in spite of its many uses, is the position of the delinquent at the bottom of the power structure in society. Delinquent groups in British society, in contrast to the Mafia in Sicily, have little power. They are commonly rated low in social status and their control over public affairs is of little consequence.

Our Bristol experience led us to emphasize the principle of *starting at the top rather than at the bottom of the power structure and of working most closely at the start of a project with those who are in positions of authority in the society.* Social policy is influenced more effectively by those at the top than by those at the bottom of the ladder and, conversely, opposition to change from those at the top may lead to stronger resistance.

It follows from this that the understanding of the top policy-makers constitutes the initial phase, and that failure to secure a measure of consensus at this level will give rise to obstacles at a later stage.

The Ethics of Action Research

By contrast with conventional social research, special questions of ethics are involved in action research. The position of the team in relation to the client in action research is in many respects analogous to the relationship of doctor and patient. The client discloses certain confidential information as part of the process of change – a problem, for example, on which help is required. He expects his confidence to be respected.

The medical profession has developed a strict and elaborate code of ethics to deal with this and other ethical problems and the code

---

[1] Twain (1924, p. 21): 'Tom said to himself that it was not such a hollow world after all. He had discovered a great law of human action without knowing it, namely, that, in order to make a man or a boy covet a thing, it is only necessary to make the thing difficult to attain.'

is supported by a long tradition. Action research, on the other hand, has no such professional code. Its ethics have grown up piecemeal. One of the consequences of the Bristol Project has been the highlighting of the difficulties which arise for a team of social workers and sociologists who have to work out for themselves their own code to meet the particular situation.

There is a strong case, we believe, in any future project for careful planning between client and professional team along the lines adopted by the Tavistock Institute in the Glacier Metal Project. But action-research teams are not always employed directly by the client, as was the case at Glacier Metal, and the situations which may arise in a community setting are in some respects more complex than those in a single industrial firm.

Quis Custodiet?

The problem of ethics is closely related to the responsibility of the team. Where does the responsibility lie, with the team or with the client? It is important to be clear about the respective spheres of responsibility. Action research is certainly not a method of shifting responsibility to the expert working in a confidential relationship with the client. Nothing could be more dangerous in public affairs. Nor is the team introduced to strengthen the arm of a particular group, for example, a political party.

In the Glacier Metal Project the Tavistock team was most concerned that its services should not appear to the trade union members of the Works Council as an additional bargaining weapon for the management. The process of working through this issue was one of the earliest tasks in its project. In a project concerning the public life of a city it is essential that the team members should avoid any suggestion of political bias in their work. Their responsibility is to the academic discipline of which they are members. They are not a group of wirepullers or manipulators. This responsibility deserves to be made abundantly clear. An earlier suggestion that *the team's main responsibility to the client is to clarify the issues for the client, not to make decisions as to the policy to be carried out*, makes it easier for the team to fulfil a detached role.

But is the social scientist's advice worth having? The proof of this lies in the team's value to the client. Action research has still a long way to travel and a good deal of scepticism to overcome, but we are certainly confident that it is a method which justifies continued experiment. Apart from the Tavistock Institute there is no means of giving training to the worker, and the shortage of trained workers is a serious gap. Experience, moreover, has taught us that academic knowledge by itself is insufficient without a thorough acquaintance with the practical issues concerned in the field of study. Both social scientist and layman alike still have much to learn in ways of communicating with each other.

APPENDICES

APPENDIX I *Organization of the Project Main and Executive Committees*

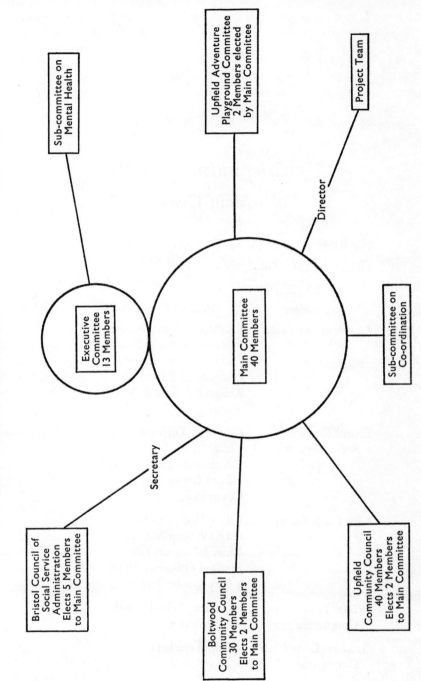

APPENDIX II

Composition of the Project Main Committee

The Right Honourable the Lord Mayor of Bristol
The Vice-Chancellor, University of Bristol

Body or Interest Represented	Status of Representatives	Remarks
University of Bristol	Lecturer in Social Studies	
	Professor of Child Health	
	Professor of Economics	
	Professor of Education	Chairman of
	Research Fellow in Youth Work	Executive
Bristol Council of Social Service	Company Director	Chairman
	Vicar	
	Community Advisory Officer	
	School Bursar	
	Councillor	
City Corporation	City Children's Officer	
	City Housing Manager	
	Chief Education Officer	
	Medical Officer of Health	
	4 City Councillors	
Bristol Youth Committee	Secretary, Bristol Youth Committee	
Teachers Consultative Committee	2 school teachers	

Churches	1 representative of each denom-ination nominated by: Church of England Bishop Roman Catholic Bishop President of the Free Church Council Bristol Council of Christian Churches Bristol Hebrew Congregation
City Constabulary	Chief Constable
Magistrates	Chairman, Juvenile Court
Women's Organizations	Housewife
Probation Committee	Chairman, Probation Committee
Co-opted Members	Director, Bristol Child Guidance Clinic Principal Probation Officer Warden, University Settlement Vicar of Upfield Vicar of Boltwood 2 representatives from Upfield 2 representatives from Boltwood
Secretary	The General Secretary of the Bristol Council of Social Service

APPENDIX III

Composition of the Project
Executive Committee

Professor of Education (Chairman)
Professor of Child Health
University Research Fellow in Youth Work
Lecturer in Social Studies
School Bursar
Company Director
City Housing Manager
City Councillor
Secretary, Bristol Youth Committee
Chairman, Juvenile Court
Warden, University Settlement
Medical Officer of Health
Director, Bristol Child Guidance Clinic

In attendance

Project Director
Project Secretary

APPENDIX IV

The Project Team

Post	Previous Experience	Dates of Employment
Director	Graduated in Modern Greats at Oxford and received a Social Science Certificate from the London School of Economics. Probation Officer, Surrey. Magistrate, Metropolitan Juvenile Courts. Lecturer in Social Science at the London School of Economics.	Oct. 1953–Sept. 1958
Secretary	Social Science Certificate, Liverpool.	Oct. 1953–Aug. 1955
Sociologist	Graduated in Sociology at the London School of Economics. Research at Leeds University into a Yorkshire mining community, published as *Coal is Our Life.*	Sept. 1954–Sept. 1958
Field worker	Hardware roundsman. Youth worker. Chairman of the International Club, Bristol Folk House.	Sept. 1954–March 1957
Field worker on the Families Research	Graduated in Moral Sciences at Cambridge; followed by Social Science Certificate at the London School of Economics.	Dec. 1954–Feb. 1956

Social worker (part-time)	Children's Aid Society in Canada. Graduated at the Toronto School of Social Work.	Jan. 1955–June 1956
Field worker	Graduated externally at London University. Colonial Administrative Service and later Community officer, Bristol Council of Social Service.	April 1955–Aug. 1955
Adventure Playground leader	Youth leader at the Barge Boys' Club and the Redvers Club, Hoxton. Trained in Youth Leadership at University of Wales, Swansea.	May 1955–June 1957
Secretary	Whitehall Secretarial College, Eastbourne.	Sept. 1955–Sept. 1958
Group worker	Youth worker in East End and Central London. Warden, Children's Neighbourhood Settlement, Social Welfare Department, Municipality of Tel-Aviv-Jaffa. Studied for one year at the London School of Economics.	Dec. 1955–April 1958
Psychiatric social worker engaged mainly on the Families Research	Read Sociology at the London School of Economics. Later returned to take a Certificate in Mental Health. Social worker at the Belmont Rehabilitation Unit.	Nov. 1956–Sept. 1958

APPENDIX V

The Responsibilities of Individual Team Members

————————— Groups to which team members belonged
—··—··—··—··— Groups with which team members came into contact
························· Groups with which team members worked

DIRECTOR
- Main Committee
- Executive Committee
- Upfield Community Council
- Boltwood Community Council
- Upfield Adventure Playground Committee
- Teachers Group
- Social Workers Group
- Meeting Rooms Management Committee
- Goslings Club Committee

SOCIOLOGIST
- Boltwood Community Council
- Boltwood Community Association and Committee
- Boltwood Youth Club and Management Committee
- Ward Labour Party
- Families through Families Research
- Individuals through living on estates
- Boltwood Football Team
- An Upfield Rugby Team
- Jehovah's Witnesses
- Toc H
- St. Paul's and St. Nicholas's Churches
- Tenants Protection Association

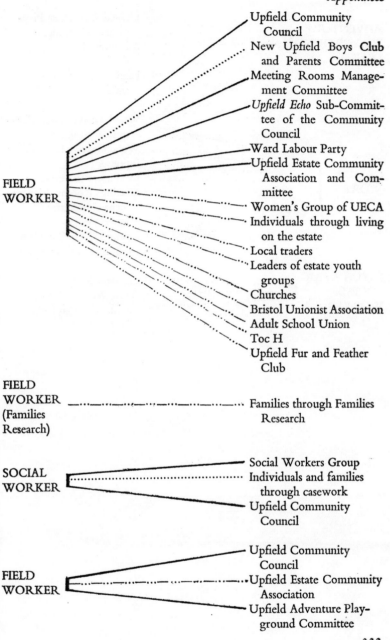

FIELD
WORKER

- Upfield Community Council
- New Upfield Boys Club and Parents Committee
- Meeting Rooms Management Committee
- *Upfield Echo* Sub-Committee of the Community Council
- Ward Labour Party
- Upfield Estate Community Association and Committee
- Women's Group of UECA
- Individuals through living on the estate
- Local traders
- Leaders of estate youth groups
- Churches
- Bristol Unionist Association
- Adult School Union
- Toc H
- Upfield Fur and Feather Club

FIELD
WORKER
(Families
Research)

- Families through Families Research

SOCIAL
WORKER

- Social Workers Group
- Individuals and families through casework
- Upfield Community Council

FIELD
WORKER

- Upfield Community Council
- Upfield Estate Community Association
- Upfield Adventure Playground Committee

333

ADVENTURE
PLAYGROUND
LEADER
— Upfield Adventure Playground Committee
— Adventure Playground children
— Families of Playground children

GROUP
WORKER
— Wood Grove Club Committee
— Wood Grove Club children
— Espressos
— Families of the Espressos
— Meeting Rooms Management Committee
— Mothers Group
— Goslings Club Committee
— Goslings and their mothers

PSYCHIATRIC
SOCIAL
WORKER
— Teachers Group
— Social Workers Group
— Families through Families Research

APPENDIX VI

Some Social Characteristics of the Estates
(compared with Bristol Wards)

Gross population

UPFIELD	12,000 (Old Upfield: 7,000; New Upfield: 5,000)
BOLTWOOD	4,000
MOUNT VIEW	11,000

Housing

UPFIELD—commenced in 1931, under the Acts of 1923-24, *not* the 1930 Act— i.e. started as 'housing shortage', *not* 'slum clearance' estate. More than half the houses were built before the 1933 Act put an end to any building but slum clearance building. Therefore pre-war UPFIELD is highly unusual (for Bristol) in that half the houses are respectable 'housing shortage' and half are 'slum clearance'. UPFIELD is composed of 1,500 pre-war houses (820 'housing shortage', 670 'slum clearance'), and 1,100 post-war houses.

BOLTWOOD—entirely post-war (built at the same time as post-war UPFIELD: 1946-53), 1,100 houses.

Distribution of the Registrar General's 'Social classes' in BOLTWOOD and UPFIELD, compared with some Bristol wards (1951 wards)

Percentage of population (males, occupied and retired) falling into Social Classes I and II		Percentage of population (males, occupied and retired) falling into Social Class V	
Redland	38	Windmill Hill	28
St. Michael's	31	**Upfield**	27
Bishopston	23	St. Paul	25
St. James	16	**Mount View**	20
Mount View	14	**Boltwood**	16
St. George E.	12	St. James	16
Windmill Hill	12	St. George E.	14
St. Paul	9	St. Michael's	8
Boltwood	7	Bishopston	6
Upfield	4.5	Redland	4
(cf. Bristol	17%	(cf. Bristol	15%
England and Wales 18%)		England and Wales 13%)	

Household structure: percentage of the population living alone

Clifton	10	Windmill Hill	4
St. Michael's	9	Eastville	3
Redland	8	Knowle	3
St. Augustine's	8	St. George E.	3
Mount View	6	Bedminster	2
District	6	Stapleton	2
St. James	6	Brislington	2
Redcliffe	6	Hillfields	2
St. Paul	5	Westbury	2
St. George W.	5	Somerset	2
St. Philip and Jacob N.	4	Avon	1
Southville	4	Horfield	1
Easton	4	Hengrove	1
St. Philip and Jacob S.	4	**Upfield**	0.6
Durdham	4	**Boltwood**	0.2
Bishopston	4		

Ages: BOLTWOOD and UPFIELD compared with some Bristol wards with regard to percentage of population aged 0-14

Boltwood	46	**Mount View**	20
Upfield	38	St. George E.	20
Hengrove	30	Bishopston	18
Westbury	28	Southville	18
Horfield	25	Windmill Hill	18
Somerset	24	St. James	16
St. Paul	22	Redland	15
Bedminster	21	St. Michael's	15
		Redcliffe	12

(cf. England and Wales 22%; Bristol 23%)

Sex distribution: BOLTWOOD and UPFIELD compared with the wards of Bristol with regard to percentage of males in the population

Brislington	51	Hillfields	47
Boltwood	51	Eastville	47
Upfield	50	**Mount View**	46
Avon	49	St. Augustine	46
St. George W.	48	Easton	46
Hengrove	48	Westbury	46
Bedminster	48	Horfield	45
Somerset	48	St. Philip and Jacob N.	45
Redcliffe	48	Bishopston	44
Southville	48	St. Michael's	42
Knowle	48	St. James	42
District	48	Durdham	41
St. George E.	48	Stapleton	39
Windmill Hill	47	Redland	38
St. Paul	47	Clifton	36

The distribution of the six main occupational groups in UPFIELD, Bristol, and England and Wales as a percentage of males in all Occupational Orders is as follows:

				UPFIELD %	Bristol %	England and Wales %
	Largest	occupational	group	20.8	14.8	14.2
2nd	,,	,,	,,	14.5	13.9	12.1
3rd	,,	,,	,,	12.0	11.5	8.8
4th	,,	,,	,,	11.4	8.7	7.8
5th	,,	,,	,,	4.9	7.0	7.0
6th	,,	,,	,,	3.7	6.7	5.9

Persons registered as mentally deficient in Bristol 13 January 1954— rate per 100,000 of the population

Old **Upfield**	614	St. George East	237
Upfield (Old and New)	428	St. George West	225
St. Paul	559	District	221
St. Philip and Jacob S.	553	Knowle	207
St. Augustine	522	Brislington	207
Windmill Hill	472	Redcliffe	195
Hengrove	440	Avon	193
St. Philip and Jacob N.	424	Stapleton	188
Easton	333	Horfield	185
Hillfields	312	Bedminster	183
Somerset	297	St. Michael's	180
Eastville	252	Clifton	143
Westbury-on-Trym	249	Redland	138
St. James	247	Bishopston	118
Southville	239	Durdham	80

Truancy cases brought before the Court, 1952-53, per 100,000
of the population aged 0-14

Upfield	1,284	Brislington	219
Hengrove	938	District	212
Boltwood	834*	St. George E.	199
Westbury	470	St. Philip and Jacob S.	177
Somerset	456	Avon	158
St. Paul	374	Easton	154
Redcliffe	350	St. George W.	153
Southville	309	Horfield	135
St. Michael's	285	Clifton	122
St. Augustine	279	Windmill Hill	93
Hillfields	254	Knowle	84
St. James	254	Bishopston	46
Bedminster	231	St. Philip and Jacob N.	42
Eastville	225	Durdham	Nil
Stapleton	221	Redland	Nil

* Nearly all from hutted camp—now abandoned.

Crime: males convicted of crimes in 1955 per 100,000 of the population

Age-group	England and Wales	Bristol	UPFIELD	BOLTWOOD
5-9	380	143	—	—
10-14	1,393	1,150	1,610	1,500
15-19	1,228	1,030	1,020	3,000
20-24	916	578	500	1,110
25-29	680	485	1,840	555
30-34	}478	379	1,300	—
35-39		267	500	800
40-44	}265	212	476	2,310
45-49		141	590	—
50-54	}153	128	834	2,000
55-59		79	—	—
60 and over	55	29	—	—
Total	502	313*	647	611

* Bristol's law-abidingness can also be seen in the phenomenally low drunkenness offence rate—e.g. in 1956 Bristol's rate was 30 per 100,000 as compared with the average of 174 for England and Wales.

Crime: all persons convicted of crimes in Bristol in 1955
per 100,000 of the population

St. Paul	454	Avon	177
Upfield	415	Redcliffe	171
St. James	357	St. Philip and Jacob N.	160
St. Philip and Jacob S.	353	Horfield	130
Hengrove	349	St. George East	116
Mount View	342	Brislington	112
Boltwood	336	Eastville	109
Westbury-on-Trym	282	Windmill Hill	101
St. Augustine	267	Bedminster	97
District	258	Stapleton	94
Somerset	243	Clifton	79
Hillfields	204	Bishopston	76
Easton	201	Redland	57
St. Michael's	198	Knowle	53
Southville	183	St. George West	51(?)
		Durdham	33

Mental illness: all diagnoses
First admissions to Bristol Mental Hospitals, 1949-53,
per 100,000 of the population over 15 (all diagnoses)

Redland	1,250	Hillfields	940
St. Michael's	1,240	Stapleton	940
Durdham	1,170	St. Augustine	920
St. James	1,150	St. Philip and Jacob N.	920
Clifton	1,140	Horfield	910
Westbury	1,090	Eastville	890
St. Paul	1,090	Hengrove	860
District	1,070	Brislington	840
Bishopston	1,020	Somerset	820
Redcliffe	1,020	St. George East	820
Knowle	990	St. George West	790
Southville	990	Bedminster	750
St. Philip and Jacob S.	960	Avon	720
Easton	940		

All cases of mental illness (first admissions 1949-53) for the whole of Bristol = 3,304, out of total population of 442,994.

Therefore, would 'expect' 53.5 cases from Old UPFIELD (population 7,185). 'Actual' number of cases = 47.

For whole of UPFIELD would 'expect' 70 cases; but 'actual' number found is 84.

Schizophrenia

It is not possible to standardize for age and sex in Old UPFIELD, because we do not possess figures, but rough comparison can be made. In 1949-53 there were 472 first admissions for schizophrenia (so diagnosed) for the city as a whole—total population 442,994. Would 'expect' (on random hypothesis) 7.5 cases out of Old UPFIELD's population of 7,185. In fact there were only 5 cases.

For the whole of UPFIELD (Old and New) would 'expect' 10.4 cases of schizophrenia; 'actual' number is 7.

REFERENCES

In addition to the references listed below, which are those referred to in the text, a short bibliography of works dealing with group work and adventure playgrounds is appended.

PART I

ARGYLE, M. (1957). *The Scientific Study of Social Behaviour*. London: Methuen.

COSER, L. (1956). *Functions of Social Conflict*. Glencoe, Ill.: The Free Press.

CURLE, ADAM. (1947). 'Transitional Communities and Social Reconnection.' *Human Relations*, **1**, 42.

JAQUES, ELLIOTT. (1951). *The Changing Culture of a Factory*. London: Tavistock.

MAIR, L. P. (1956). 'Applied Anthropology and Development Policies.' *British Journal of Sociology*, **7**, 120.

MERTON, R. K. (1949). *Social Theory and Social Structure*. Glencoe, Ill.: The Free Press.

MERTON, R. K., READER, GEORGE & KENDALL, PATRICIA L. (1957). *The Student-Physician*. Cambridge, Mass.: Harvard University Press.

MOGEY, J. (1956). *Family and Neighbourhood*. London: Oxford University Press.

MYRDAL, GUNNAR. (1953). 'Relation between Social Theory and Social Policy.' *British Journal of Sociology*, **4**, 210.

PARSONS, TALCOTT. (1951). *The Social System*. Glencoe, Ill.: The Free Press.

Report (Sixth) on the Work of the Children's Department, May 1951 (1951). London: H.M.S.O.

ROSS, MURRAY G. (1955). *Community Organization—Theory and Principles*. New York: Harper.

References

SIMEY, T. S. (1949). In *Why Delinquency? The Case for Operational Research*. London: National Association for Mental Health. Pp. 43–51.

Social Service Quarterly (1957). Editorial. Winter, **31**, 98.

SPROTT, W. J. H. (1958). *Human Groups*. Harmondsworth: Penguin Books.

THRASHER, F. M. (1937). *The Gang*. Chicago: University of Chicago Press.

TURNER, M. L. I. (1953). *Ships without Sails*. London: University of London Press.

TUXFORD, JOY & DENNIS, NORMAN (1958). 'Research and Social Work.' *Social Work*, **15**, 462.

WHYTE, WILLIAM H., Jr. (1956). *The Organization Man*. New York: Simon & Schuster; London: Cape (1957).

WILSON, A. T. M. (1947). 'Some Implications of Medical Practice and Social Case-Work for Action Research.' *Journal of Social Issues*, **3**, 11.

WILSON, A. T. M. (1949). 'Some Reflections and Suggestions on the Prevention and Treatment of Marital Problems.' *Human Relations*, **2**, 233.

PART II

FRANKENBERG, RONALD. (1957). *Village on the Border*. London: Cohen & West.

RICHARDS, AUDREY I. (1956). '*Chisungu*'—*A girl's initiation ceremony among the Bemba of Northern Rhodesia*. London: Faber & Faber.

WILSON, BRYAN R. (1962). 'The Teacher's Role—A Sociological Analysis.' *British Journal of Sociology*, **13**, 15.

PART III

COHEN, A. K. (1956). *Delinquent Boys*. London: Routledge & Kegan Paul.

CRAWFORD, PAUL L., MALAMUD, DANIEL I. & DUMPSON, JAMES R. (1950). *Working with Teen-Age Gangs*. New York: Welfare Council of New York City.

FORD, D. (1957). *The Delinquent Child and the Community*. London: Constable.

344

JAHODA, M. (1956). 'Toward a Social Psychology of Mental Health.' In Arnold M. Rose (Ed.), *Mental Health and Mental Disorder.* London: Routledge & Kegan Paul. Pp. 556–77.

MEAD, MARGARET. (1943). *Coming of Age in Samoa.* Harmondsworth: Penguin Books.

MILLS, C. WRIGHT. (1956). *The Power Elite.* London: Oxford University Press.

NEW YORK CITY YOUTH BOARD. (1952). *Reaching the Unreached.* New York: New York City Youth Board.

NEW YORK CITY YOUTH BOARD. (1960). *Reaching the Fighting Gang.* New York: New York City Youth Board.

TITMUSS, RICHARD M. (1958). *Essays on 'The Welfare State'.* London: George Allen & Unwin.

WILSON, ROGER. (1952). 'Homes, Schools and the Social Services.' *Social Service,* Autumn, **26,** 54.

PART IV

BLOM, H. (1958). Paper to United Nations European Seminar on 'Playground Activities, Objectives, and Leadership in Sweden.' (May/June.)

GOLDING, WILLIAM. (1954). *Lord of the Flies.* London: Faber & Faber.

MAYS, JOHN B. (1957). *Adventure in Play.* Liverpool: Council of Social Service.

MORRIS, T. P. (1958). *The Criminal Area.* London: Routledge & Kegan Paul.

SIMEY, T. S. (1952). 'The Contributions of the Social Sciences to the Solution of Administrative Problems.' *Public Administration,* **30,** 13.

PART V

HALMOS, P. (Ed.) (1962). *The Canford Families: A study in social casework and group work.* Keele, Staffs.: The Sociological Review: Monograph No. 6.

HOLLINGSHEAD, A. B. & REDLICH, F. C. (1958). *Social Class and Mental Illness.* New York: John Wiley.

KUENSTLER, PETER. (1956). In *European Seminar on The Principles and Practice of Group Work,* Leicester. Geneva: United Nations, UN/TAA/SEM/1956/REP. 1.

KUPER, L., *et al.* (1953). *Living in Towns.* London: Cresset Press.

References

MORRIS, T. P. (1958). *The Criminal Area*. London: Routledge & Kegan Paul.

MORRIS T. P. (1959). 'The Carrot Out of Reach.' *Listener*, **61**, 982.

ROSS, MURRAY G. (1955). *Community Organization—Theory and Principles*. New York: Harper.

SUTHERLAND, J. D. (1957). 'The Study Group Method of Training.' (Paper to Training Conference in Group Relations, Tavistock Institute, Sept.)

TAYLOR, G. BROOKE. (1959). 'Community Life in New Town.' *Social Service Quarterly*, **32**, 148.

THRASHER, F. M. (1937). *The Gang*. Chicago: University of Chicago Press.

TITMUSS, RICHARD M. (1957). In *European Seminar on the Relation between Research, Planning and Social Welfare Policy*, The Hague. Geneva: United Nations, UN/TAA/SEM/1957/REP. 3.

TURQUET, PIERRE. (1949). In *Why Delinquency? The Case for Operational Research*. London: National Association for Mental Health. Pp. 60-1.

TWAIN, MARK. (1876). *The Adventures of Tom Sawyer*. London: Harrap, 1924.

WHYTE, WILLIAM H., JR. (1956). *The Organization Man*. New York: Simon & Schuster; London: Cape (1957).

WOOTTON, BARBARA. (1959). *Social Science and Social Pathology*. London: George Allen & Unwin.

YOUNGHUSBAND, EILEEN L. (1959). *Report of the Working Party on Social Workers in the Local Authority Health and Welfare Services*. London: H.M.S.O.

GROUP WORK

COYLE, GRACE. (1947). *Group Experience and Democratic Values*. New York: Women's Press.

KLEIN, ALAN F. (1953). *Society, Democracy and the Group*. New York: Women's Press and W. Morrow.

KLEIN, JOSEPHINE. (1961). *Working with Groups—The Social Psychology of Discussion and Decision*. London: Hutchinson.

KONOPKA, GISELA. (1963). *Social Group Work*. New Jersey: Prentice Hall.

KUENSTLER, PETER. (1955). *Social Group Work in Great Britain*. London: Faber & Faber.

SULLIVAN, DOROTHY F. (1952). *Readings in Group Work*. New York: Association Press.

UNITED NATIONS. (1956). *European Seminar on the Principles and Practice of Group Work*, Leicester. Geneva: United Nations, UN/TAA/SEM/1956/REP. I.

WILSON, GERTRUDE & RYLAND, GLADYS. (1949). *Social Group Work Practice*. Boston: Houghton Mifflin.

ADVENTURE PLAYGROUNDS

'Adventure Playgrounds in Britain.' (1955). *Playing Fields*. April-June.

ALLEN, LADY, OF HURTWOOD. (1955). 'Adventure Playgrounds.' *Bulletin* of the National Froebel Foundation, December.

ALLEN, LADY, OF HURTWOOD. (1960). 'Adventure Playgrounds.' National Playing Fields Association.

BENJAMIN, JOE. (1961). *In Search of Adventure—A Study of the Junk Playground*. London: National Council of Social Service.

BOOKER, ILYS. (1957). 'What Puts the "Play" into a Playground?' *Housing Review*, May-June.

Housing Centre Review. (1953). Play Areas Number, No. 6.

'Junk Playgrounds.' (1948). *The Lancet*. 28 August.

NATIONAL PLAYING FIELDS ASSOCIATION. (1953). 'Playgrounds for Blocks of Flats.' December.

NATIONAL UNDER-FOURTEENS' COUNCIL. (1948). 'Junk Playgrounds'.

SAVE THE CHILDREN FUND. (1952). 'Play Needs of the Town Child.' London.

Index